University Texts in the Mathematical Sciences

Textbooks in this series cover a wide variety of courses in mathematics, statistics and computational methods. Ranging across undergraduate and graduate levels, books may focus on theoretical or applied aspects. All texts include frequent examples and exercises of varying complexity. Illustrations, projects, historical remarks, program code and real-world examples may offer additional opportunities for engagement. Texts may be used as a primary or supplemental resource for coursework and are often suitable for independent study.

Md Aquib

Advanced LaTeX

Springer

Md Aquib
Department of Mathematics and
Statistics
Imam Mohammad ibn Saud
Islamic University
Riyadh, Saudi Arabia

ISSN 2731-9318 ISSN 2731-9326 (electronic)
University Texts in theMathematical Sciences
ISBN 978-981-96-9321-4 ISBN 978-981-96-9322-1 (eBook)
https://doi.org/10.1007/978-981-96-9322-1

Mathematics Subject Classification: 65Y99, 68U35, 68N15, 97U50, 00A66, 68U05, 00A35

This Springer imprint is published by the registered company Springer Nature Singapore Pte Ltd.
The registered company address is: 152 Beach Road, #21-01/04 Gateway East, Singapore 189721, Singapore

To my beloved mother,
whose unwavering support and prayers have been my strength,

and to the memory of my late father,
whose guidance and values continue to inspire me every day.

Foreword

As users grow more confident in LaTeX, they often begin to explore its more sophisticated capabilities, producing technical illustrations, managing large collaborative documents, designing posters and presentations, and customizing layouts to fit the exact needs of their field. At this stage, LaTeX is no longer just a tool, it becomes an extension of the author's intention, offering precision, scalability, and control unmatched by conventional word processors.

Advanced LaTeX is a response to that journey. It is written for those who have mastered the fundamentals and are ready to take full advantage of LaTeX's advanced features. This book explores domain-specific packages, complex graphics with TikZ and PGFPlots, scientific poster creation, multilingual typesetting, and best practices for managing large projects. It also dives into the often overlooked areas of troubleshooting and optimization, skills essential to efficient LaTeX authorship.

Rather than treating advanced topics in isolation, this book integrates them into real-world scenarios, aiming to provide not just technical know-how but also strategic insights into how LaTeX can be molded to serve different academic and professional disciplines. Whether you are an engineer creating circuit diagrams, a linguist preparing multilingual texts, or a researcher presenting data in complex plots, this book is tailored to your needs.

School of Mathematics
Hangzhou Normal University
Hangzhou 311121, China

Yanlin Li

Preface

As users of LaTeX grow more familiar with its core features, they often encounter the need for deeper control, customization, and the ability to manage complex documents. From dynamic presentations and multilingual typesetting to algorithm formatting, circuit diagrams, and package development, LaTeX is capable of meeting highly specialized needs across academic and professional domains. *Advanced Topics in LaTeX and Applications* is the second installment in this two-volume series. It is intended for readers who have mastered the fundamentals and are now ready to engage with LaTeX's full potential. This volume investigates complex aspects that extend the basic LaTeX skillset: creating presentations with Beamer, designing posters, defining custom commands and environments, developing packages, and typesetting documents in multiple languages, including Arabic, Chinese, and Russian. It also addresses common challenges in compilation, document scaling, and collaborative workflows using Git or Overleaf. The structure of this volume emphasizes clarity and practical application. Each chapter is supported by real code examples, visual outputs, and best-practice suggestions that reflect how LaTeX is used in research and publishing environments today. By working through this volume, readers will not only expand their command over LaTeX but will also gain the tools necessary to adapt it to the specific demands of their field, be it engineering, computer science, linguistics, or the humanities. The preparation of this volume has been greatly informed by the vibrant and resourceful LaTeX community. We express our gratitude to all contributors, past and present, whose open tools, discussions, and documentation have helped shape this advanced guide.

Riyadh, Saudi Arabia Md Aquib

Acknowledgments Writing an advanced-level LaTeX book is only possible by standing on the shoulders of giants. The authors express their sincere gratitude to the LaTeX developers and community maintainers whose tireless efforts make this ecosystem as rich and versatile as it is today. From comprehensive documentation to actively maintained packages, their contributions form the backbone of this work.

I am especially thankful to my academic peers and collaborators who shared their expertise and reviewed early drafts of this manuscript. Your critical insights and technical suggestions strengthened the depth and scope of the book.

I would also like to acknowledge the many LaTeX enthusiasts and experts who publish tutorials, maintain forums, and respond to questions across platforms. You make the learning curve less steep for all of us. Heartfelt thanks to my family and loved ones for their enduring patience and understanding throughout this long but fulfilling process. Lastly, I would like to thank Prof. Yanlin Li for writing foreword for this book.

Competing Interests The author has no competing interests to declare that are relevant to the content of this manuscript.

Contents

Chapter 1

Managing Large Projects

Contents

Md. Aquib, *Advanced LaTeX*, University Texts in the Mathematical Sciences,
https://doi.org/10.1007/978-981-96-9322-1_1

Abstract: As LaTeX continues to serve as the tool of choice for writing technical documents, users often transition from short articles and reports to more complex and extended projects such as theses, books, manuals, and collaborative research papers. Managing these larger projects requires not only a sound understanding of LaTeX's structure but also effective strategies for modularization, error handling, and content organization. This chapter is designed to guide readers through the process of working with large LaTeX documents in a scalable and efficient way.

Keywords: Large documents, Document structuring, `\input` and `\include`, LaTeX errors, Project organization, Indexing and glossaries

We begin with a quick review of LaTeX's fundamental structure to reinforce the basic document architecture. From there, we introduce the use of `\input` and `\subfile` commands for breaking a large document into manageable components. Subsequent sections focus on best practices for organizing content, handling frequent compilation errors, and implementing robust indexing and glossary features. By mastering these tools and conventions, users will be well-equipped to undertake and maintain sophisticated LaTeX projects with clarity, precision, and control.

1.1 Structuring LaTeX Documents: A Quick Review

Before delving into advanced techniques for managing large LaTeX projects, it is useful to briefly revisit the fundamental structure of a LaTeX document. Understanding how a LaTeX file is organized helps maintain clarity and consistency, especially as documents grow in size and complexity.

A typical LaTeX document consists of two main parts: the preamble and the document body. The preamble is the portion that appears before `\begin{document}`, and it includes commands for setting up the document class, loading packages, defining macros, and configuring formatting. For example:

Sample Preamble

```
\documentclass[12pt]{article}
\usepackage{amsmath, graphicx, hyperref}
\title{Sample Document}
\author{Author Name}
\date{\today}
```

The document body, enclosed between `\begin{document}` and `\end{document}`, contains the actual content, including sections, paragraphs, equations, figures, and references:

Sample Document Body

```
\begin{document}

\maketitle

\section{Introduction}
This is a simple LaTeX document.

\end{document}
```

LaTeX provides a hierarchical structure for organizing content. The most common sectional commands are:

`\part`	Top-level division (mainly for books or reports)
`\chapter`	Major division (only in `book` and `report` classes)
`\section`	Standard heading
`\subsection`	Subdivision under a section
`\subsubsection`	Further subdivision
`\paragraph`	Smaller division (not numbered by default)

The `article` class, commonly used for short documents and academic papers, does not support `\chapter` by default. In contrast, `report` and `book` classes offer deeper structure for long-form writing.

It is important to use this structural hierarchy logically and consistently, as it directly impacts features like the table of contents, cross-references, and numbering of sections and equations.

1.2 Complex Document Management with Subfiles and Input

As your LaTeX projects grow in complexity, managing large documents efficiently becomes increasingly important. Instead of placing all content in one main file, you can break your document into smaller, manageable parts and then combine them. This approach improves readability, collaboration, and maintainability. LaTeX offers two main commands for handling such modular document structures: `input` and `subfiles`. In this section, we will explore how to use these commands effectively to manage complex LaTeX projects.

1.2.1 Using the `input` and Include Commands

To incorporate external files, LaTeX provides two primary methods: the input and include commands. The `input` command allows you to break your document into smaller files and then include them in the main document. Each file can represent a chapter, section, or any logical part of your document. When `input` is used, LaTeX processes the included file as if its contents were written directly in the main file.

The basic syntax of the `input` command is as follows:

```
\input{filename}
```

`filename` refers to the name of the file that you want to include. You do not need to specify the file extension (`.tex`) as LaTeX automatically assumes that the file is a LaTeX file. Here is how you would set up the main file and input.

```
\documentclass{article}
\begin{document}

\input{introduction}
% Includes the content of introduction.tex
\input{chapter1}
% Includes the content of chapter1.tex
\input{chapter2}
% Includes the content of chapter2.tex

\end{document}
```

This approach makes it easy to keep chapters or sections in separate files while compiling everything into a single document. One key advantage of `input` is that LaTeX treats the included file as if it were part of the main file, so the numbering (e.g., section numbers, equation numbers) flows seamlessly.

On the other hand, the `include` command processes each file separately and ensures that a new page begins before each included file. This method is well suited for books and theses, where each chapter is expected to start on a fresh page. An example of its usage is:

```
\documentclass{book}
\begin{document}

\include{chapters/introduction}
\include{chapters/chapter1}

\end{document}
```

A notable advantage of `include` is its ability to selectively compile specific sections using the `{\includeonly}` command. By enabling only certain files, one can significantly reduce compilation time, especially in large documents. For example:

```
\includeonly{chapters/chapter1}
```

This approach ensures that only `chapter1.tex` is processed while ignoring all other files, making it a useful feature when working on revisions of specific sections.

1.2.2 Using the `subfiles` Package

For more complex documents, especially those involving collaboration or individual compilation of parts, the `subfiles` package is a more versatile option. It allows each file (subfile) to be compiled independently or as part of the main document, providing greater flexibility.

To use the `subfiles` package, first, include it in the preamble of your main file as:

```
\usepackage{subfiles}
```

Next, you can divide your document into separate subfiles, where each subfile can be compiled on its own. The `subfiles` package allows for local preambles and independent testing of each subfile without the need to compile the entire project.

Here is how you would set up the main file and a subfile.

Main file (e.g., `main.tex`)

```
\documentclass{article}
\usepackage{subfiles}

\begin{document}

\subfile{introduction}
% Includes introduction.tex as a subfile
\subfile{chapter1}
% Includes chapter1.tex as a subfile
\subfile{chapter2}
% Includes chapter2.tex as a subfile

\end{document}
```

Subfile (e.g., `chapter1.tex`)

```
\documentclass[main]{subfiles}

\begin{document}

\section{Chapter 1}
This is the content of Chapter 1.

\end{document}
```

In the example above, `chapter1.tex` can be compiled as a standalone document, or it can be included in `main.tex` as part of the larger document. When compiling the subfile independently, LaTeX uses its own local preamble (inherited from `main.tex`), making it possible to test each chapter or section individually.

1.2.3 Advantages of Using `input` and `subfiles`

Both `input` and `subfiles` provide useful features for complex document management:

- **Modularity**: Breaking your document into smaller files makes it easier to manage, debug, and collaborate with others. Each file represents a logical unit, such as a chapter or section.
- **Collaboration**: In collaborative projects, each author can work on separate files independently. Using `subfiles`, team members can compile their parts without affecting the entire document.
- **Efficiency**: You can compile only the subfile you are working on without compiling the entire document, saving time when dealing with large projects.
- **Consistency**: With both `input` and `subfiles`, the document structure remains consistent. Numbering of sections, equations, figures, and tables flows smoothly throughout the document, regardless of whether you are working with individual files or the main document.

1.3 Common Errors and How to Fix Them

Even though LaTeX is a powerful tool, it is common to encounter errors during the document compilation process.

These errors can be frustrating, but most of them have straightforward fixes once you understand their cause. In this section, we will discuss some of the most common LaTeX errors and how to resolve them effectively.

1.3.1 Error: `! LaTeX Error: Missing \begin{document}`

This is one of the most common LaTeX errors and occurs when LaTeX cannot find the command that starts the document environment. Every LaTeX document must contain the `\begin{document}` command, which tells LaTeX where the content of the document begins. It may also cause due typo in `\begin{document}` command or if you forget to close an environment you started.

Solution Ensure that your document includes both the `\begin{document}` and `\end{document}` commands and there is no typo. Also, ensure that every environment has start and end command. Here is an example of a minimal LaTeX structure:

```
\documentclass{article}

\begin{document}
This is the content of the document.
\end{document}
```

If either the `\begin{document}` or `\end{document}` command is missing, LaTeX will produce this error.

1.3.2 Error: `! Undefined control sequence`

This error occurs when LaTeX encounters a command that it does not recognize. It usually happens when there is a typo in the command or when a required package has not been loaded.

Solution

- Double-check that the command is spelled correctly. For example, `\it` will produce an error because the correct command for italics is `\textit`.
- Ensure that you have loaded the correct package if the command comes from a specific package. For example, `\includegraphics` requires the `graphicx` package.

1.3.3 Error: `! Misplaced \{ or \}`

This error occurs when curly braces {} are not placed properly within the LaTeX code. Curly braces are used to group content, and a mismatch between opening and closing braces can cause this error.

Solution Check that every opening brace { has a corresponding closing brace }.

Example 1.3.1
```
\textbf{This is bold}   % Correct
\textbf{This is bold
% Incorrect: Missing closing brace
```

LaTeX expects matching braces to enclose content correctly, and forgetting to close a brace is a common mistake that causes this error.

1.3.4 Error: `! Package inputenc Error: Unicode character`

This error is generated when LaTeX encounters a character that it cannot interpret because the document does not support Unicode characters. It typically occurs when special characters, such as accented letters, are used without the appropriate encoding package.

Solution Load the `inputenc` package with the `utf8` option in the preamble of your document. This allows LaTeX to interpret UTF-8 characters, which include most common Unicode characters.

```
\usepackage[utf8]{inputenc}
```

If you are using XeLaTeX or LuaLaTeX, you do not need `inputenc` because these engines support Unicode natively.

1.3.5 Error: `Overfull hbox`

This warning occurs when a line of text is too long to fit within the margins, and LaTeX cannot break it into multiple lines. An `Overfull hbox` warning usually results in text overflowing into the margin.

Solution

- Manually break the line using \\ to force a line break.
- Alternatively, you can reduce the width of the text box using the `sloppy` or `raggedright` command:

```
\sloppy
% Allows LaTeX to adjust spacing more
     liberally
```

1.3.6 Error: `! LaTeX Error: Too many unprocessed floats`

This error occurs when you have too many figures, tables, or other floating environments that LaTeX has not been able to place. LaTeX maintains a list of floats and places them in appropriate positions in the document, but if the list grows too long, it will produce this error.

Solution Use the `[H]` option from the `float` package to force LaTeX to place the float exactly where it appears in the code as:

```
\usepackage{float}
\begin{figure}[H]
    \centering
    \includegraphics{example-image}
    \caption{Example Image}
\end{figure}
```

This forces LaTeX to place the figure or table “here” instead of waiting for the next suitable location.

1.3.7 Error: `! Missing \endcsname inserted`

This error can be difficult to diagnose, but it usually occurs when there is a mistake with macro expansion or when a command is incorrectly defined. This often happens in more complex LaTeX code, especially when dealing with custom commands or environments.

Solution Check for any custom macros or environments and ensure that they are defined correctly. If the error occurs after defining a custom command, verify that all arguments are handled properly and that braces are balanced.

1.3.8 Error: `! LaTeX Error: There's no line here to end`

This error occurs when you attempt to insert a line break using \\ in a place where LaTeX does not expect one. For example, trying to force a line break between two paragraphs or in a floating environment can trigger this error.

Solution Remove the extraneous \\ or ensure that you are using it in an appropriate place, such as inside a paragraph or a table environment. If you need additional vertical spacing, use the `\vspace` command instead.

```
\vspace{10pt}  % Adds 10 points of vertical
      space
```

1.3.9 General Tips for Debugging LaTeX Errors

When debugging LaTeX errors, it is important to:

- **Read the error message carefully**: LaTeX's error messages often provide clues about what went wrong. The line number mentioned in the error message will help you locate the problematic code.
- **Check the log file**: LaTeX generates a log file during compilation. This file contains detailed information about errors and warnings. You can use it to identify issues that are not immediately visible in the output.
- **Use minimal examples**: When debugging a difficult error, try to create a minimal working example (MWE) by stripping down your document to the smallest version that still produces the error. This will help you isolate the issue.

1.3.10 Full LaTeX Example with Common Errors Resolved

```
\documentclass{article}
\usepackage[utf8]{inputenc}
% Ensure UTF-8 encoding is used

\begin{document}
\title{Handling Common LaTeX Errors}
\author{Author Name}
\date{\today}
\maketitle

\section{Introduction}
This document addresses common LaTeX errors
and how to fix them.

\section{Example of a Correct Figure}
\usepackage{graphicx}
\begin{figure}[H]
% Use float package to force placement
    \centering
    \includegraphics{example-image}
    \caption{An example image}
\end{figure}

\section{Conclusion}
By understanding common errors, you can
resolve issues and compile
your document smoothly.

\end{document}
```

1.4 Indexing and Glossaries

In larger documents like books or theses, it is often useful to include an index and a glossary to help readers quickly find terms, concepts, or specific sections. LaTeX provides powerful tools for automating the creation of both an index and a glossary. In this section, we will explore how to generate these elements using LaTeX packages.

1.4.1 Creating an Index

In extensive documents, an **index** plays a crucial role in helping readers locate important terms, definitions, and references efficiently. Instead of manually compiling an index, LaTeX provides automated tools to generate one dynamically. This ensures that as the document expands or undergoes modifications, the index remains accurate and up to date. The process involves marking terms within the text, compiling the index separately, and integrating it into the final document.

Setting Up Indexing in LaTeX

To begin, the `makeidx` package must be loaded in the document's preamble. Additionally, the `\makeindex` command must be included to enable indexing:

Example: Enabling Indexing

LaTeX Code:

```
\documentclass{book}
\usepackage{makeidx}
\makeindex
```

With these commands, LaTeX prepares the document for indexing. However, merely enabling indexing is not sufficient; specific terms must be **marked within the text** to be included in the index.

Marking Index Entries

To include a word or phrase in the index, the `\index` command is used immediately after the term. For example:

Example: Indexing a Single Word

LaTeX Code:

```
LaTeX is a powerful typesetting
system\index{LaTeX}.
```

This marks the term "LaTeX" for inclusion in the index, and its corresponding page number will be listed in the generated index.

For better organization, **subentries** can also be created. This is particularly useful when grouping related topics under broader terms:

Example: Creating a Subentry

LaTeX Code:

```
LaTeX\index{LaTeX!typesetting system}
```

In this case, "LaTeX" is the main entry, and "typesetting system" is listed as a subcategory under it. The final index will display:

```
LaTeX
    typesetting system, 12
```

Printing the Index

Once the terms have been indexed throughout the document, the compiled list must be printed at the end. This is done using the `\printindex` command, which should be placed at the desired location in the document:

Example: Printing the Index

LaTeX Code:

```
\printindex
```

This command instructs LaTeX to generate the index and place it at the specified position in the document, typically at the end of a book or thesis.

Compiling the Document with an Index

Unlike standard LaTeX compilation, **indexing requires additional processing** to generate the final index correctly. The process consists of the following steps:

1. Run `pdflatex` (or `latex`) on your document.
2. Run the `makeindex` command to process the index entries.
3. Run `pdflatex` again to incorporate the generated index.

For users working with Overleaf or TeXShop, this process may be automated in the compilation settings.

Complete Example of Indexing

The following example illustrates the entire process of indexing in LaTeX, from defining the index to generating the final compiled output.

Example: Complete Indexing Process

LaTeX Code:

```
\documentclass{book}
\usepackage{makeidx}
\makeindex

\begin{document}

\chapter{Introduction}
LaTeX is a powerful typesetting
system\index{LaTeX}.

\chapter{Advanced Topics}
We will discuss various LaTeX
packages\index{packages}.

\printindex

\end{document}
```

1.4.2 Creating a Glossary

A glossary is a structured list of key terms and their definitions, commonly found in academic and technical documents. It serves as a reference for readers who may be unfamiliar with specific terminology. In LaTeX, the `glossaries` package provides an efficient way to define, reference, and automatically generate a glossary.

Setting Up the Glossaries Package

To begin using a glossary in a LaTeX document, the `glossaries` package must be loaded in the preamble. Additionally, the command `\makeglossaries` is required to enable glossary generation. The package allows the inclusion of acronyms alongside standard glossary entries if the `acronym` option is specified. The setup is as follows:

Example: Loading the Glossaries Package

LaTeX Code:

```
\documentclass{article}
\usepackage[acronym]{glossaries}
\makeglossaries
```

This prepares the document for glossary creation and ensures that all defined terms are automatically collected for compilation.

Defining Glossary Terms

Glossary terms must be explicitly defined using the `\newglossaryentry` command. Each term is assigned a unique identifier, a display name, and a description. The following example demonstrates the definition of a term:

Example: Defining a Glossary Entry

LaTeX Code:

```
\newglossaryentry{latex}{name=LaTeX,
description={a typesetting system
used for creating professional
documents}
}
```

Here, the term LaTeX is defined with a corresponding explanation. Whenever this term is referenced in the document, it will appear in the glossary.

Defining Acronyms

Apart from standard glossary terms, the `glossaries` package also allows the definition of acronyms, which can be expanded upon first use. Acronyms are defined using the `\newacronym` command:

Example: Defining an Acronym

LaTeX Code:

```
\newacronym{html}{HTML}
{Hypertext Markup Language}
```

This command creates the acronym "HTML," which will appear as "Hypertext Markup Language (HTML)" the first time it is referenced in the document and simply as "HTML" thereafter.

Using Glossary Entries in Text

Once glossary terms and acronyms are defined, they can be referenced throughout the document using the `\gls` command. This command automatically ensures that the term is properly formatted and, if applicable, the acronym expansion occurs on first use.

For example:

Example: Referencing a Glossary Entry

LaTeX Code:

```
LaTeX is a powerful tool for document
preparation, as explained by
\gls{latex}. It is often used together
with \gls{html} for web-related tasks.
```

This ensures that LaTeX and HTML are properly linked to their respective glossary definitions.

Generating and Printing the Glossary

At the location where the glossary should be displayed, the command `\printglossary` must be included. Similarly, to generate a separate list of acronyms, the command `\printglossary[type={acronymtype}]` is used:

Example: Printing the Glossary

LaTeX Code:

```
\printglossary
\printglossary[type=\acronymtype]
```

The first command prints the main glossary, while the second prints a separate list of acronyms if the `acronym` option is enabled.

Compiling the Document with a Glossary

Unlike standard LaTeX documents, generating a glossary requires an additional compilation step. The recommended workflow is:

1. Run `pdflatex` (or `latex`) on the document.
2. Run the command `makeglossaries` to process glossary entries.
3. Run `pdflatex` again to incorporate the glossary into the final document.

Users working with Overleaf or other LaTeX editors may have the glossary compilation integrated into their build process.

Complete Glossary Example

Below is a fully functional LaTeX example that includes glossary terms, acronyms, and references:

Example: Full Glossary Implementation

LaTeX Code:

```
\documentclass{article}
\usepackage[acronym]{glossaries}
\makeglossaries

\newglossaryentry{latex}{
name=LaTeX,
description={a typesetting system used
for creating professional documents}
}

\newacronym{html}{HTML}
{Hypertext Markup Language}

\begin{document}

LaTeX is a powerful tool for document
preparation, as explained by
\gls{latex}. It is often used together
with \gls{html} for web-related tasks.

\printglossary
\printglossary[type=\acronymtype]

\end{document}
```

1.4.3 Best Practices for Indexing and Glossaries

- **Consistency**: Use consistent labels for both your index entries and glossary terms. This ensures clarity and prevents duplicate entries.

- **Case Sensitivity**: LaTeX is case-sensitive when it comes to indexing and glossary entries. Be sure to match the case exactly when using the `\index` and `\gls` commands.

- **Acronym First Use**: When using acronyms, it is good practice to define them in full the first time they are used. The `glossaries` package handles this automatically, displaying the full term on the first use and the acronym on subsequent uses.

1.4.4 Full LaTeX Example

Full LaTeX Example

```
\documentclass{article}
\usepackage[acronym]{glossaries}
\usepackage{makeidx}
\makeindex
\makeglossaries

\newglossaryentry{latex}{ name=LaTeX,
description={a typesetting system used for
creating professional documents}
}

\newacronym{html}{HTML}
{Hypertext Markup Language}

\begin{document}

\section{Introduction}
LaTeX is a powerful typesetting
system\index{LaTeX}, widely used in
academia. It integrates well with \gls{html}.
```

```
\section{Advanced Topics}
We will discuss various LaTeX packages
\index{packages}.

\printindex
\printglossary
\printglossary[type=\acronymtype]

\end{document}
```

Exercises for Chap. 1: Managing Large Projects

1.2 Complex Document Management with Subfiles and Input

1. **Using `input` for Multiple Files**: Write a LaTeX document that uses the `input` command to manage multiple sections of a document. Break the document into several smaller files (e.g., `introduction.tex`, `conclusion.tex`) and compile them together using `input`.

2. **Using `subfiles` for Large Projects**: Use the `subfiles` package to manage a complex document, such as a book or thesis. Write a main document that includes at least three chapters, each written in a separate file. Compile individual chapters independently using the `subfiles` package.

3. **Cross-Referencing Between Files**: Create a LaTeX project where you cross-reference figures, sections, or equations between different files. Ensure that the references work correctly when compiled using `subfiles`.

1.3 Common Errors and How to Fix Them

1. **Identifying Common Errors**: Write a LaTeX document that intentionally contains three common errors (e.g., missing `\begin{document}`, mismatched braces, unrecognized commands). Compile the document and identify the errors in the log file. Explain how to fix each error.

2. **Dealing with Undefined References**: Create a LaTeX document with an undefined reference (e.g., referencing a section that does not exist). Identify the error in the log file and explain how to resolve the issue.

3. **Overfull and Underfull Boxes**: Write a LaTeX document that demonstrates both overfull and underfull `hbox` warnings. Modify the document to eliminate these warnings and explain how you corrected the layout.

1.4 Indexing ans Glossaries

1. **Creating an Index**: Write a LaTeX document that includes an index. Use the `makeidx` package to add entries to the index and compile the document to generate the index at the end.

2. **Glossary Entries**: Create a glossary for your LaTeX document using the `glossaries` package. Add at least five terms to the glossary and generate the glossary section in the final output.

3. **Adding Acronyms**: Add acronyms to your LaTeX document using the `glossaries` package. Ensure that the acronym is explained the first time it appears and is abbreviated in subsequent uses. Compile the document to display the list of acronyms.

Chapter 2

Advanced Figures and Graphics

Contents

Md. Aquib, *Advanced LaTeX*, University Texts in the Mathematical Sciences,
https://doi.org/10.1007/978-981-96-9322-1_2

Abstract: While the foundational aspects of including figures and basic image manipulation in LaTeX have been explored in the first volume, this chapter moves beyond the basics to explore the sophisticated tools LaTeX offers for creating technical and domain-specific graphics. LaTeX's drawing capabilities, through packages like `PSTricks`, `TikZ`, and `PGFPlots`, enable the creation of high-quality vector diagrams, mathematical illustrations, data plots, and electrical circuit schematics with remarkable precision. These tools are especially valuable in disciplines where clarity of structure, spatial relationships, or data representation is essential. This chapter guides you through constructing intricate visuals natively within LaTeX, offering fine control over every element of the diagram and ensuring seamless integration with the surrounding content. Whether you are drawing function graphs, flowcharts, or electrical circuits, the techniques discussed here will equip you with the knowledge to produce publication-grade graphics tailored to your field.

Keywords: TikZ graphics, PGFPlots, PSTricks diagrams, Technical illustrations, 2D and 3D plotting, Circuit diagrams

2.1 Creating Diagrams with `PSTricks`

Diagrams and illustrations play an essential role in mathematical and scientific documents. LaTeX provides several tools for creating high-quality vector-based figures, and among them, PSTricks stands out for its precision and flexibility. Unlike rasterized image formats, which can lose quality when scaled, PSTricks produces scalable PostScript graphics that integrate seamlessly with LaTeX.

With PSTricks, users can generate a wide variety of graphical elements, including geometric shapes, mathematical plots, circuit diagrams, and flowcharts. Its syntax is highly structured, offering fine control over positioning, transformations, and styling. This chapter introduces PSTricks and explores its key features, beginning with basic setup and drawing commands.

2.1.1 Setting Up the PSTricks Environment

Before using PSTricks, it is necessary to configure the LaTeX compiler appropriately. Unlike modern packages that work with direct PDF output, PSTricks requires a PostScript-compatible workflow. A standard compilation sequence follows:

```
latex -> dvips -> ps2pdf
```

Alternatively, users working with xelatex can generate PostScript-based output directly.

To load PSTricks, include the following packages in the document preamble:

Preamble Setup

```
\usepackage{pstricks}
\usepackage{pst-plot, pst-node}
% Additional utilities
```

The core environment for creating diagrams is the `pspicture` environment, which defines a coordinate system for positioning graphical elements. The syntax follows:

Basic Syntax

```
\begin{pspicture}(x0,y0)(x1,y1)
    % Drawing commands go here
\end{pspicture}
```

The parameters `(x0,y0)` and `(x1,y1)` specify the lower-left and upper-right corners of the coordinate system, allowing precise placement of objects.

2.1.2 Basic Drawing Commands

Drawing Lines and Arrows

Lines and arrows are fundamental components of most diagrams. In `PSTricks`, the `\psline` command creates straight lines, while the same command with an arrow style modifier produces directional arrows. The following example illustrates a basic diagram with these elements.

Drawing Lines and Arrows

```
\begin{pspicture}(0,0)(5,5)
    \psline(0,0)(4,4) % Diagonal line
    \psline[linewidth=1.5pt]{->}(1,1)(3,4)
    % Thick arrow
\end{pspicture}
```

Drawing Shapes: Circles, Rectangles, and Ellipses

`PSTricks` provides commands for generating geometric figures, including circles, rectangles, and ellipses. These shapes are defined using their respective center points, corner coordinates, or dimensions.

The following example demonstrates how to construct a circle, an ellipse, and a rectangle within the `pspicture` environment.

Drawing Shapes

```
\begin{pspicture}(0,0)(6,6)
    \pscircle(3,3){1.5}          % Circle
    \psellipse(2,2)(3,1)         % Ellipse
    \psframe(0,0)(2,3)           % Rectangle
\end{pspicture}
```

2.1.3 Adding Text and Labels

In most diagrams, textual labels play a crucial role in identifying key components, marking coordinates, or annotating important sections. `PSTricks` provides a flexible way to add text at precise locations using the `\rput` command. This command allows text to be placed at specified coordinates relative to the diagram's coordinate system, ensuring alignment and readability.

The syntax for adding text follows a straightforward pattern:

Syntax for Placing Text

```
\rput(x, y){Text}
```

Here, `x` and `y` represent the positions in the coordinate system where the text is placed. The argument inside the curly brackets defines the text content.

To illustrate the use of `\rput`, consider a simple diagram that includes a circle with labeled points. The following example demonstrates how labels can be added at specific positions within the figure.

Adding Labels to a Diagram

```
\begin{pspicture}(0,0)(4,4)
    \pscircle(2,2){1.5}
    % Draws a circle
    \rput(2,2){Center}
    % Places label at the center
    \rput(3,3){Label A}
    % Adds a label at coordinate (3,3)
\end{pspicture}
```

Aligning Text within Diagrams

By default, `\rput` centers the text at the specified coordinates. However, in some cases, text needs to be aligned relative to a specific edge or adjusted for better readability. `PSTricks` provides an alternative command, `\urput`, which aligns text with respect to its reference point.

Consider a diagram where labels need to be offset from their reference points to prevent overlap:

Adjusting Text Alignment

```
\begin{pspicture}(0,0)(4,4)
    \psline(1,1)(3,3)
    % Draws a diagonal line
    \rput[bl](1,1){Start}
    % Aligns label to bottom-left
    \rput[tr](3,3){End}
    % Aligns label to top-right
\end{pspicture}
```

In this example, the `[bl]` (bottom-left) and `[tr]` (top-right) options control the text positioning relative to the reference point. This method ensures that labels do not overlap with diagram elements.

Rotating and Scaling Text

In some cases, labels may need to be rotated for better alignment with diagram components or scaled for emphasis. The \rput command allows transformations such as rotation and scaling using an additional argument.

The following example demonstrates how text can be rotated and resized:

Rotating and Scaling Text

```
\begin{pspicture}(0,0)(4,4)
\pscircle(2,2){1.5}            % Draws a circle
\rput{45}(2,3){Rotated Text}
% Rotates text by 45 degrees
\rput[bl](1,1){\scalebox{1.5}
{Scaled Text}} % Enlarges text
\end{pspicture}
```

The \rput{angle} option rotates text by the specified degrees, while \scalebox{factor} enlarges or shrinks the text proportionally.

2.1.4 Connecting Elements with Nodes

In many diagrams, especially flowcharts, network structures, and circuit designs, elements need to be connected using directed or undirected lines. The pst-node package in PSTricks provides a robust way to define and manipulate nodes, allowing for precise control over connections between labeled components.

A node acts as a reference point within the diagram, which can be labeled and connected to other nodes using lines or arrows. This method ensures that elements remain aligned correctly, even when the diagram is resized or adjusted.

To use nodes, the pst-node package must be included in the document preamble:

Loading the pst-node Package

```
\usepackage{pst-node}
```

Creating and Connecting Nodes

A basic connection between two nodes involves defining their positions and using a connector to establish a relationship between them. The `\rput` command places the nodes at specific coordinates, and the `\ncline` command draws a line or arrow between them.

Consider the following example, where two labeled nodes are connected by a directed arrow:

Connecting Two Nodes

```
\begin{pspicture}(0,0)(5,5)
\rput(1,1){\psframebox{Start}}  % First node
\rput(4,4){\psframebox{End}}    % Second node
\ncline{->}{1,1}{4,4}   % Directed connection
\end{pspicture}
```

In this example, the two labeled elements, "Start" and "End," are enclosed in rectangular frames using the `\psframebox` command. The `\ncline` command establishes a directed connection between them with an arrow indicating directionality.

Using Named Nodes for Clarity

While placing nodes using coordinates is effective, defining named nodes improves readability and allows for dynamic positioning. Named nodes are assigned using the `\pnode` command and referenced in connections, making it easier to modify diagrams.

The following example demonstrates how named nodes simplify connections:

Using Named Nodes

```
\begin{pspicture}(0,0)(5,5)
    \pnode(1,1){A}          % Define first node
    \pnode(4,4){B}          % Define second node
    \ncline{->}{A}{B}       % Connect the nodes
\end{pspicture}
```

Named nodes provide a structured approach to defining elements and their connections. When modifying the diagram, it becomes easier to adjust node positions without rewriting the connection commands.

Adding Labels to Connections

Connections between nodes often require labels to specify relationships, directions, or additional information. The `\naput` and `\nbput` commands place labels above or below the connecting line, respectively.

In the following example, a label is added to indicate the nature of the connection:

Labeling a Connection

```
\begin{pspicture}(0,0)(5,5)
    \pnode(1,1){A}
    \pnode(4,4){B}
    \ncline{->}{A}{B}
    \naput{Transition}
    % Places label above the line
\end{pspicture}
```

The `\naput` command ensures the label appears above the connecting arrow, improving clarity.

Using Multiple Connections in a Diagram

Complex diagrams often require multiple nodes connected in structured layouts, such as state machines, organizational charts, or hierarchical structures. Multiple nodes can be connected using a combination of the techniques described earlier.

Consider a simple three-node diagram with multiple directed connections:

Connecting Multiple Nodes

```
\begin{pspicture}(0,0)(6,6)
    \pnode(1,1){A}
    \pnode(4,1){B}
    \pnode(2.5,4){C}

    \ncline{->}{A}{B}
    \naput{Step 1}

    \ncline{->}{B}{C}
    \naput{Step 2}

    \ncline{->}{A}{C}
    \naput{Direct Path}
\end{pspicture}
```

2.1.5 Plotting Graphs with PSTricks

Graphs play a crucial role in mathematical and scientific documentation. The pst-plot package extends the capabilities of PSTricks by enabling function plotting directly within the pspicture environment. This section explores how to create and customize plots using pst-plot, focusing on function graphs, coordinate axes, and enhancements for better visualization.

To begin using function plotting in PSTricks, include the pst-plot package in the document preamble:

Loading the pst-plot Package

```
\usepackage{pst-plot}
```

Basic Function Plotting

To plot a function, the \psplot command is used within the pspicture environment. The syntax follows:

```
\psplot{x_min}{x_max}{expression}
```

where x_min and x_max define the range of the independent variable, and expression specifies the mathematical function to be plotted.

Consider the example below, which plots the function $y = x^2$ over the interval $0 \leq x \leq 5$, along with labeled coordinate axes.

Plotting a Function

```
\begin{pspicture}(0,-1)(5,5)
    \psaxes{->}(0,0)(5,5)
    % Draws coordinate axes
    \psplot{0}{5}{x 2 exp}
    % Plots y = x^2
\end{pspicture}
```

In this example, the coordinate axes are drawn with arrowheads, and the function $y = x^2$ is plotted smoothly from $x = 0$ to $x = 5$.

Customizing Graph Appearance

A graph can be customized by adjusting its color, line style, and thickness. The following options modify the appearance of the plotted function:

```
\psplot[linecolor=blue, linewidth=1.5pt,
linestyle=dashed]{0}{5}{x 2 exp}
```

This customization applies a blue dashed line with increased thickness to the function plot.

Customizing Graph Appearance

```
\begin{pspicture}(0,-1)(5,5)
    \psaxes{->}(0,0)(5,5)
    \psplot[linecolor=blue, linewidth=1.5pt,
    linestyle=dashed]{0}{5}{x 2 exp}
\end{pspicture}
```

Adding Grid Lines for Better Readability

Grid lines improve the readability of graphs by providing reference markers along the axes. The `\psgrid` command generates a background grid, aiding in visualizing function behavior over specific intervals.

```
\psgrid[subgriddiv=1,griddots=10,
       gridlabels=7pt](0,0)(5,5)
```

This command adds a grid with one subdivision per unit, small grid dots for clarity, and labels with a font size of 7pt.

Adding Grid Lines

```
\begin{pspicture}(0,-1)(5,5)
    \psaxes{->}(0,0)(5,5)
    \psgrid[subgriddiv=1,griddots=10,
    gridlabels=7pt](0,0)(5,5)
    \psplot[linecolor=red]{0}{5}{x 2 exp}
\end{pspicture}
```

Plotting Multiple Functions in a Single Graph

To compare functions, multiple plots can be included within the same `pspicture` environment. Each function is assigned different colors and styles for clear distinction.

Plotting Multiple Functions

```
\begin{pspicture}(0,-1)(5,5)
    \psaxes{->}(0,0)(5,5)
    \psplot[linecolor=blue]{0}{5}{x}
    \psplot[linecolor=red, linestyle=dasheds]
    {0}{5}{x 2 exp}
\end{pspicture}
```

In this case, the function $y = x$ is plotted as a solid blue line, while $y = x^2$ appears as a dashed red curve. This allows for direct comparison between linear and quadratic growth.

2.1.6 Best Practices for Using `PSTricks`

When working with the `PSTricks` package, it is important to follow a few best practices to ensure high-quality diagrams and compatibility across different compilation methods. Since `PSTricks` relies on PostScript commands, users must compile their documents using methods that support PostScript rendering, such as `latex` → `dvips` → `ps2pdf` or by using XeLaTeX. Attempting to compile with `pdflatex` directly will typically result in errors unless additional support packages are used.

Before constructing a diagram, it is advisable to define an appropriate coordinate system that fits the scope and scale of the drawing. This makes it easier to place elements precisely and maintain proportion.

Color and labeling should be employed thoughtfully to enhance the interpretability of diagrams. Distinct colors can help differentiate components, while well-placed labels provide immediate context for readers. It is equally important to optimize line styles, thickness, and scaling so that figures look clean, professional, and consistent with the rest of the document.

By adhering to these guidelines, users can leverage the full power of `PSTricks` to create precise and visually compelling illustrations in their LaTeX documents.

2.2 Creating Diagrams with TikZ

LaTeX offers powerful tools for creating high-quality diagrams and plots directly within your document. Two of the most widely used packages for creating diagrams are **TikZ** and **PGFPlots**. These packages allow you to create everything from simple geometric shapes to complex plots and 3D surfaces. In this section, we will explore how to use both TikZ and PGFPlots to create a variety of diagrams.

2.2.1 Introduction to TikZ

TikZ is a powerful tool for creating high-quality diagrams, graphs, and illustrations in LaTeX. Unlike graphical user interfaces that rely on point-and-click interactions, TikZ enables users to define graphics using precise code. This approach ensures that all elements remain fully scalable, consistent, and easy to modify, making TikZ particularly valuable in scientific and technical documents.

To use TikZ, the package must be included in the document preamble:

Loading the TikZ Package

```
\usepackage{tikz}
```

Once the package is loaded, diagrams are created using the `tikzpicture` environment. Everything inside this environment follows a structured syntax for defining shapes, lines, and other graphical elements.

2.2.2 Drawing Basic Shapes with TikZ

TikZ allows for the creation of simple geometric shapes, such as lines, rectangles, and circles, using minimal code. Each element is placed within the coordinate system, where the origin $(0,0)$ represents the bottom-left corner by default.

The following example illustrates how to draw a straight line, a rectangle, and a circle.

Basic Shapes in TikZ

```
\begin{tikzpicture}
    \draw (0,0) -- (2,0);
    % Drawing a line

    \draw (3,0) rectangle (5,1);
    % Drawing a rectangle

    \draw (7,0.5) circle (1cm);
    % Drawing a circle
\end{tikzpicture}
```

The display is (Fig. 2.1):

Figure 2.1: Line, rectangle and circle

This simple illustration highlights three essential TikZ drawing commands:

- The command `\draw (0,0) -- (2,0);` creates a straight line from the coordinate $(0,0)$ to $(2,0)$.

- The command `\draw (3,0) rectangle (5,1);` defines a rectangle with its bottom-left corner at $(3, 0)$ and top-right corner at $(5, 1)$.

- The command `\draw (7,0.5) circle (1cm);` generates a circle centered at $(7, 0.5)$ with a radius of 1 cm.

2.2.3 Combining Shapes to Create More Complex Diagrams

Once the basic shapes are understood, they can be combined to construct more intricate diagrams. By strategically placing elements and modifying their sizes, TikZ can be used to design structured figures.

The following example demonstrates how to combine a rectangle, a circle, and a connecting line into a single diagram.

LaTeX Code:

```
\begin{tikzpicture}
\draw (0,0) rectangle (2,1);
% Rectangle
\draw (3,0.5) circle (0.5cm);
% Circle
\draw (2,0.5) -- (2.5,0.5);
% Connecting line
\end{tikzpicture}
```

Output:

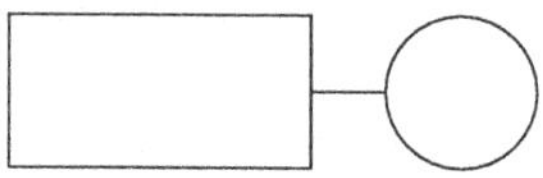

```
%
%\begin{tikzpicture}
%\draw (0,0) rectangle (2,1);  % Rectangle
%\draw (3,0.5) circle (0.5cm);  % Circle
%\draw (2,0.5) -- (2.5,0.5);
% Connecting line
%\end{tikzpicture}
%
```

This example introduces the concept of linking elements within a diagram. A rectangle and a circle are drawn separately, and a horizontal line is used to connect them. Such connections are fundamental when designing flowcharts, process diagrams, and network schematics.

2.2.4 Adjusting Position and Size of Shapes

TikZ allows for precise control over positioning by specifying coordinates and relative placements. The ability to scale shapes while maintaining proportions is particularly useful for structuring diagrams.

To adjust positioning, one can modify the coordinates in the drawing commands. Alternatively, shapes can be shifted relative to existing elements using the `shift` option.

The following example demonstrates how to position shapes dynamically while maintaining consistency in alignment.

LaTeX Code:

```
\begin{tikzpicture}
\draw (0,0) rectangle (2,1);
\draw [shift={(3,0.5)}]
 circle (0.5cm);
\draw (2,0.5) -- (2.5,0.5);
\end{tikzpicture}
```

Output:

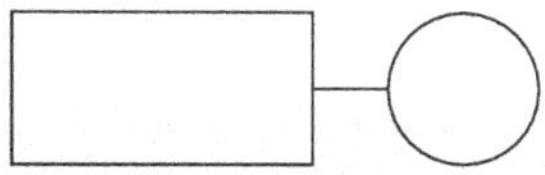

```
%
%\begin{tikzpicture}
%\draw (0,0) rectangle (2,1);
%\draw [shift={(3,0.5)}]
% circle (0.5cm);
%\draw (2,0.5) -- (2.5,0.5);
%\end{tikzpicture}
%
```

By using `shift={(3,0.5)}`, the circle is repositioned relative to its original coordinates. This approach simplifies diagram creation, especially when working with multiple interconnected elements.

2.2.5 Adding Colors and Styles in TikZ

Visual appeal is an important aspect of creating diagrams, and TikZ offers extensive customization options for adding colors, line styles, and fills. These features enhance the clarity of illustrations and make different components easily distinguishable.

TikZ provides a range of predefined colors such as `red`, `blue`, `green`, and `yellow`. In addition to these, custom colors can be defined using the `xcolor` package. Besides color, line thickness and stroke styles can be adjusted. For example, a line can be set to different thickness levels such as `thin`, `thick`, or `ultra thick`, while strokes can be modified to appear as dashed, dotted, or solid lines.

The example below demonstrates different ways to apply colors and styles. A red line, a thick dashed rectangle, and a filled circle with a blue border and yellow fill are drawn.

Applying Colors and Line Styles in TikZ

```
\begin{tikzpicture}
% Drawing a red line
\draw[red] (0,0) -- (2,0);
% Drawing a thick, dashed rectangle
\draw[thick, dashed] (3,0) rectangle (5,1);
% Drawing a filled circle with a blue border
\filldraw[fill=yellow, draw=blue] (7,0.5)
circle (1cm);
\end{tikzpicture}
```

The output of the above code is shown below (Fig. 2.2):

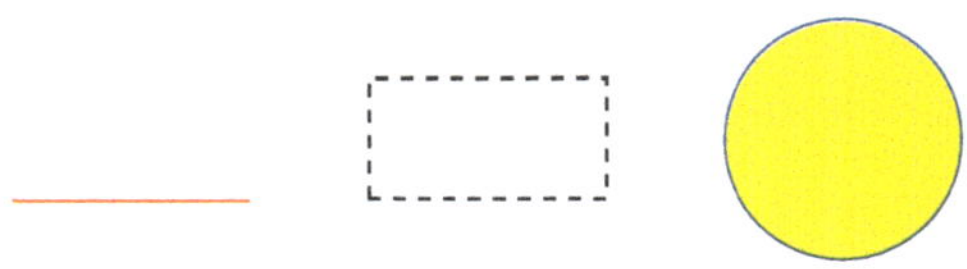

Figure 2.2: Line, rectangle, and circle with color and style

Custom colors can also be defined. The `xcolor` package allows users to create colors using RGB or CMYK values. For instance, defining a shade of orange is achieved with the following command:

Defining a Custom Color

```
\definecolor{myorange}{RGB}{255,165,0}
```

This newly defined color, `myorange`, can be used just like any predefined color within TikZ.

Besides color customization, line thickness and stroke styles also add variety to diagrams. The following example demonstrates solid, dotted, and dashed lines.

Custom Line Styles

```
\begin{tikzpicture}
    % Solid thick line
    \draw[thick] (0,0) -- (2,0);

    % Dotted line
    \draw[dotted] (3,0) -- (5,0);

    % Dashed line
    \draw[dashed] (6,0) -- (8,0);
\end{tikzpicture}
```

The output of the above code is (Fig. 2.3):

Figure 2.3: Different line styles in TikZ

Shapes in TikZ can also be filled with different colors. The `\fill` command allows filling a shape without a border, while `\filldraw` enables both filling and outlining. The following example demonstrates three shapes: a blue-filled rectangle, an ellipse with a green fill and black border, and a red circle without a border.

Filling Shapes with Custom Colors

```
\begin{tikzpicture}
    % Filled rectangle
    \fill[blue!40] (0,0) rectangle (2,1);

    % Filled ellipse with border
    \filldraw[fill=green!50, draw=black]
    (4,0.5) ellipse(1.5 and 0.7);

    % Filled circle with no border
    \fill[red!70] (7,0.5) circle (1cm);
\end{tikzpicture}
```

The output of the above code is (Fig. 2.4):

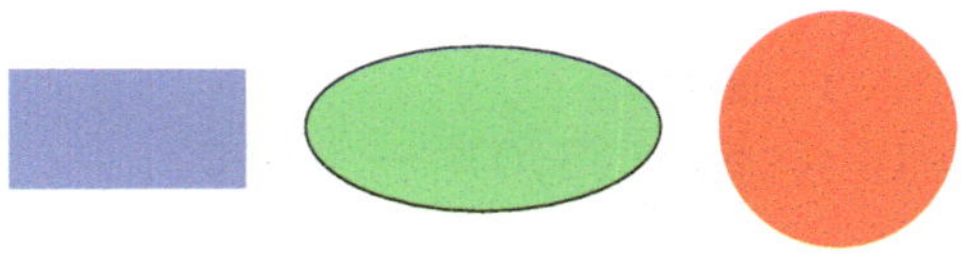

Figure 2.4: Filled shapes in TikZ

This example demonstrates how shapes can be visually customized. The rectangle has a blue fill at 40% opacity. The ellipse has a green fill at 50% opacity with a black outline. The red circle is filled at 70% opacity but has no border.

By incorporating colors and styles, diagrams in TikZ become more visually informative and appealing. Adjusting line thickness, fill opacity, and stroke styles enhances readability and ensures clarity in complex illustrations. The ability to use predefined colors, custom RGB values, and varying opacities makes TikZ a powerful tool for graphical representation in LaTeX.

The next sections will explore more advanced applications of TikZ, including structured diagrams, flowcharts, hierarchical trees, and mind maps.

2.3 Creating Advanced Diagrams with TikZ

In addition to drawing basic shapes and simple illustrations, TikZ can be used to create more complex and detailed diagrams. TikZ's strength lies in its ability to combine geometrical precision with flexibility, allowing users to create everything from flowcharts and trees to mind maps and circuit diagrams. In this subsection, we will explore some advanced features and techniques of TikZ.

2.3.1 Creating Flowcharts

Flowcharts are an essential tool for representing workflows, decision-making processes, and algorithms in a structured manner. TikZ provides a powerful way to create flowcharts by utilizing its `node` and `draw` commands to define elements such as process steps, decisions, and directional flows. The ability to customize shapes, arrows, and labels makes TikZ an excellent choice for producing professional-quality flowcharts.

A basic flowchart consists of different types of nodes: rectangular nodes representing standard processes, diamond-shaped nodes indicating decision points, and directional arrows that define the flow between elements. The `node` command is used to define these elements, while `draw` commands create the connecting lines and arrows.

The following example demonstrates how to construct a simple flowchart with a start node, a process node, a decision node, and an endpoint. The diagram illustrates a basic decision-making process where, based on a condition, the workflow either proceeds to the end or loops back to a previous step.

Basic Flowchart in TikZ

```
\begin{tikzpicture}[node distance=2cm]
% Define nodes
\node (start) [rectangle, draw] {Start};
node (process) [rectangle, draw,
below of=start] {Process};
\node (decision) [draw, diamond, aspect=2,
below of=process] {Decision};
\node (end) [rectangle, draw,
below of=decision] {End};

% Draw arrows
\draw[->] (start) -- (process);
\draw[->] (process) -- (decision);
\draw[->] (decision) -- node[right]
{Yes} (end);
\draw[->] (decision) -| node[above]
{No} (process.west);
\end{tikzpicture}
```

The generated output from this code is displayed below (Fig. 2.5):

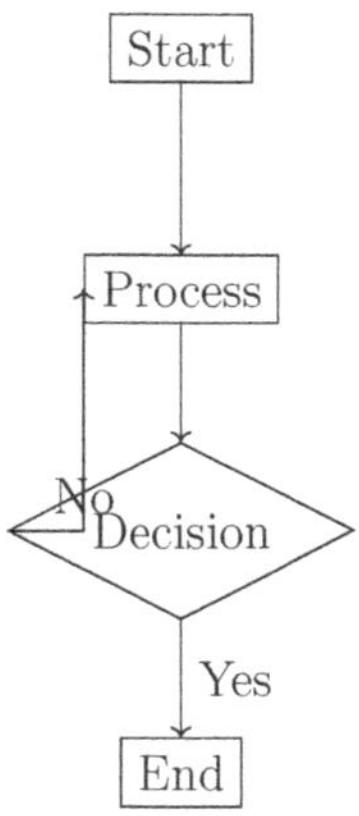

Figure 2.5: Basic flowchart

In this flowchart, the process begins at the "Start" node and moves downward to a process step. The decision node evaluates a condition, directing the flow either toward an "End" state if the condition is satisfied ("Yes") or looping back to the process node if the condition is not met ("No").

The `node` command defines each step in the flowchart, assigning specific shapes to distinguish between process steps and decision points. By default, nodes are spaced evenly using the `node distance` property, which in this case ensures a uniform 2 cm gap between each step. The `rectangle` option is applied to standard process steps, while `diamond, aspect=2` is used for the decision node, ensuring a proportionally wider diamond shape.

Arrows, created using the `\draw[->]` command, establish the connections between nodes. Labels are added along these arrows to indicate conditions such as "Yes" or "No," helping clarify the branching logic of the flowchart. The use of `-|` instead of a straight arrow in one of the connections allows the arrow to make a right-angle turn, visually reinforcing the loop back to the process step.

Flowcharts created in TikZ can be customized extensively. Users can modify line styles, adjust the spacing between elements, and incorporate colors to differentiate various steps. For example, coloring decision nodes differently from process nodes can help improve readability. Additionally, dashed lines can be used to indicate alternative paths or optional steps within the workflow.

By combining these fundamental TikZ features, flowcharts of varying complexity can be constructed, ranging from simple procedural representations to intricate multipath decision trees. The next section will explore how similar principles apply to the construction of hierarchical diagrams, such as mind maps and tree structures.

2.3.2 Creating Mind Maps

Mind maps provide a structured way to visually organize concepts and their relationships. They are particularly useful for brainstorming ideas, outlining topics, and demonstrating hierarchical structures. In LaTeX, the `TikZ` package, along with its **`mindmap`** library, enables the easy creation of visually appealing and well-structured mind maps. By defining a central concept and connecting it to various related subtopics, we can illustrate complex ideas in an intuitive manner.

To use the mind map functionality, we first load the necessary `mindmap` library within TikZ. The central concept is typically represented as a large node, with its branches extending outward to child nodes. These child nodes can have further subbranches, creating a hierarchical structure.

A basic example of a mind map is shown below. Here, "LaTeX" is placed as the central concept, with key-related topics such as "TikZ," "PGFPlots," "Beamer," and "BibTeX" branching out.

Basic Mind Map in TikZ

```
\begin{tikzpicture}
\mindmap[concept color=blue!40, text=white]
{\node [concept] {LaTeX}
child[concept color=green!60]
{ node {TikZ} }
child[concept color=red!60]
{ node {PGFPlots} }
child[concept color=orange!60]
{ node {Beamer} }
child[concept color=yellow!60]
```

```
{ node {BibTeX} };
;
\end{tikzpicture}
```

This mind map will generate a circular central node labeled "LaTeX," with four branches extending outward, each representing a key feature related to LaTeX (Fig. 2.6).

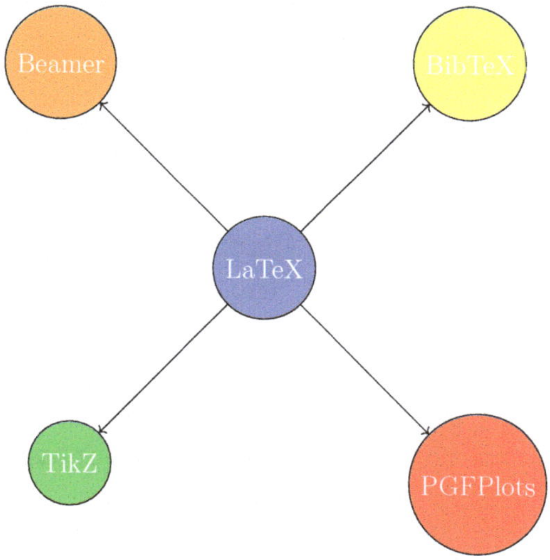

Figure 2.6: Basic mind map

Customizing Mind Maps Mind maps in TikZ are highly customizable. The `concept color` option allows each node to be colored uniquely, making it visually easier to distinguish different branches. Additionally, text within each node can be formatted using the `text` option to improve readability. The positioning of branches can also be adjusted, ensuring a balanced and aesthetically pleasing structure.

If we want to create a more detailed mind map with subcategories, we can extend the basic structure by adding subbranches. The following example demonstrates a hierarchical mind map where "LaTeX" has secondary branches, and each of those branches has further subdivisions.

Hierarchical Mind Map in TikZ

```
\begin{tikzpicture}
\mindmap[concept color=blue!40, text=white]{
    \node [concept] {LaTeX}
            child[concept color=green!60] {
                node {Document Preparation}
                child {node {Sections}}
                child {node {Tables}}
                child {node {Figures}}
            }
            child[concept color=red!60] {
                node {Mathematics}
                child {node {Equations}}
                child {node {Symbols}}
                child {node {Alignments}}
            }
            child[concept color=orange!60] {
                node {Graphics}
                child {node {TikZ}}
                child {node {PGFPlots}}
            }
            child[concept color=yellow!60] {
                node {Referencing}
                child {node {BibTeX}}
                child {node {Citations}}
            };
    };
\end{tikzpicture}
```

The hierarchical mind map extends the previous example by adding multiple levels of branches, demonstrating the interconnections between different LaTeX features (Fig. 2.7).

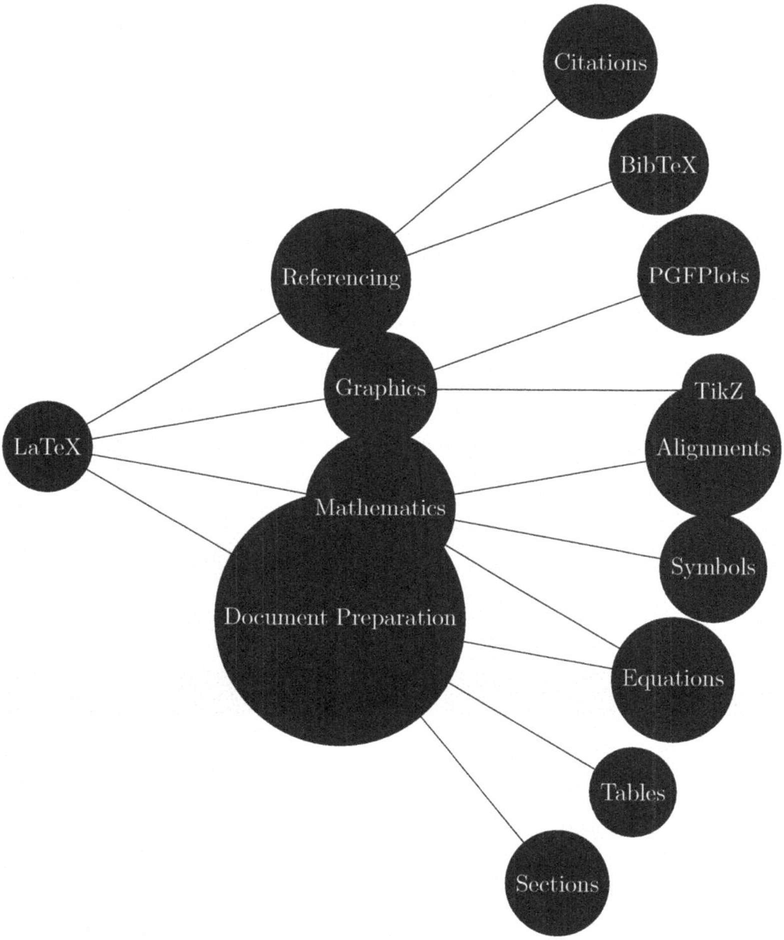

Figure 2.7: Hierarchical mind map

This example demonstrates how TikZ can be used to create detailed and well-structured mind maps. The ability to layer multiple levels of branches makes it a powerful tool for organizing complex information visually.

2.3.3 Drawing Trees

Tree diagrams play an essential role in representing hierarchical structures across different fields, such as computer science, decision analysis, and organizational planning. In LaTeX, tree diagrams can be created using either TikZ or the `forest` package. While TikZ provides a straightforward way to construct trees, the `forest` package offers extensive customization options and an intuitive syntax.

The simplest form of a tree consists of a root node with branches leading to child nodes. Using TikZ, trees can be constructed by defining a root node and attaching children through the `child` command. The following example illustrates a basic binary tree, where a central root node connects to two children.

Example: Basic Binary Tree

```
\begin{tikzpicture}
    \node {Root}
    child {node {Left}}
    child {node {Right}};
\end{tikzpicture}
```

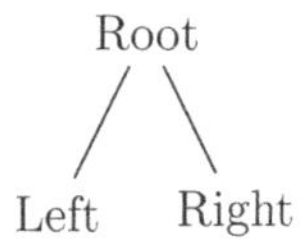

Figure 2.8: Simple binary tree

This tree consists of a root node labeled "Root," from which two branches extend to the nodes labeled "Left" and "Right." The layout is automatically structured by TikZ to maintain clarity and proper spacing between nodes (Fig. 2.8).

For more complex hierarchical structures, the `forest` package offers a more advanced approach. This package simplifies the process of defining trees by organizing nodes within a bracketed structure. To use the package, it must first be included in the document preamble with the command:

```
\usepackage{forest}
```

The syntax of the `forest` environment follows a nested format, where each level of the hierarchy is enclosed within brackets. The next example demonstrates a multilevel tree, where each node branches out to additional sub-nodes.

Example: Multilevel Tree

```
\begin{forest}
  [Root
    [Left Child
      [Left Subchild]
      [Right Subchild]
    ]
    [Right Child
      [Left Subchild]
      [Right Subchild]
    ]
  ]
\end{forest}
```

This tree extends the binary structure by adding another level, where each child node branches further into two sub-nodes. The result is a well-structured hierarchy with uniform spacing (Fig. 2.9).

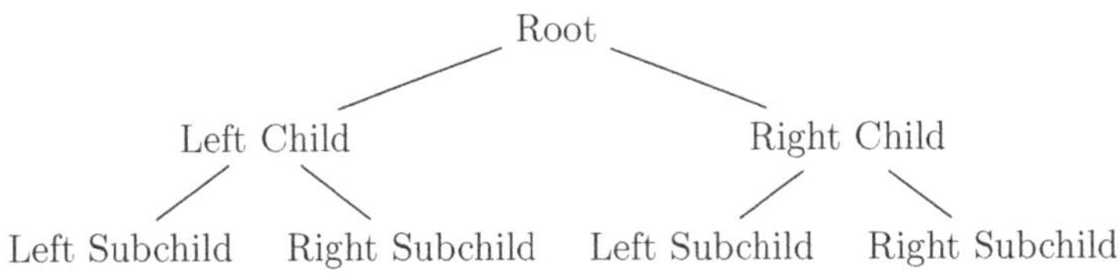

Figure 2.9: Multilevel tree

Customization plays a significant role in enhancing tree diagrams, especially when visual clarity is required. The `forest` package supports various styling options, including node shapes, colors, and edge formatting. In the following example, nodes are customized with circular shapes and filled with different colors. The tree structure is arranged horizontally instead of vertically, and directed arrows are used to connect the nodes.

Example: Styled Tree with Colors

```
\begin{forest}
  for tree={
    grow=east,
    draw,
    circle,
    minimum size=1.5em,
    edge={thick, ->},
    l sep+=10pt,
    s sep+=10pt,
  }
  [A
    [B, fill=red
      [D]
      [E]
    ]
    [C, fill=blue
      [F]
      [G]
```

```
    ]
  ]
\end{forest}
```

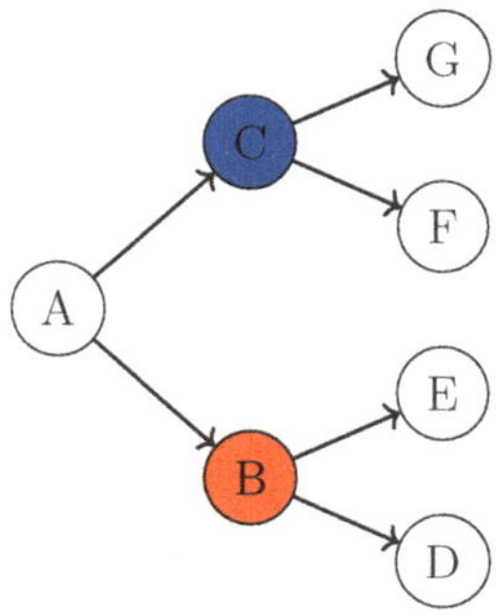

Figure 2.10: Styled tree with colors

In this example, the tree grows horizontally rather than vertically, which can be useful for certain types of visualizations. Each node is circular and filled with a distinct color. The edges are thicker, and arrows indicate directionality, making the relationships between elements more explicit (Fig. 2.10).

Another important aspect of tree diagrams is the ability to label edges. In cases where connections between nodes need to be annotated, edge labels provide additional clarity. The next example demonstrates a tree where each edge carries a descriptive label.

Example: Tree with Edge Labels

```
\begin{forest}
  for tree={
    draw,
    l sep+=10pt,
    s sep+=10pt,
  }
  [Parent
```

```
    [Child 1, edge label={node[midway, left]
    {Edge 1}}]
    [Child 2, edge label={node[midway, right]
    {Edge 2}}]
    [Child 3, edge label={node[midway, above]
    {Edge 3}}]
  ]
\end{forest}
```

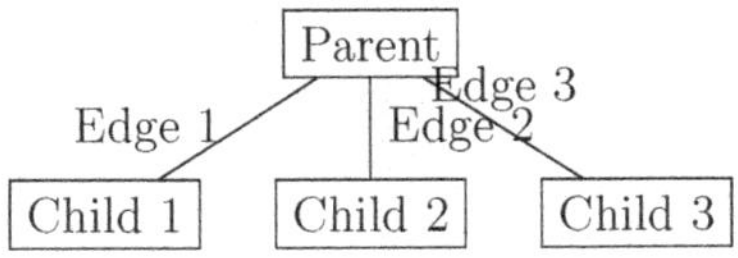

Figure 2.11: Tree with edge labels

The tree consists of a "Parent" node connected to three children. Each edge is labeled midway along its length, describing the relationship between the nodes. The positioning of labels can be adjusted to ensure readability, depending on the complexity of the tree (Fig. 2.11).

Tree diagrams in LaTeX offer a structured and flexible way to represent hierarchical relationships. TikZ provides a simple approach for basic structures, while the `forest` package extends functionality by enabling intuitive customization. Whether representing binary trees, decision trees, or more intricate hierarchical structures, these tools provide a versatile framework for creating professional -quality diagrams.

Customizing the Layout The `forest` package provides many options for customizing the layout of trees:

- **Node Shape**: Use `circle`, `rectangle`, or other shapes.
- **Edge Style**: Add arrows (`->`), change thickness (`thick`), or use dashed edges (`dashed`).

- **Separation**: Control sibling and level separation using `l sep` and `s sep`.
- **Colors**: Use `fill=<color>` for node backgrounds and `edge color=<color>` for edges.

Remark 2.3.1 *The* `forest` *package is highly versatile and supports several advanced features that are particularly useful for creating complex diagrams. One of its key strengths is the ability to construct nested trees, which allows users to represent deeply layered or hierarchical structures with ease. Additionally,* `forest` *integrates seamlessly with TikZ, enabling users to customize nodes and edges with the full power of TikZ's styling and drawing capabilities. Another useful feature is the support for anchors and labels, which makes it possible to annotate specific parts of a diagram for reference, explanation, or interaction with other TikZ elements.*

2.4 Drawing Circuit Diagrams

Electronic circuit diagrams are essential in electrical and electronics engineering, illustrating circuit functionality with clarity and precision. Instead of using external software, LaTeX provides a built-in way to create circuit diagrams using the `circuitikz` package. This package supports standard electrical symbols, such as resistors, capacitors, inductors, diodes, voltage sources, and operational amplifiers. The ability to produce scalable, high-quality circuit diagrams directly in LaTeX makes `circuitikz` a valuable tool for researchers, engineers, and students.

2.4.1 Setting Up TikZ and circuitikz

To use `circuitikz`, the package must be included in the document preamble as follows:

```
\usepackage{circuitikz}
```

Once loaded, circuit diagrams can be drawn within the `circuitikz` environment. The basic syntax for connecting components follows a straightforward pattern:

```
\begin{circuitikz}
    \draw (0,0) to[component] (3,0);
\end{circuitikz}
```

This notation defines a circuit component between two points, ensuring automatic alignment.

2.4.2 Basic Circuit Components

Circuit diagrams consist of various standard components, each with a corresponding representation in `circuitikz`.

Resistors, Capacitors, and Inductors

Resistors can be drawn in either American or European notation, as shown in the following example (Fig. 2.12):

Example: Resistors in Different Notations

```
\begin{circuitikz}
    \draw (0,0) to[american, R=$R_1$] (3,0);
    \draw (4,0) to[european, R=$R_2$] (7,0);
\end{circuitikz}
```

Figure 2.12: Resistors in American and European notation

Capacitors and inductors follow a similar approach (Fig. 2.13):

Example: Standard and Polar Capacitors

```
\begin{circuitikz}
    \draw (0,0) to[C=$C_1$] (3,0);
    \draw (4,0) to[C, polar, l=$C_2$] (7,0);
\end{circuitikz}
```

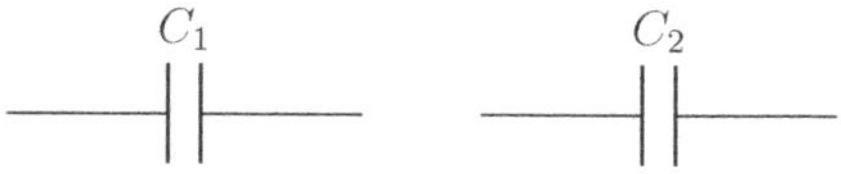

Figure 2.13: Standard and polar capacitors

Voltage and Current Sources

Sources provide the required power in circuits. The following example demonstrates how to include independent and sinusoidal voltage sources in a circuit (Fig. 2.14):

Example: Voltage and Current Sources

```
\begin{circuitikz}
    \draw (0,0) to[V, l=$V_s$] (3,0);
    \draw (4,0) to[sV, l=$V_{sin}$] (7,0);
\end{circuitikz}
```

Figure 2.14: Voltage sources (independent and sinusoidal)

Diodes, LEDs, and Zener Diodes

Diodes are crucial components in circuits, ensuring unidirectional current flow. Various types of diodes, including standard, Zener, and LEDs, can be incorporated (Fig. 2.15).

Example: Diodes, Zener Diodes, and LEDs

```
\begin{circuitikz}
    \draw (0,0) to[Do] (3,0);
    \draw (4,0) to[Do, zener] (7,0);
    \draw (0,-2) to[leD, l=LED] (3,-2);
\end{circuitikz}
```

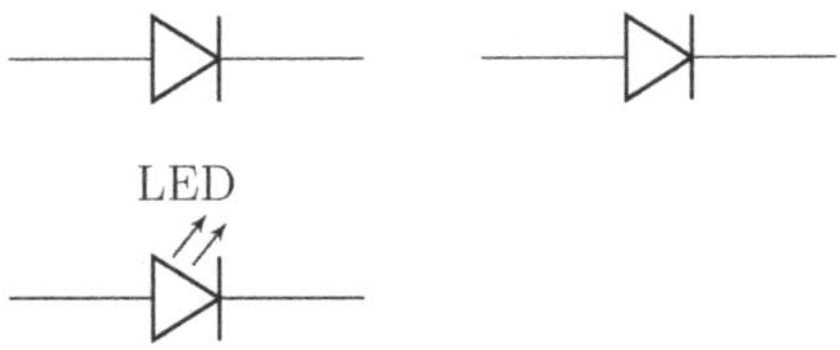

Figure 2.15: Different types of diodes

Switches

Switches control circuit connections and can be open or closed (Fig. 2.16).

Example: Open and Closed Switches

```
\begin{circuitikz}
    \draw (0,0) to[switch] (3,0);
    \draw (4,0) to[switch, o-o] (7,0);
\end{circuitikz}
```

Figure 2.16: Open and closed switches

2.4.3 Building a Complete Circuit: RC Circuit and Op-Amp Circuit

A basic RC circuit consists of a voltage source, resistor, and capacitor connected in series (Fig. 2.17).

Example: A Simple RC Circuit with Two Resistors

```
\begin{circuitikz}
    \draw
    (0,0) to[battery] (0,2)
    to[resistor, l=$R_1$] (2,2)
    to[resistor, l=$R_2$] (4,2)
    -- (4,0) -- (0,0);
\end{circuitikz}
```

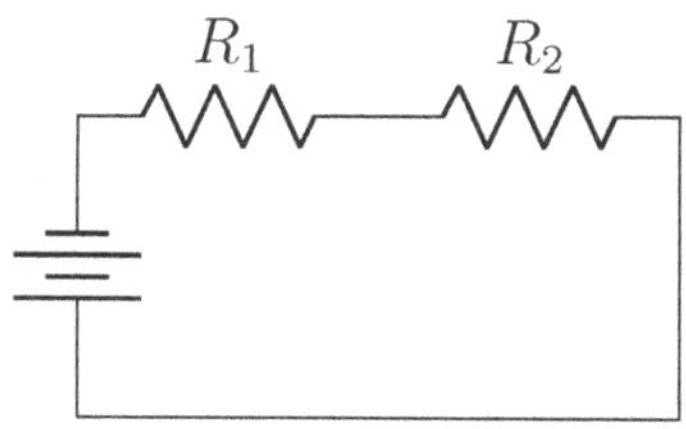

Example: A Simple RC Circuit with a Resistor, Capacitor, and Voltage

```
\begin{circuitikz}
    \draw (0,0) to[V, l=$V_s$] (0,3)
          to[R, l=$R$] (3,3)
          to[C, l=$C$] (3,0)
          -- (0,0);
\end{circuitikz}
```

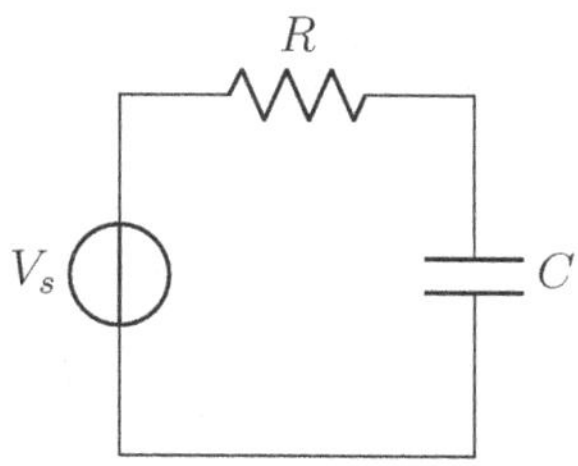

Figure 2.17: A simple RC circuit

The following code demonstrates how to draw an operational amplifier (op-amp) circuit with labeled input and output terminals:

Example: Op-amp Circuit Diagram Capacitor and Voltage

```
\begin{circuitikz}
% Draw op-amp
\draw (0,0) node[op amp] (opamp) {};
\draw (opamp.+) -- ++(-1,0) node[left]{$V_+$};
% Non-inverting input
\draw (opamp.-) -- ++(-1,0) node[left]{$V_-$};
% Inverting input
\draw (opamp.out) -- ++(1,0) node[right]
{$V_\text{out}$};
% Output

% Connect power
\draw (opamp.up) -- ++(0,0.5) node[above]
{$+V_\text{cc}$};
\draw (opamp.down) -- ++(0,-0.5) node[below]
{$-V_\text{ee}$};
\end{circuitikz}
```

This produces an op-amp circuit diagram as shown in Fig. 2.18.

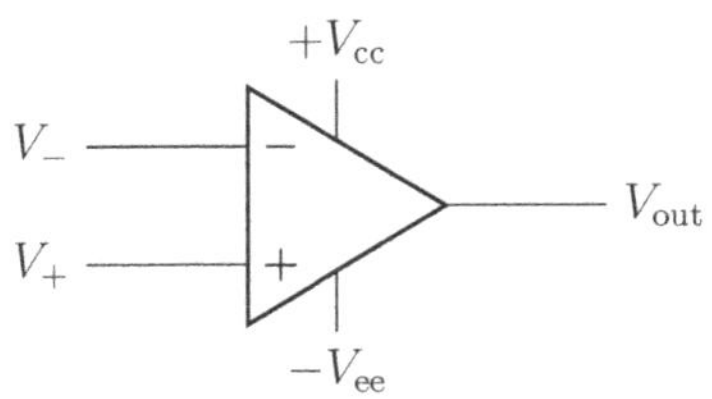

Figure 2.18: An operational amplifier circuit diagram

2.4.4 Plotting Graphs

Mathematical graphs are an essential tool for visualizing relationships between objects. Whether representing networks, dependency structures, or directed flows, graphs help convey connections in a structured manner. In LaTeX, TikZ provides an intuitive way to create graphs, and the `graphs` library simplifies their construction.

To get started, include the following package in the document preamble:

```
\usetikzlibrary{graphs}
```

With this library, graphs can be described in a compact format while allowing customization of node shapes, edges, and labels.

Creating a Simple Directed Graph

A directed graph consists of nodes connected by arrows, indicating a one-way relationship between elements. Consider a scenario where node A connects to both B and C, while B further connects to C. The following example demonstrates how to define such a structure.

Example: A Simple Directed Graph

```
\begin{tikzpicture}
\graph [nodes={circle, draw}, edges={->}] {
        A -> B -> C,
        A -> C
    };
\end{tikzpicture}
```

This diagram consists of three nodes, arranged in a structure where: Node A points to both B and C. Node B points to C, reinforcing the hierarchical flow.

The graph is defined using the `graph` command. The `nodes` option ensures all nodes are styled as circles with drawn borders. The `edges` setting applies an arrow (`->`) to all connections, making the graph directed.

Creating an Undirected Graph

Unlike directed graphs, an undirected graph represents mutual relationships between nodes, where connections have no specific direction. Consider a three-node structure where all nodes are interconnected without arrows.

Example: An Undirected Graph

```
\begin{tikzpicture}
\graph [nodes={circle, draw}, edges={-}] {
        A -- B -- C -- A
    };
\end{tikzpicture}
```

Here, the edges are represented using `--`, indicating bidirectional relationships. The absence of arrows makes it clear that each connection is symmetric.

Adding Edge Labels

To enhance the readability of graphs, labels can be added to edges, indicating weights or dependencies. Suppose the previous directed graph represents a workflow where transitions have different priorities or costs. Labels can be included using the `node[midway]` option.

Example: A Weighted Graph with Edge Labels

```
\begin{tikzpicture}
\graph [nodes={circle, draw}, edges={->}] {
        A ->["5"] B ->["3"] C,
        A ->["7"] C
    };
```

```
\end{tikzpicture}
```

Each arrow now carries a numerical label that describes the cost or weight associated with the transition. For instance:

- The edge from A to B has a weight of 5.
- The edge from B to C has a weight of 3.
- The direct connection from A to C has a weight of 7.

Customizing Node Positions

By default, TikZ arranges nodes automatically, but layouts can be customized manually. The following example positions nodes explicitly, ensuring clear alignment.

Example: Manually Positioned Graph

```
\begin{tikzpicture}
    \node (A) [draw, circle] at (0,0) {A};
    \node (B) [draw, circle] at (2,1) {B};
    \node (C) [draw, circle] at (4,0) {C};

    \draw[->] (A) -- (B);
    \draw[->] (B) -- (C);
    \draw[->] (A) to[out=20, in=160] (C);
\end{tikzpicture}
```

The output is (Fig. 2.19):

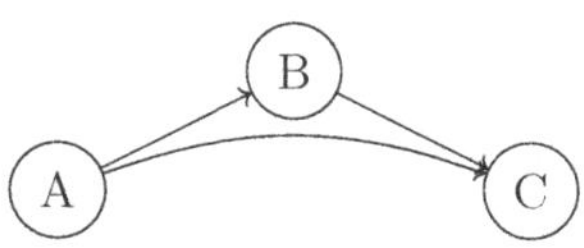

Figure 2.19: A manually positioned graph

This technique ensures precise node placement by defining positions manually, rather than relying on automatic layouts.

2.4.5 Venn Diagrams

Venn diagrams are widely used in mathematics, particularly in set theory and probability, to illustrate relationships between different sets. They visually represent intersections, unions, and differences between groups, making them an effective tool for understanding logical relationships.

Using LaTeX, Venn diagrams can be created efficiently with the TikZ package. Circles represent sets, and their overlapping regions depict common elements between those sets. Labels are used to distinguish each set and its intersection.

Creating a Basic Two-Set Venn Diagram

A simple Venn diagram consists of two overlapping circles, each representing a set. The overlapping region signifies the intersection of the two sets.

Example: A Basic Two-Set Venn Diagram

```
\begin{tikzpicture}
    \draw (0,0) circle (1.5cm);  % Set A
    \draw (2,0) circle (1.5cm);  % Set B
    \node at (-1,0.5) {A};  % Label for Set A
    \node at (3,0.5) {B};   % Label for Set B
    \node at (1,0) {A $\cap$ B};
    % Label for Intersection
\end{tikzpicture}
```

The output of the above code produces the following Fig. 2.20:

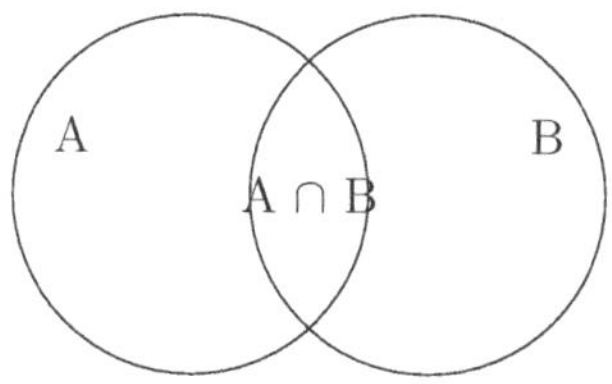

Figure 2.20: Basic two-set Venn diagram

This diagram consists of two circles, representing Set A and Set B. The overlapping region represents their intersection $A \cap B$. Labels are added to indicate the individual sets and the overlapping section.

Adding Colors to Different Regions

To make Venn diagrams more visually appealing and easier to interpret, colors can be added to different regions. The following example demonstrates how to shade different parts of the diagram using the `fill` option.

Example: A Colored Venn Diagram

```
\begin{tikzpicture}
    \begin{scope}
        \clip (0,0) circle (1.5cm);
        \fill[red!40] (2,0) circle (1.5cm);
    \end{scope}
\draw (0,0) circle (1.5cm) node[left] {A};
% Set A
\draw (2,0) circle (1.5cm) node[right] {B};
% Set B
\end{tikzpicture}
```

This code generates the following output (Fig. 2.21):

In this case, the overlapping region is shaded red, highlighting the intersection of Set A and Set B. This is achieved using the `clip` command, which restricts the filled region to the area of intersection.

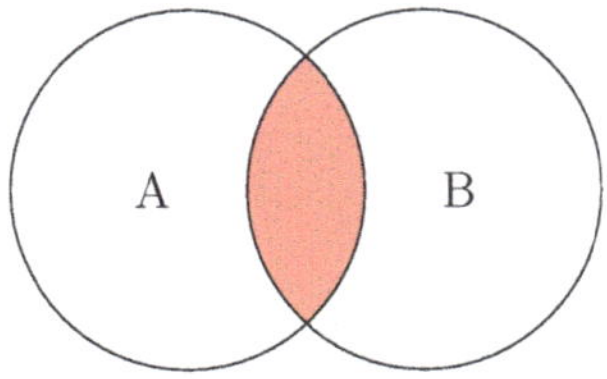

Figure 2.21: A colored Venn diagram

Extending to Three-Set Venn Diagrams

A three-set Venn diagram extends this concept by introducing a third set, C, represented by an additional overlapping circle. The following example shows how three sets interact.

Example: A Three-Set Venn Diagram

```
\begin{tikzpicture}
% Filling regions with different colors
\begin{scope}
    \clip (0,0) circle (1.5cm);
    \fill[red!30] (1.5,0.8) circle (1.5cm);
\end{scope}
\begin{scope}
    \clip (3,0) circle (1.5cm);
    \fill[blue!30] (1.5,0.8) circle (1.5cm);
\end{scope}
\begin{scope}
    \clip (1.5,0.8) circle (1.5cm);
    \fill[green!30] (0,0) circle (1.5cm);
\end{scope}

% Drawing circles
\draw (0,0) circle (1.5cm) node[left] {A};
\draw (3,0) circle (1.5cm) node[right] {B};
\draw (1.5,0.8) circle (1.5cm)
```

```
node[above] {C};
\end{tikzpicture}
```

The output is shown below (Fig. 2.22):

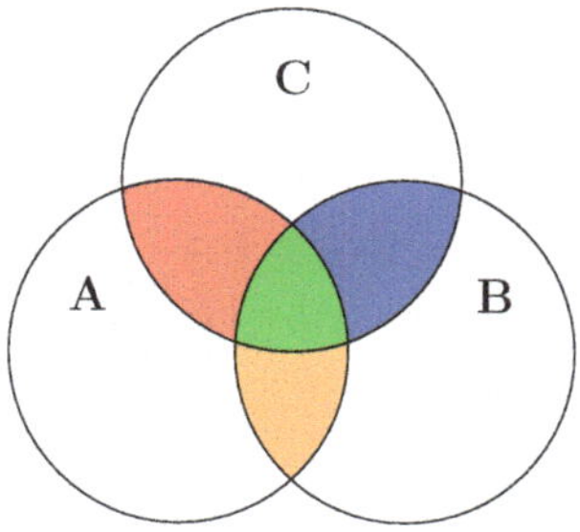

Figure 2.22: Three-set Venn diagram

Here, each set is represented by a circle, and the overlapping areas are shaded to highlight different intersections:

- **Red** represents the overlap of Sets A and Set C.
- **Blue** represents the overlap of Set B and Set C.
- **Orange** represents the overlap of Set A and Set B.
- **Green** represents the overlap of Set A, B and Set C.

2.5 Plotting with PGFPlots (2D and 3D)

Mathematical plotting and data visualization are essential in scientific and technical documents. `PGFPlots` is a powerful package in LaTeX that allows users to create high-quality 2D and 3D plots with fine control over axes, labels, colors, and styles. Built on top of `TikZ`, PGFPlots simplifies the process of generating professional-looking graphs directly in LaTeX without needing external software.

To begin using PGFPlots, the package must be loaded in the document preamble:

Loading PGFPlots

```
\usepackage{pgfplots}
```

Once the package is loaded, the `axis` environment serves as the main framework for defining plots. Within this environment, different plotting styles, axis labels, titles, and various options can be specified.

2.5.1 Basic Plotting with PGFPlots

A simple example of plotting a set of discrete points is shown below. This illustrates how to create a straightforward 2D plot using coordinate pairs.

Example: Simple 2D Plot

LaTeX Code:

```
\begin{tikzpicture}
    \begin{axis}[
        xlabel={$x$-axis}, ylabel={$y$-axis},
        title={Simple Plot of Discrete Data}
    ]
    \addplot coordinates {(0,0) (1,1) (2,4)
    (3,9)};
    \end{axis}
\end{tikzpicture}
```

The output of the above code is (Fig. 2.23):

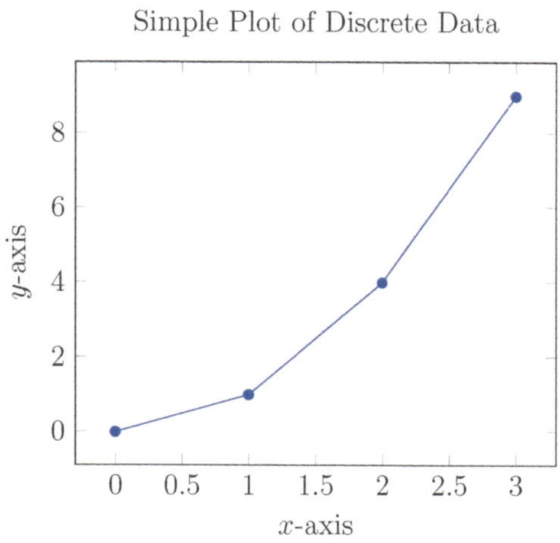

Figure 2.23: A simple 2D plot

This example demonstrates how PGFPlots works. The `axis` environment defines the plotting area, while the `xlabel` and `ylabel` options label the axes. The `title` command adds a heading above the plot. The actual data points are plotted using the `\addplot` command, which connects them with a default line style.

If only individual points are required without connecting lines, the plotting style can be modified:

Example: Scatter Plot

LaTeX Code:

```
\begin{tikzpicture}
    \begin{axis}[
        xlabel={$x$}, ylabel={$y$},
        title={Scatter Plot of Discrete Data}
    ]
    \addplot[only marks] coordinates {(0,0)
    (1,1) (2,4) (3,9)};
    \end{axis}
```

```
\end{tikzpicture}
```

The resulting plot is (Fig. 2.24):

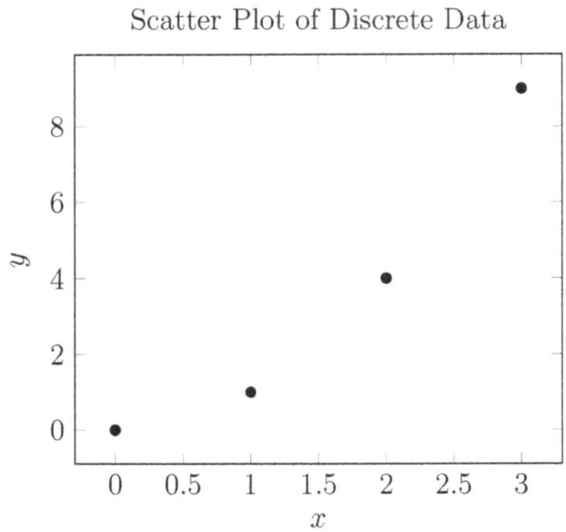

Figure 2.24: Scatter plot of discrete data

Here, the `only marks` option ensures that only points are displayed without connecting lines. This is particularly useful for visualizing experimental data points where continuous connections might not be meaningful.

2.5.2 Plotting a Continuous Function

Instead of plotting discrete points, PGFPlots also allows users to graph continuous functions. Rather than specifying individual coordinate pairs, the function can be provided directly.

Example: Plotting a Function

LaTeX Code:

```
\begin{tikzpicture}
    \begin{axis}[
```

```
        xlabel={$x$}, ylabel={$y$},
        title={Plot of $y = x^2$}
    ]
    \addplot[domain=-2:2, samples=100, thick,
    red] {x^2};
    \end{axis}
\end{tikzpicture}
```

The output of this code is (Fig. 2.25):

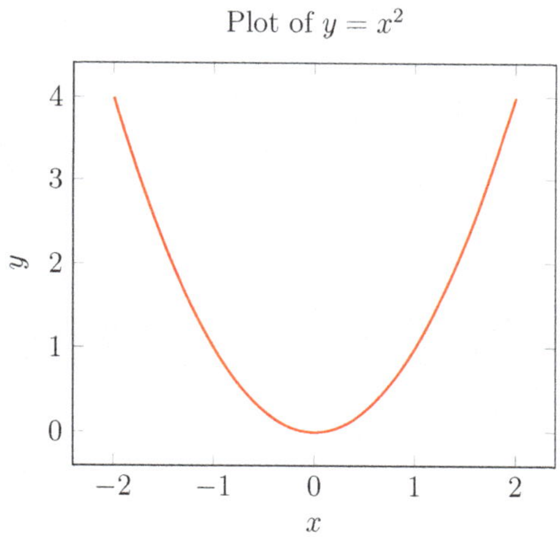

Figure 2.25: Plot of the quadratic function $y = x^2$

This example shows how PGFPlots can generate function graphs dynamically. Instead of manually providing data points, the function $y = x^2$ is plotted over the domain $[-2, 2]$. The `samples=100` argument ensures a smooth curve by evaluating the function at 100 points between -2 and 2. The `thick` option increases the line width for better visibility, while the `red` color makes the graph more distinct.

PGFPlots is widely used in mathematics, engineering, and physics for data visualization and function plotting. While this section introduced simple 2D plotting, PGFPlots supports advanced features such as 3D surface plots, logarithmic axes, multiple plots on the same graph, and various data interpolation techniques.

2.5.3 Plotting Functions with PGFPlots

Beyond plotting discrete data points, PGFPlots provides the ability to visualize continuous mathematical functions with ease. This capability makes it particularly useful for representing trigonometric, polynomial, and other analytic functions directly within a LaTeX document. By specifying a function formula instead of discrete coordinates, PGFPlots automatically computes and renders smooth curves.

One of the most commonly plotted functions is the sine function, which oscillates between -1 and 1 periodically. The following example demonstrates how to plot the function $y = \sin(x)$ over a default domain.

Example: Plotting the Sine Function

LaTeX Code:

```
\begin{tikzpicture}
    \begin{axis}[
        xlabel={$x$}, ylabel={$\sin(x)$},
        title={Plot of the Sine Function}
    ]
    \addplot {sin(deg(x))};
    \end{axis}
\end{tikzpicture}
```

The output of this code is (Fig. 2.26):

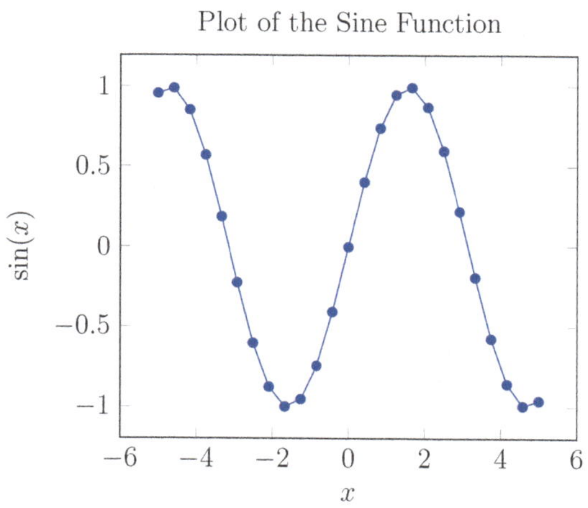

Figure 2.26: Graph of the sine function

This example illustrates how PGFPlots automatically computes function values and plots them as a smooth curve. The `addplot` command specifies the function to be plotted, where `sin(deg(x))` ensures that the sine function is evaluated in degrees rather than radians, as PGFPlots assumes radian input by default.

While the above plot provides a simple visualization of $\sin(x)$, the domain and appearance of the graph can be customized further. Consider a modified version that restricts the domain to $[-2\pi, 2\pi]$ and includes additional features such as grid lines and color styling.

Example: Customizing the Sine Function Plot

LaTeX Code:

```
\begin{tikzpicture}
\begin{axis}[
domain=-6.28:6.28, samples=100,
grid=both, xlabel={$x$}, ylabel={$\sin(x)$},
title={Sine Function Over $[-2\pi, 2\pi]$},
xtick={-6.28, -3.14, 0, 3.14, 6.28},
```

```
xticklabels={$-2\pi$, $-\pi$, $0$, $\pi$,
$2\pi$}
]
\addplot[thick, red] {sin(deg(x))};
\end{axis}
\end{tikzpicture}
```

The output of this code is (Fig. 2.27):

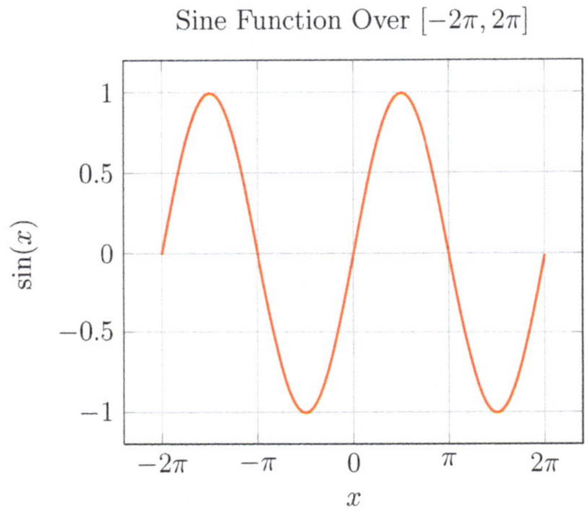

Figure 2.27: Customized sine function plot

In this improved version, several enhancements are applied:

- The domain is explicitly defined as $[-2\pi, 2\pi]$, ensuring that the graph extends symmetrically on both sides of the origin.
- The `samples=100` option increases the number of computed points, resulting in a smoother curve.
- A grid is added for better readability.
- The x-axis tick labels are manually set to multiples of π, making the graph more mathematically interpretable.

- The sine curve is displayed in red with increased thickness for better visibility.

Plotting Multiple Functions on the Same Graph

PGFPlots allows the visualization of multiple functions simultaneously by using multiple `addplot` commands. For example, the following plot compares the sine and cosine functions on the same set of axes.

Example: Plotting Sine and Cosine Together

LaTeX Code:

```
\begin{tikzpicture}
\begin{axis}[
domain=-6.28:6.28, samples=100,
grid=both, xlabel={$x$}, ylabel={$y$},
title={Comparison of $\sin(x)$ and $\cos(x)$},
legend pos=north east,
xtick={-6.28, -3.14, 0, 3.14, 6.28},
xticklabels={$-2\pi$, $-\pi$, $0$, $\pi$,
$2\pi$}
]
\addplot[blue, thick] {sin(deg(x))};
\addlegendentry{$\sin(x)$};
\addplot[green, dashed, thick] {cos(deg(x))};
\addlegendentry{$\cos(x)$};
\end{axis}
\end{tikzpicture}
```

The output of this code is (Fig. 2.28):

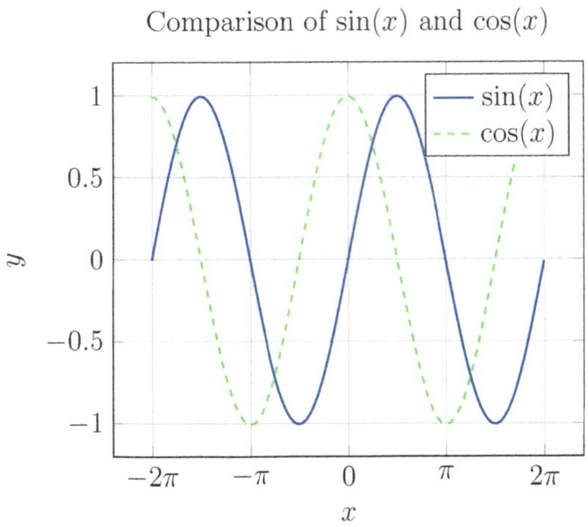

Figure 2.28: Comparison of sine and cosine functions

This example plots both the sine and cosine functions, highlighting their periodic relationship. The sine curve appears in solid blue, while the cosine function is represented by a green dashed line. The legend ensures that both functions are properly identified.

These examples demonstrate how PGFPlots can be used to visualize mathematical functions with high precision and flexibility. In the next sections, we will explore how to extend these techniques to 3D plotting and further customization options.

2.5.4 Creating 3D Plots with PGFPlots

Beyond 2D plotting, PGFPlots is capable of generating 3D plots, making it a powerful tool for visualizing three-dimensional surfaces, parametric functions, and data sets. This capability is particularly useful for illustrating mathematical concepts in calculus, geometry, and physics.

A basic 3D plot in PGFPlots is created using the `axis` environment with the `addplot3` command. The additional `surf` key enables surface plotting, allowing functions of two variables to be visualized in three dimensions.

The following example illustrates how to plot the function $z = x^2 + y^2$, which represents a simple parabolic surface.

Example: Plotting a 3D Surface

LaTeX Code:

```
\begin{tikzpicture}
    \begin{axis}[
        view={60}{30},
        % Sets the viewing angle
        xlabel={$x$}, ylabel={$y$},
        zlabel={$z$},
        title={3D Surface Plot of
        $z = x^2 + y^2$}
    ]
    \addplot3[surf] {x^2 + y^2};
    \end{axis}
\end{tikzpicture}
```

The corresponding output is (Fig. 2.29):

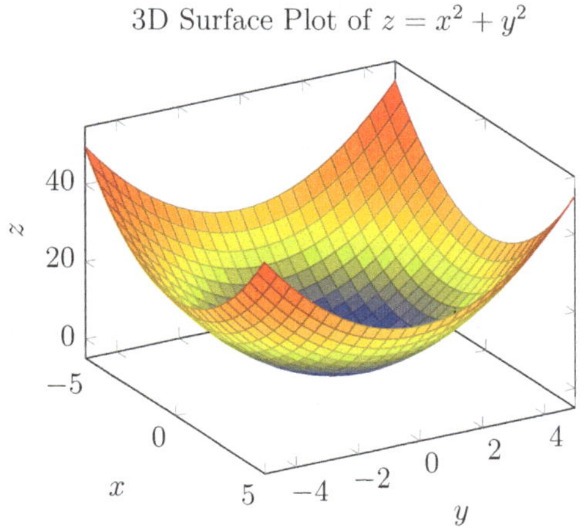

Figure 2.29: 3D surface plot of $z = x^2 + y^2$

This visualization presents a parabolic surface where the height z increases as x and y move further from the origin. The `view` option specifies the viewing angle, with 60° for elevation and 30° for rotation, ensuring a well-balanced perspective.

While the above example demonstrates a basic surface plot, PGFPlots also allows for more refined control over plot resolution, colors, and contour representation. The next example improves the visualization by defining a finer mesh grid and using a color gradient to enhance depth perception.

Example: Refining the 3D Surface Plot

LaTeX Code:

```
\begin{tikzpicture}
\begin{axis}[
view={60}{30}, % Viewing angle
colormap/viridis , % Color gradient
domain=-2:2, y domain=-2:2,
% Defines the domain of x and y
samples=30, % Increases resolution
xlabel={$x$}, ylabel={$y$}, zlabel={$z$},
title={Enhanced 3D Plot of
$z = x^2 + y^2$}
]
\addplot3[surf] {x^2 + y^2};
\end{axis}
\end{tikzpicture}
```

The refined plot is displayed below (Fig. 2.30):

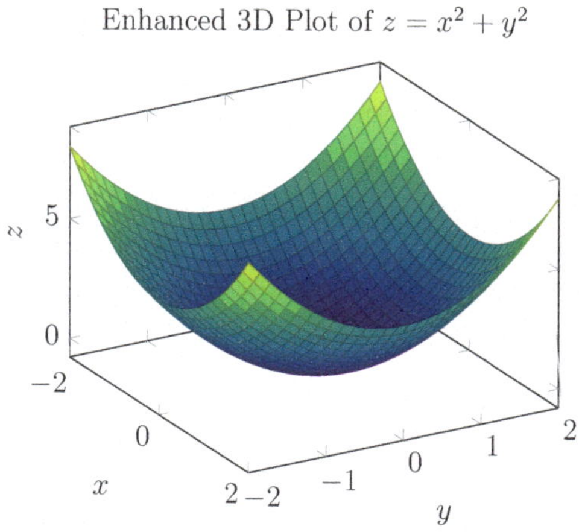

Figure 2.30: Refined 3D surface plot with enhanced resolution

The key improvements in this version include a higher number of samples, which results in a smoother surface, and the use of the `colormap/viridis` option to apply a visually appealing gradient.

PGFPlots supports a variety of surface styles beyond simple mesh-based rendering. Contour lines, wireframe models, and transparent surfaces can also be incorporated to better represent three-dimensional structures.

For cases where a function is not defined explicitly but data points are available, PGFPlots can interpolate and visualize scattered data in three dimensions. This makes it a useful tool for applications in engineering, data science, and computational simulations.

With these techniques, PGFPlots provides an efficient and elegant way to visualize complex mathematical surfaces, allowing for precise customization of graphical representations.

2.5.5 Customizing Plots in PGFPlots

PGFPlots allows extensive customization of plots, making it a versatile tool for producing professional-quality visualizations. Adjusting colors, grid lines, markers, and line styles enhances the readability and effectiveness of a plot. This section explores some common customization techniques with examples.

One of the simplest ways to modify a plot is by changing the color of the plotted function. PGFPlots supports a range of predefined colors and allows custom-defined colors. The following example illustrates how to plot the function $y = x^2$ using a red curve.

Example: Changing Line Color

LaTeX Code:

```
\begin{tikzpicture}
\begin{axis}[
xlabel={$x$}, ylabel={$y$},
title={Plot of $y = x^2$ with Red Line}
]
\addplot[red] {x^2};
\end{axis}
\end{tikzpicture}
```

The corresponding output is (Fig. 2.31):

The `red` argument within `\addplot` modifies the function's color. Other colors, such as `blue`, `green`, and `cyan`, can also be used. PGFPlots allows defining custom RGB colors if predefined ones are insufficient.

Another useful feature is adding grid lines to improve readability, especially when interpreting values from a plot. The following example includes major grid lines by enabling the `grid=major` option in the axis settings.

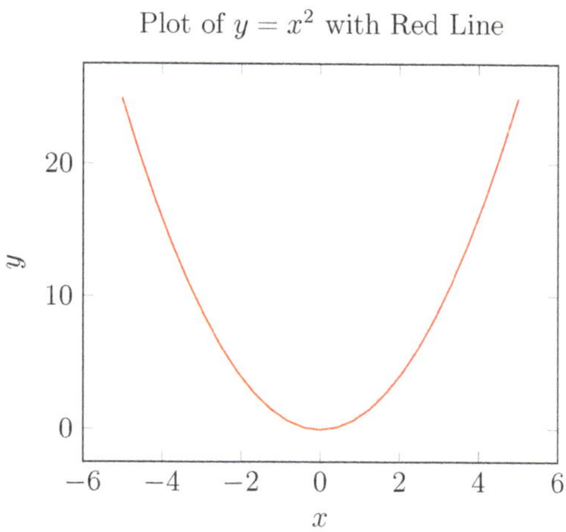

Figure 2.31: Changing line color in a plot

Example: Adding Grid Lines

LaTeX Code:

```
\begin{tikzpicture}
    \begin{axis}[
        grid=major,
        xlabel={$x$}, ylabel={$y$},
        title={Plot with Grid Lines}
    ]
    \addplot {x^2};
    \end{axis}
\end{tikzpicture}
```

The corresponding output is (Fig. 2.32):

The `grid=major` option generates grid lines at major tick marks. If finer granularity is required, `grid=both` enables both major and minor grid lines, aiding in precision reading.

Besides modifying line styles and grid lines, PGFPlots supports different markers to highlight data points. Markers help distinguish multiple data series within a plot. The

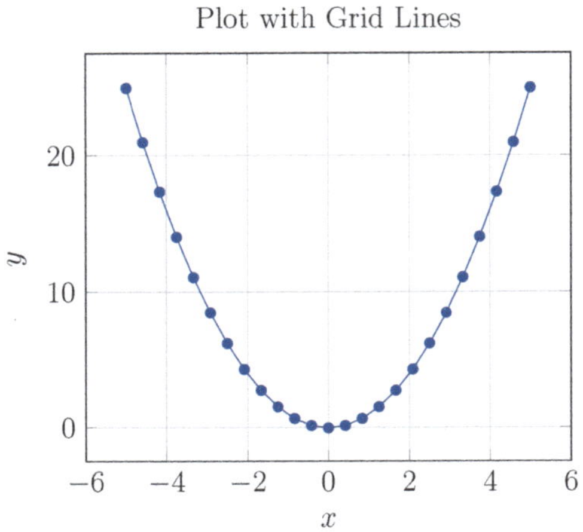

Figure 2.32: Adding grid lines to a plot

next example plots a set of discrete points, marking each with a filled square.

Example: Changing Marker Styles

LaTeX Code:

```
\begin{tikzpicture}
\begin{axis}[xlabel={$x$}, ylabel={$y$},
    title={Plot with Square Markers}]
\addplot[mark=square*,blue]
coordinates {(0,0) (1,1) (2,4) (3,9)};
\end{axis}
\end{tikzpicture}
```

The corresponding output is (Fig. 2.33):

The `mark=square*` option specifies that each data point should be marked with a filled square. The `blue` color argument ensures the points are highlighted distinctly. PGF-Plots supports various markers, such as circles, triangles, and stars, which can be changed by modifying the `mark` argument.

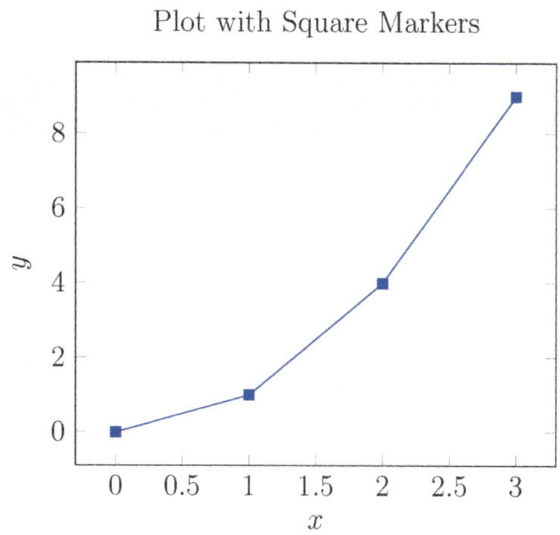

Figure 2.33: Using square markers in a plot

Beyond these fundamental customizations, PGFPlots offers control over font sizes, legend placement, tick mark spacing, and background styles. By adjusting these settings, users can tailor plots to fit the requirements of different scientific publications, presentations, and reports.

With these customization tools, PGFPlots transforms simple plots into highly readable and aesthetically pleasing visual representations.

2.5.6 More Examples with PGFPlots

PGFPlots is a powerful tool for visualizing mathematical functions and data. It provides extensive features for creating a wide range of plots, from simple 2D functions to complex 3D surfaces. This section presents 20 different examples showcasing the versatility of PGFPlots.

Plotting a Quadratic Function

Example: Quadratic Function

LaTeX Code:

```
\begin{tikzpicture}
    \begin{axis}[
        xlabel={$x$}, ylabel={$y$},
        title={$y = x^2$},
        domain=-2:2, samples=100
    ]
    \addplot {x^2};
    \end{axis}
\end{tikzpicture}
```

See Fig. 2.34.

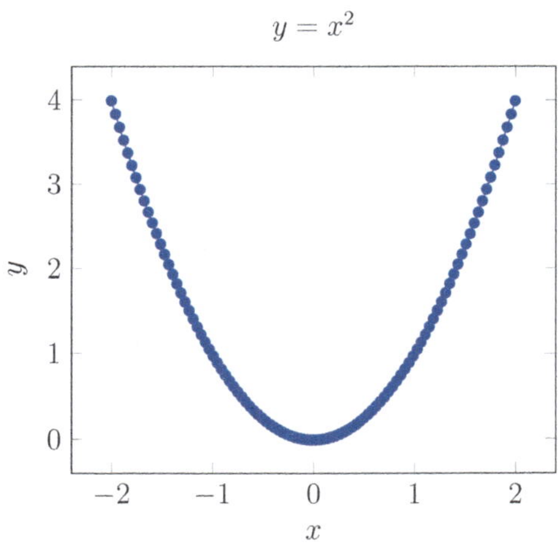

Figure 2.34: Quadratic function

Plotting the Sine Function

Example: Sine Function

LaTeX Code:

```
\begin{tikzpicture}
    \begin{axis}[
        xlabel={$x$}, ylabel={$y$},
        title={$y = \sin(x)$},
        domain=0:6.28, samples=100
    ]
    \addplot {sin(deg(x))};
    \end{axis}
\end{tikzpicture}
```

See Fig. 2.35.

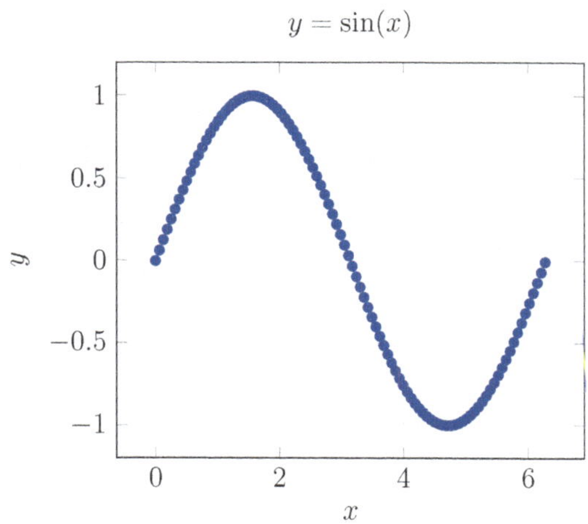

Figure 2.35: Sine function

Plotting an Exponential Function

Example: Exponential Function

LaTeX Code:

```
\begin{tikzpicture}
    \begin{axis}[
        xlabel={$x$}, ylabel={$y$},
        title={$y = e^x$},
        domain=-2:2, samples=100
    ]
    \addplot {exp(x)};
    \end{axis}
\end{tikzpicture}
```

See Fig. 2.36.

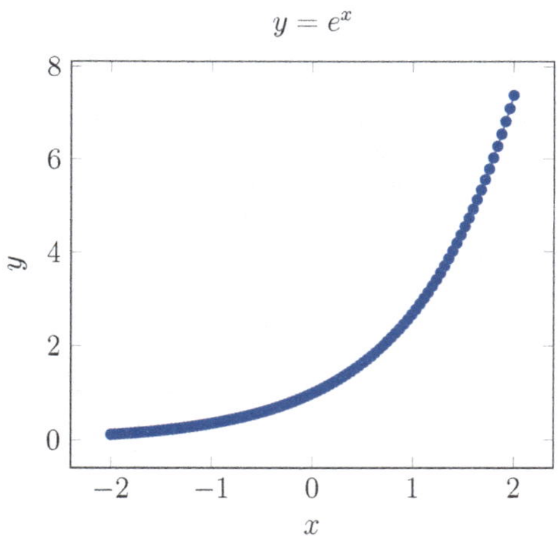

Figure 2.36: Exponential function

Plotting a Logarithmic Function

Example: Logarithmic Function

LaTeX Code:

```
\begin{tikzpicture}
    \begin{axis}[
        xlabel={$x$}, ylabel={$y$},
        title={$y = \ln(x)$},
        domain=0.1:5, samples=100
    ]
    \addplot {ln(x)};
    \end{axis}
\end{tikzpicture}
```

See Fig. 2.37.

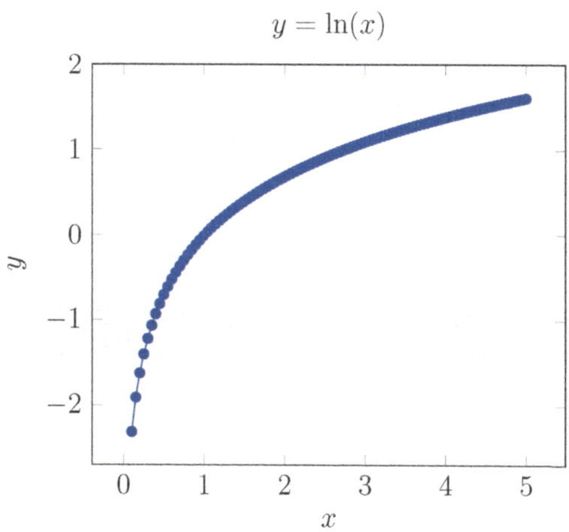

Figure 2.37: Logarithmic function

Example: Intersecting Lines

LaTeX Code:

```
\begin{tikzpicture}
```

```
\draw[gray, thick] (-1,2) -- (2,-4);
\draw[gray, thick] (-1,-1) -- (2,2);
\filldraw[black] (0,0) circle (3pt)
node[anchor=west]{Intersection point};
\end{tikzpicture}
```

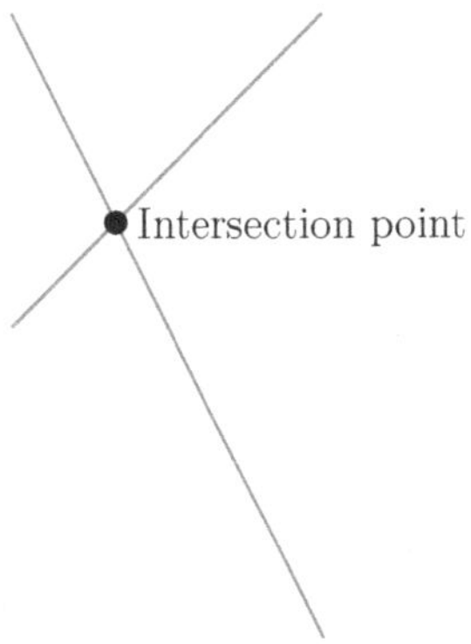

Figure 2.38: Intersecting lines

See Fig. 2.38.

Example: Curves and Lines

LaTeX Code:

```
\begin{tikzpicture}
\draw (-2,0) -- (2,0);
\filldraw [gray] (0,0) circle (2pt);
\draw (-2,-2)..controls(0,0) .. (2,-2);
\draw (-2,2)..controls (-1,0) and
(1,0)..(2,2);
\end{tikzpicture}
```

See Fig. 2.39.

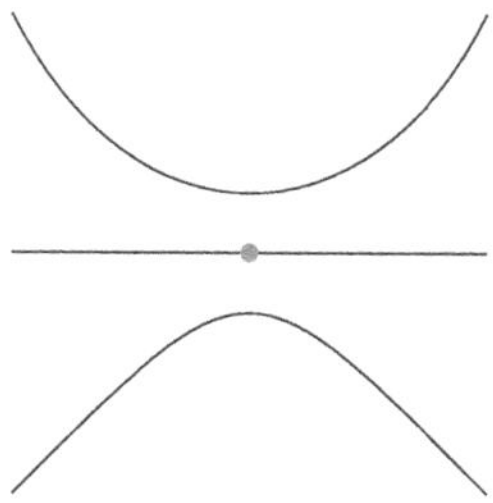

Figure 2.39: Curves and line

Example: More Curves

LaTeX Code:

```
\begin{figure}[H]
\centering
\begin{tikzpicture}[smooth cycle]
  \draw plot[tension=0.2]
coordinates{(0,0) (1,1) (2,0) (1,-1)};
 \draw[yshift=-2.25cm]
plot[tension=0.5]
coordinates{(0,0) (1,1) (2,0) (1,-1)};
\draw[yshift=-4.5cm] plot[tension=1]
coordinates{(0,0) (1,1) (2,0) (1,-1)};
\end{tikzpicture}
\includegraphics{figure.eps}
\caption{Some closed curve}
    \label{fig:3dplot11}
\end{figure}
```

See Fig. 2.40.

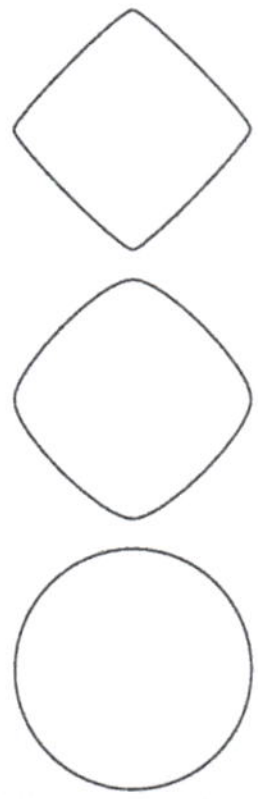

Figure 2.40: Some closed curve

Example: Closed Curves

LaTeX Code:

```
\begin{tikzpicture}
\filldraw[color=green!60, fill=green!5,
very thick]
(-1,0) circle (1.5);
\fill[red!50] (2.5,0)
ellipse (1.5 and 0.5);
\draw[ultra thick, ->]
(6.5,0) arc (0:220:1);
\end{tikzpicture}
```

See Fig. 2.41.

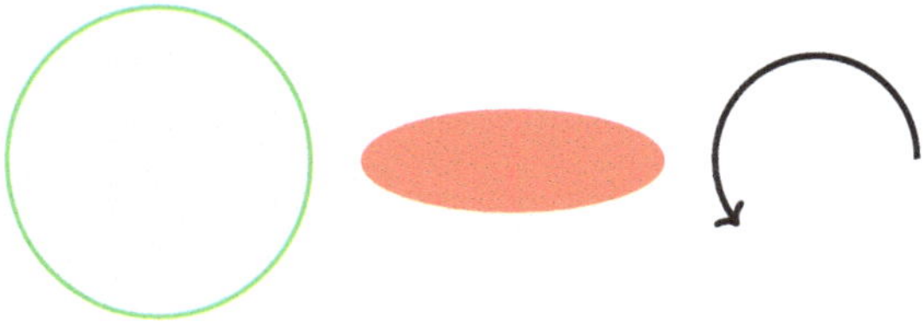

Figure 2.41: Circle, ellipse, and arc

Example: Plotting Nodes

LaTeX Code:

```
\begin{tikzpicture}[
roundnode/.style={circle, draw=blue!60,
fill=blue!5,very thick,minimum size=7mm},
squarednode/.style={rectangle,
draw=green!60, fill=green!5,
very thick, minimum size=5mm},
]
%Nodes
\node[squarednode]
(maintopic)
{2};
\node[roundnode]
(uppercircle)
[above=of maintopic] {1};
\node[squarednode]
(rightsquare)
[right=of maintopic] {3};
\node[roundnode]
(lowercircle)
[below=of maintopic] {4};

%Lines
\draw[->] (uppercircle.south)
-- (maintopic.north);
\draw[->] (maintopic.east)
-- (rightsquare.west);
\draw[->] (rightsquare.south)
.. controls +(down:7mm)
and +(right:7mm)
.. (lowercircle.east);
\end{tikzpicture}
```

See Fig. 2.42.

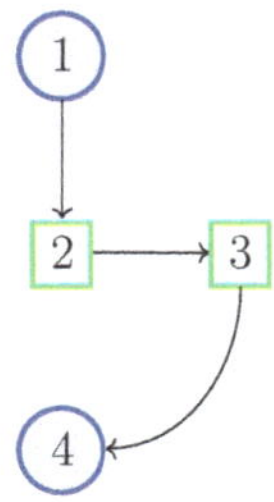

Figure 2.42: Piloting nodes

Example: 3D Surface Plot

LaTeX Code:

```
\begin{tikzpicture}
    \begin{axis}[
        xlabel=$x$,
        ylabel=$y$,
        zlabel=$z$,
    ]
    \addplot3[surf] {-x^2 - y^2};
    \end{axis}
\end{tikzpicture}
```

See Fig. 2.43.

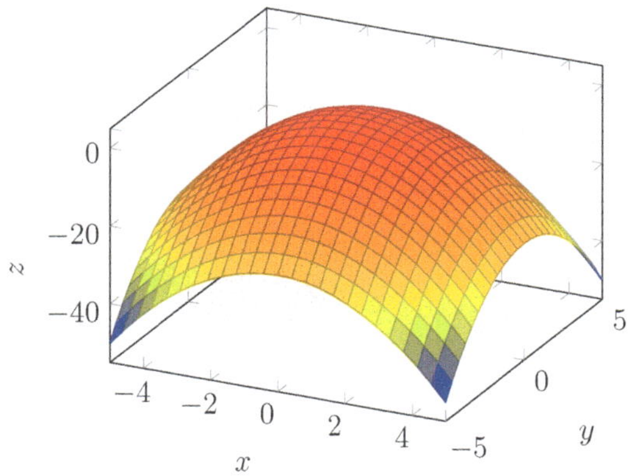

Figure 2.43: 3D surface plot

Example: Parametric 3D Shere

LaTeX Code:

```
\begin{tikzpicture}
    \begin{axis}[view={60}{30},
        xlabel=$x$,
        ylabel=$y$,
        zlabel=$z$,
    ]
    \addplot3[
        surf,
        samples=30,
        domain=0:360,
        y domain=0:180
    ]
    ({cos(x)*sin(y)}, {sin(x)*sin(y)},
    {cos(y)});
    \end{axis}
\end{tikzpicture}
```

See Fig. 2.44.

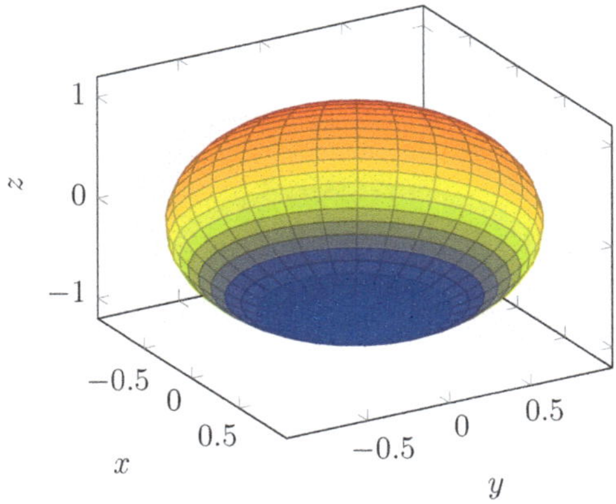

Figure 2.44: Parametric 3D sphere

Example: Another 3D Surface

LaTeX Code:

```
\begin{tikzpicture}
    \begin{axis}[
        xlabel=$x$,
        ylabel=$y$,
        zlabel=$z$,
        colormap/jet
    ]
    \addplot3[
        surf,
        samples=30,
        domain=-3:3,
        y domain=-3:3,
    ]
    {x^2 - y^2};
    \end{axis}
\end{tikzpicture}
```

See Fig. 2.45.

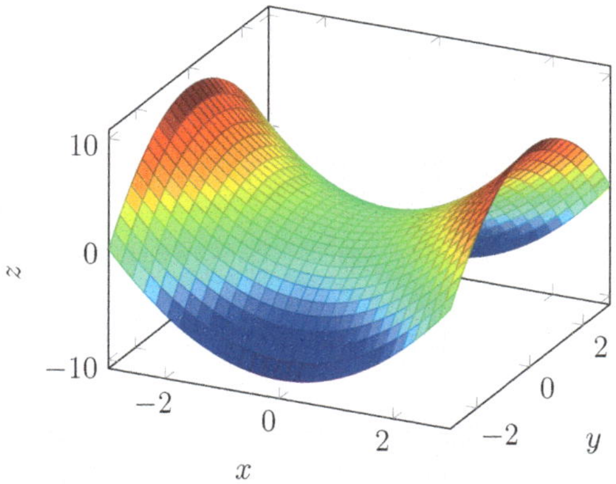

Figure 2.45: A 3D plot of the function $z = x^2 - y^2$

Example: Another 3D Surface

LaTeX Code:

```
\begin{tikzpicture}
\begin{axis}[
    hide axis,
    colormap/cool,
]
\addplot3[
    mesh,
    samples=50,
    domain=-8:8,
]
{sin(deg(sqrt(x^2+y^2)))/sqrt(x^2+y^2)};
%\addlegendentry{\(\frac{sin(r)}{r}\)}
\end{axis}
\end{tikzpicture}
```

See Fig. 2.46.

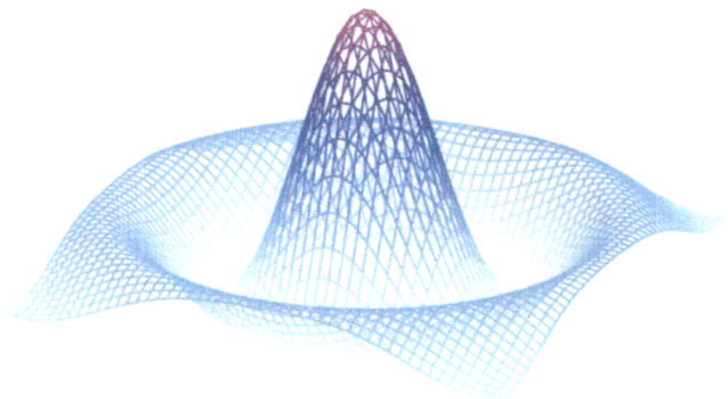

Figure 2.46: Plot $\frac{sin(r)}{r}$

Example: Another 3D Surface

LaTeX Code:

```
\begin{tikzpicture}
    \begin{axis}[
        xlabel=$x$,
        ylabel=$y$,
        zlabel=$z$,
    ]
    \addplot3[
        surf,
        samples=30,
        domain=0:2*pi,
        y domain=0:2*pi
    ]
    {sin(deg(x)) * cos(deg(y))};
    \end{axis}
\end{tikzpicture}
```

See Fig. 2.47.

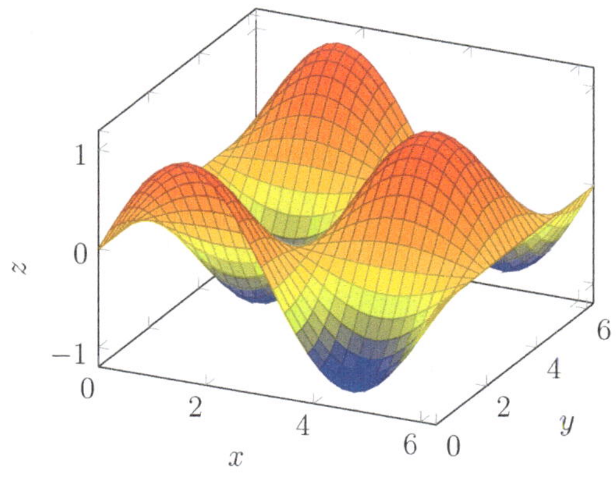

Figure 2.47: 3D sine ans cosine plot

Creating a Simple Bar Chart

Example: Bar Chart

LaTeX Code:

```
\begin{tikzpicture}
    \begin{axis}[
        ybar,
        symbolic x coords={A, B, C, D},
        xtick=data,
        ylabel={Value},
    ]
    \addplot coordinates {(A,3) (B,5)
    (C,2) (D,6)};
    \end{axis}
\end{tikzpicture}
```

See Fig. 2.48.

Example: Histogram

LaTeX Code:

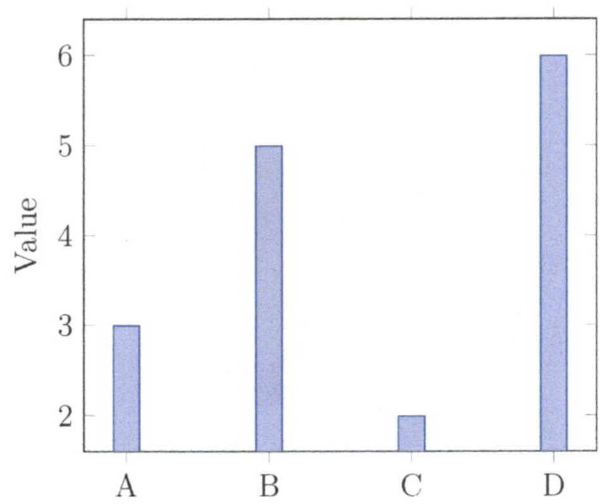

Figure 2.48: Simple bar chart

```
\begin{tikzpicture}
    \begin{axis}[
        ybar interval,
        ymin=0,
        xlabel={$x$}, ylabel={Frequency},
    ]
    \addplot coordinates {(1,2) (2,5)
    (3,7) (4,4) (5,6)};
    \end{axis}
\end{tikzpicture}
```

See Fig. 2.49.

Example: Bar Graph

LaTeX Code:

```
\begin{tikzpicture}
\begin{axis}[
x tick label style={
/pgf/number format/1000 sep=},
        ylabel=Year,
        enlargelimits=0.05,
```

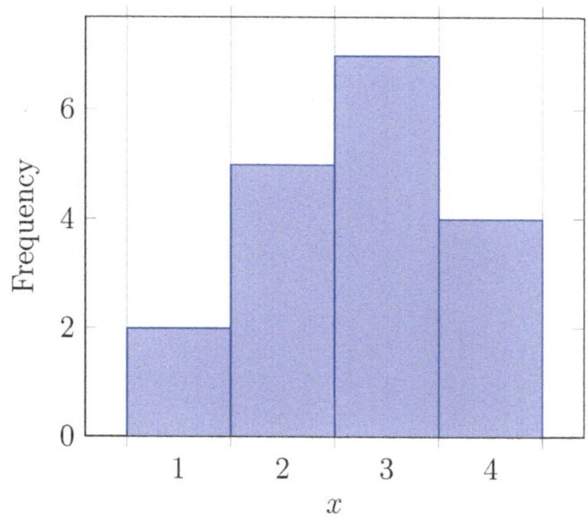

Figure 2.49: Histogram

```
        legend style={at={(0.5,-0.1)},
        anchor=north,legend columns=-1},
        ybar interval=0.5,
]
\addplot
coordinates {(2012,408184)
(2011,408348) (2010,414870)
(2009,412156)};
\addplot
coordinates {(2012,388950)
(2011,393007) (2010,398449)
(2009,395972)};
\legend{Export,Import}
\end{axis}
\end{tikzpicture}
```

See Fig. 2.50.

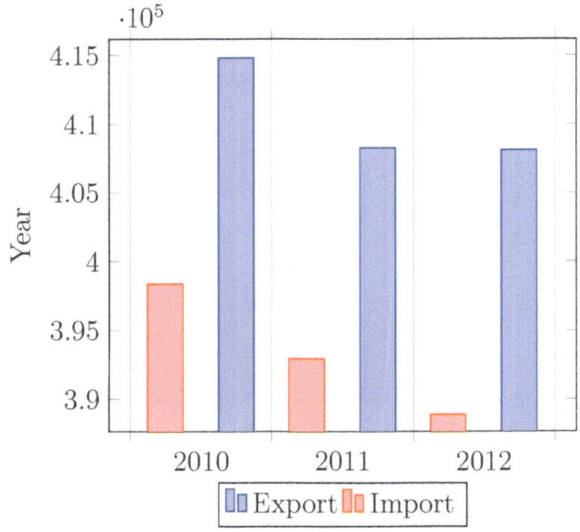

Figure 2.50: Bar graph

3D Surface with Grid Lines

LaTeX Code:

```
\begin{tikzpicture}
    \begin{axis}[
        grid=both,
        xlabel=$x$,
        ylabel=$y$,
        zlabel=$z$,
    ]
    \addplot3[
        surf,
        samples=30,
        domain=-3:3,
        y domain=-3:3,
    ]
    {exp(-x^2 - y^2)};
    \end{axis}
\end{tikzpicture}
```

See Fig. 2.51.

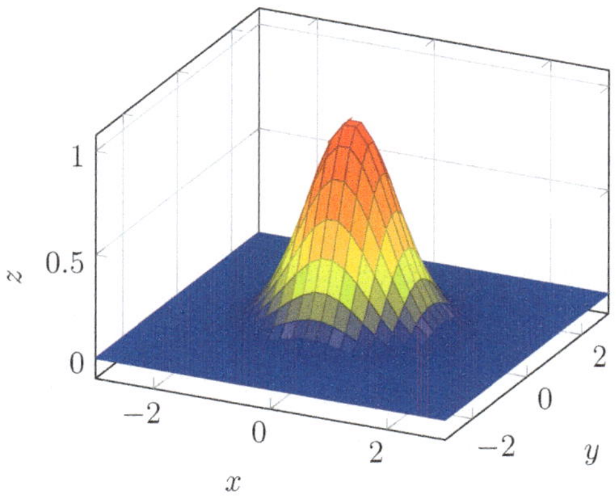

Figure 2.51: 3D surface with grid lines

Exercises for Chap. 2: Advanced Figures and Graphics

2.1 Creating Diagrams with PSTricks

1. **Basic Diagram with Shapes**: Create a simple PSTricks diagram that includes a circle, rectangle, and line segment. Use commands like `\pscircle`, `\psframe`, and `\psline`.

2. **Coordinate-Based Drawing**: Draw a coordinate grid and place labeled points at specific coordinates. Use `\psaxes` and mark points using `\psdot` and `\uput` for annotations.

3. **Styling and Color**: Modify one of your diagrams to include customized line styles (dashed, dotted), fill colors, and node labels. Use optional arguments for `\psline` and `\psframe` to apply styling.

2.2 Creating Advanced Diagrams with TikZ

1. **Basic TikZ Drawing**: Use TikZ to draw a triangle with labeled vertices and angles. Include grid lines and coordinate axes using `\draw` and `\node` commands.

2. **Flowchart Creation**: Create a simple flowchart with at least three steps and directional arrows using TikZ shapes (e.g., `rectangle`, `diamond`) and path connectors.

3. **Custom Styles**: Define and apply a custom TikZ style that changes color, line thickness, and font size. Apply this style to a diagram of your choice.

2.3 Drawing Circuit Diagrams with `circuitikz`

1. **Basic Electrical Circuit**: Draw a simple circuit using `circuitikz` with a voltage source, two resistors in series, and ground. Use appropriate symbols and labels.

2. **Parallel Circuit**: Create a diagram of a parallel resistor circuit with labeled current and voltage across each component. Use annotations to enhance clarity.

3. **Realistic Layout**: Build a circuit with mixed series-parallel components, including at least one capacitor and an inductor. Emphasize realistic placement and alignment.

2.4 Plotting with PGFPlots (2D and 3D)

1. **Plotting a 2D Function**: Use the `pgfplots` package to plot the function $y = \sin(x)$ for $x \in [0, 2\pi]$. Label the axes and title the graph.

2. **Multiple Curves in One Plot**: Plot $y = \sin(x)$ and $y = \cos(x)$ on the same axes with different colors and a legend. Customize tick marks and grid lines.

3. **3D Surface Plot**: Create a 3D plot of the function $z = \sin(x)\cos(y)$ using PGFPlots. Adjust the view angle and mesh density for a smoother appearance.

Chapter 3

Advance Presentations and Posters

Contents

Md. Aquib, *Advanced LaTeX*, University Texts in the Mathematical Sciences, https://doi.org/10.1007/978-981-96-9322-1_3

Abstract: In the first volume, we introduce the fundamentals of crafting professional presentations using the `beamer` class, covering basic structure, frames, lists, blocks, and the integration of figures and mathematical content. This chapter takes a step further by focusing on advanced techniques that enhance the clarity and visual appeal of scientific communication. We explore how to incorporate dynamic content such as animations and overlays to enrich presentations and improve audience engagement. Additionally, we provide comprehensive guidance on creating scientific posters using dedicated LaTeX classes such as `beamerposter` and `baposter`. These tools allow researchers to design visually effective, print-ready posters within the LaTeX environment, maintaining consistency in style and content. The chapter concludes with a comparative discussion of poster creation approaches and best practices to help you select the most suitable framework for your research presentations. Whether you are preparing for a conference talk or poster session, this chapter equips you with the tools and insights to deliver compelling, professional-quality materials.

Keywords: Beamer presentations, Scientific posters, Beamerposter class, Poster design, Animations in Beamer, Poster templates

3.1 Animations and Overlays

Beamer offers powerful tools to create animations and overlays, making your presentations more dynamic and interactive. Overlays allow you to reveal content gradually on the same slide, which is particularly useful for guiding your audience step-by-step through a concept or process. In this section, we will explore how to use animations, overlays, and incremental reveals in Beamer to enhance your presentation.

3.1.1 Basic Overlay and Incremental Content

One of Beamer's most valuable features is its support for overlays, which allow content to appear incrementally rather than all at once. This technique is especially useful in guiding the audience's focus and pacing the delivery of complex material. Whether it is a list, a set of equations, or parts of a diagram, overlays let the presenter introduce elements step-by-step.

A simple and effective use of overlays is in itemized lists. This is done using overlay specifications in the form of angle brackets, `<n->`, attached to each list item. The syntax tells Beamer when that particular item should become visible during the progression of the slide. The number `n` corresponds to the slide's overlay step, and the dash (`-`) indicates that once the item is shown, it should remain visible in all subsequent overlays of that slide.

The following example demonstrates a frame with an incrementally revealed list:

Incremental List Example

LaTeX Code:

```
\begin{frame}
\frametitle{Advantages of LaTeX}
\begin{itemize}
    \item<1-> High-quality typesetting
    \item<2-> Easy to create complex
    documents
    \item<3-> Extensive mathematical
    capabilities
\end{itemize}
\end{frame}
```

In this code, the first item appears on the first click or advancement during the presentation, the second on the next, and so on. The incremental reveal not only helps in building suspense or emphasis but also avoids overwhelming the audience with too much information at once.

This overlay method is versatile and can be used with other environments beyond itemized lists, such as within text, blocks, or even figures.

3.1.2 Controlling Slide Transitions with `\onslide`

While overlay specifications such as `<1->` are commonly applied within environments like `itemize`, there are situations where finer control over the appearance of specific content is needed. The `\onslide` command is designed precisely for this purpose. It allows authors to explicitly dictate when a particular portion of content should appear, independent of list environments or structural elements.

The `\onslide` command takes an overlay specification as an argument. This specification determines the visibility of the content that follows. Unlike commands like `\pause` which simply create a break, `\onslide` selectively reveals content in a deterministic sequence.

Below is a clear illustration of how `\onslide` can be used to introduce a sequential narrative across a single frame:

Slide: Using `\onslide` for Stepwise Explanation

LaTeX Code:

```
\begin{frame}
\frametitle{Step-by-Step Process}
\onslide<1-> First, introduce the
concept.
\onslide<2-> Then, explain the details.
\onslide<3-> Finally, summarize the key
points.
\end{frame}
```

Explanation:

In this example, the slide begins by revealing only the first sentence. With each subsequent click or advancement, additional content is displayed. This gives the presenter control over pacing and allows the audience to absorb each idea before moving on to the next.
The `<1->` syntax specifies that the line should appear on the first overlay and remain visible thereafter. Similarly, `<2->` and `<3->` delay the appearance of their respective lines until the second and third overlays.

The `\onslide` command is particularly effective when you wish to interleave regular text with incremental control, something not easily accomplished with list-based overlays. It can also be combined with math, blocks, images, or custom environments, making it a flexible tool for dynamic presentations.

3.1.3 Overlay Specifications for Different Content

Overlay specifications in Beamer are not limited to controlling the appearance of list items. They can be applied just as effectively to other content types, such as equations, figures, tables, or even custom environments. This flexibility allows for highly tailored and dynamic presentations where content can be revealed progressively, maintaining the audience's focus and avoiding cognitive overload.

Slide: Incremental Reveal of Equations

LaTeX Code:

```
\begin{frame}
\frametitle{Incremental Equation}
  \[  E = mc^2  \]
```

```
  \onslide<2->
  \[ F = ma    \]
\end{frame}
```

Explanation:
This slide introduces two separate equations. The first, Einstein's mass-energy equivalence formula, appears immediately. Upon advancing to the next overlay, Newton's second law of motion is displayed. The use of `\onslide<2->` ensures that the second equation does not appear until the second step, while the first equation remains visible.

This technique is especially helpful when guiding your audience through multiple related formulas without presenting all of them at once. Each equation receives dedicated attention, and the presenter can provide verbal context before transitioning to the next.

Similarly, overlays are useful in incrementally displaying figures or diagrams. For example, a side-by-side comparison of two images, where the second is only revealed after discussion of the first, keeps the visual space uncluttered and focused.

Slide: Overlay with Two Sequential Figures

LaTeX Code:

```
\begin{frame}
\frametitle{Revealing Figures}
\begin{figure}
\centering
\onslide<1->{
\includegraphics[width=
0.4\textwidth]{image1.png}
}
\onslide<2->{
\includegraphics[width=
```

```
0.4\textwidth]{image2.png}
}
\end{figure}
\end{frame}
```

Explanation:
This slide uses the same overlay technique to display two images. The first image appears when the slide is initially shown. After clicking the second overlay, the second image appears next to the first. The use of `\onslide` keeps control granular and avoids the use of multiple frames for simple content sequencing.

Overlay specifications like these provide a great deal of flexibility for managing pacing and narrative clarity. They can be applied to virtually any content that can be placed in a frame, including aligned equations, figures, blocks, or even table rows, without needing to restructure your entire layout.

3.1.4 Pausing Content with \pause

In Beamer, controlling the flow of content within a single frame is crucial for pacing your presentation effectively. One of the most accessible and widely used tools for this purpose is the `\pause` command. It allows you to sequentially reveal blocks of content, one step at a time, as you advance through a slide.

The primary benefit of `\pause` lies in its simplicity; it does not require overlay specifications or additional complexity in syntax. Instead, it acts as a natural delimiter in the content stream. Everything before `\pause` is visible on the initial overlay of the slide, and each subsequent `\pause` command causes the following content to appear on the next overlay.

This is particularly effective when you are presenting key points, ideas, or steps in a process, and you want the audience to focus on one element at a time before moving on to the next.

Slide: Using the \pause Command

LaTeX Code:

```
\begin{frame}

  \frametitle{Using Pause}
  First point.
  \pause

  Second point.
  \pause

  Final point.

\end{frame}
```

Explanation:
This simple frame introduces three statements. When the slide first appears, only “First point.” is shown. Pressing the forward key once reveals “Second point.” on the same slide, and a second press reveals “Final point.” The effect creates a linear, readable delivery, ideal for structured exposition or suspense.

It is important to note that `\pause` is evaluated in the order it appears in the source code, and it divides the slide into a sequence of overlays. However, it cannot be used in environments that create a box (e.g., inside `align`, `equation`, or `itemize` in older Beamer versions) unless the environment itself supports overlays. In such cases, overlay specifications or commands like \onslide or \only should be preferred for finer control.

3.1.5 Using \only for More Complex Animations

In Beamer, the \only command serves as a powerful overlay tool that enables precise control over when content is shown, and just as importantly, when it is hidden. Unlike \pause, which simply delays content, or \onslide, which allows content to appear and then persist, the \only command ensures that content appears exclusively at the specified overlay step and is not present on any other step. This behavior makes \only ideal for creating dynamic transitions or simulating content replacement within a single slide.

The syntax of the \only command is straightforward: \only¡overlay specification¿content. The angle-bracketed number indicates the step at which the content will appear. At all other overlay steps, this content will be entirely suppressed.

To understand how \only works in practice, consider a scenario where you want to replace a line of content with a different one at each step of the slide. This can be accomplished by using a series of \only commands, each tied to a different overlay.

Slide: Step-by-Step Replacement with \only

LaTeX Code:

```
\begin{frame}

  \frametitle{Using Only}
  \only<1>{This content is shown
  on the first step.}
```

```
  \only<2>{This content replaces
  the previous content.}

  \only<3>{And now, a third piece
  of content appears.}

\end{frame}
```

Explanation:
On overlay 1, the first message is displayed. On the second overlay, it disappears and is replaced by the second message. On the third overlay, only the final message is visible. No two pieces of content appear simultaneously on the same frame, allowing a true "replacement" effect.

This selective behavior is particularly useful in instructional presentations, where you want to revise or build upon previous ideas without visual clutter. For example, you might use `\only` to walk through progressively simplified or rewritten versions of a mathematical expression or to simulate movement in a diagram.

It is also worth noting that, while `\only` is powerful, it should be used thoughtfully. Because it completely hides the content from the PDF output except during the specified overlay, it can cause confusion if the transitions are too abrupt or if there is no visual cue that something changed. Combining `\only` with elements like `\alert`, colored boxes, or minimal animation can help keep the viewer oriented.

3.1.6 Animations with `beamer` Animations

In Beamer, animations refer to the ability to progressively reveal or alter content across multiple overlay steps within a single slide. These animations are not "animated" in the sense of motion graphics or timeline-based effects, but rather refer to logical transitions, such as text appearing step-by-step, objects being replaced, or visual layers being shown conditionally, through the use of overlays.

At its core, Beamer achieves animation-like behavior by compiling multiple overlay stages into separate versions of the same frame. As the presenter advances through the slides, these overlays are rendered sequentially to simulate animated transitions. This mechanism is built entirely on LaTeX's typesetting logic, without relying on external graphic engines.

For instance, consider a slide in which you want three separate visual objects to appear one after the other. This can be done through basic overlay techniques like `\onslide`, `\only`, or the implicit `pause` command. But when coordinated carefully, particularly with layout-sensitive content such as figures, aligned equations, or layered graphics, this behavior mimics a basic animation timeline.

Beamer also supports basic graphical movement or transitions by updating the content position or visibility over overlay steps. Below is an example that illustrates this effect using text blocks revealed in a layered sequence.

Slide: Simulating Animation with Overlays

LaTeX Code:

```
\begin{frame}
\frametitle{Simulated Animation}
\begin{block}{Step 1}
\onslide<1->{Initialize the concept.}
\end{block}

\begin{block}{Step 2}
```

```
\onslide<2->{Build on the idea with a
figure or definition.}
\end{block}

\begin{block}{Step 3}
\onslide<3->{Conclude with
a key result or summary.}
\end{block}
\end{frame}
```

Explanation:
The slide introduces three blocks of content, each revealed on a different overlay step. As the user advances through the slide, the additional blocks appear without modifying the layout or resetting previous content. The result is a smooth, controlled animation-like experience.

While such overlay-based animations are sufficient for most academic or professional presentations, more sophisticated animations, such as frame-by-frame visual motion or morphing diagrams, require external packages like `animate`. This package allows actual multi-frame image sequences to be embedded and viewed within PDF readers that support animation.

However, it is important to note that the usage of such features depends on the output medium. PDF animations require viewer support (e.g., Adobe Acrobat) and are not rendered correctly in all browsers or previewers.

In practice, overlay-based animations in Beamer strike a balance between expressiveness and compatibility. When combined with structural tools like `\only`, `\alt`, or even figure layering, they provide more-than-enough visual control for most pedagogical needs.

3.1.7 Full LaTeX Example

Slide 1: Title Page

LaTeX Code:

```
\documentclass{beamer}
\usepackage{graphicx}
\title{Animations and
Overlaysin Beamer}
\author{Dr. LaTeX}
\date{\today}
\begin{document}
\begin{frame}
    \titlepage
\end{frame}
```

Output:

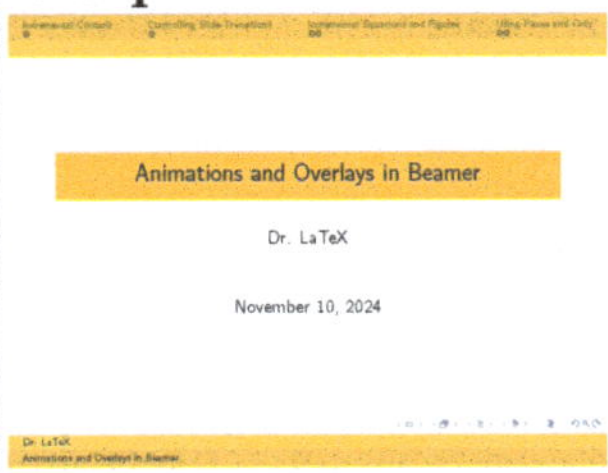

Slide 2: Incremental List

LaTeX Code:

```
\begin{frame}
\frametitle
{Advantages of LaTeX}
\begin{itemize}
\item<1-> High-quality
          typesetting
\item<2->Easy to create
    complex documents
\item<3-> Extensive
mathematical
capabilities
\end{itemize}
\end{frame}
```

Output:

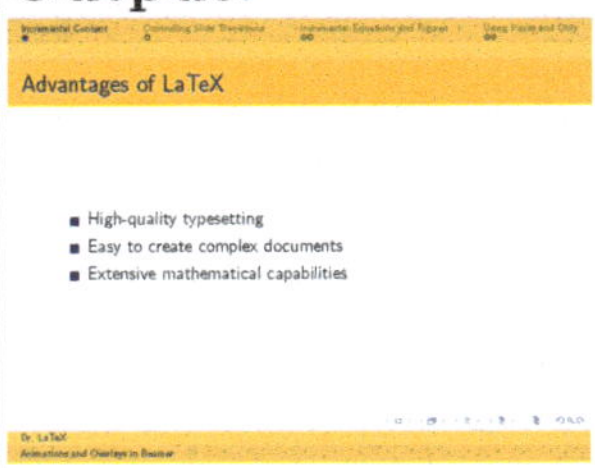

Each item appears one-by-one during presentation.

Slide 3: Incremental Equations

LaTeX Code:

```
\begin{frame}\frametitle
{Incremental Equations}
    \[ E = mc^2 \]
    \onslide<2->
    \[ F = ma \]
\end{frame}
```

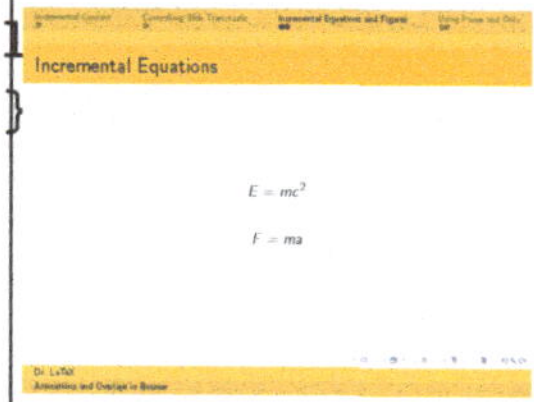

Equations appear one-by-one with overlays.

Slide 4: Step-by-Step with `\onslide`

LaTeX Code:

```
\begin{frame}\frametitle{
Step-by-Step Process}
\onslide<1-> First,
introduce the concept.
\onslide<2-> Then,
explain the details.
\onslide<3-> Finally,
summarize the key points.
\end{frame}
```

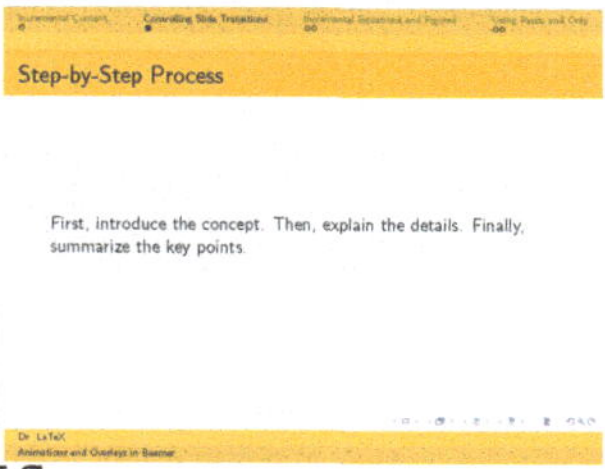

Content appears step-by-step using overlay specifications.

Slide 5: Revealing Figures

LaTeX Code:

```
\begin{frame}
\frametitle{Revealing Figures}
\begin{figure}
\centering
\onslide<1->
{\includegraphics
[width=0.4\textwidth]
{image1.png}}
\onslide<2->
{\includegraphics
[width=0.4\textwidth]
{image2.png}}
\end{figure}
\end{frame}
```

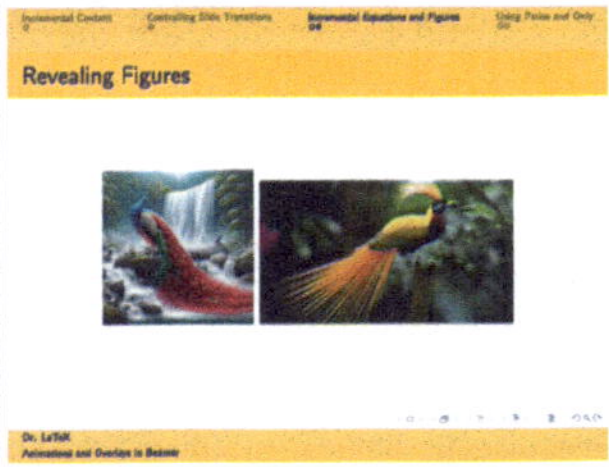

Figures appear sequentially as overlays.

Slide 6: Using

LaTeX Code:

```
\begin{frame}
\frametitle
{Using Pause}
    First point.
    \pause
    Second point.
    \pause
    Final point.
\end{frame}
```

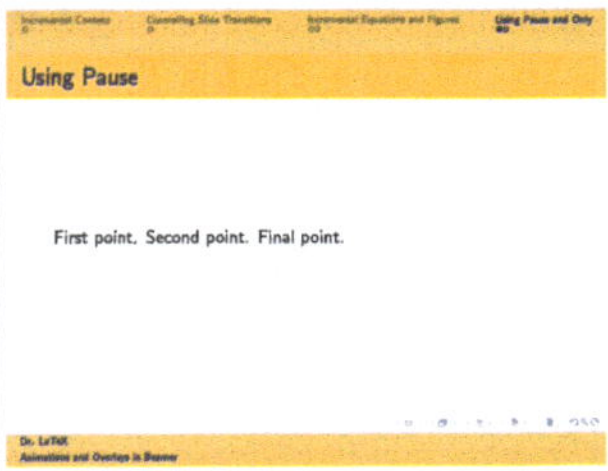

Simple stepwise reveal using .

Slides 7–9: Using \only for Replacement Animation

LaTeX Code:

```
\begin{frame}
\frametitle{Using Only}
\only<1>
{This content is shown
 on the first step.}
\only<2>
{This content replaces
the previous content.}
\only<3>
{And now, a third piece
of content appears.}
\end{frame}
```

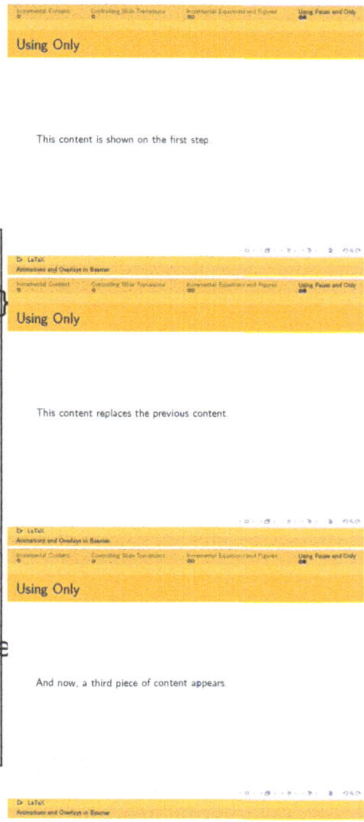

Each step replaces the previous content entirely.

3.2 Creating Scientific Posters with `beamerposter`

The `beamerposter` class is a powerful extension of the `beamer` class, designed for producing large-format academic or conference posters. It combines the intuitive structure of Beamer with specific layout capabilities suited to printed displays. Posters created using `beamerposter` are highly customizable, supporting theme-based designs, institutional logos, block-based layouts, and precise control over typography and visual presentation.

3.2.1 Getting Started with `beamerposter`

The `beamerposter` package extends the functionality of the standard `beamer` class, enabling the creation of large-format academic and scientific posters. Unlike a typical slide-based presentation, a poster is printed as a single page, often in A0 or A1 format, and must be carefully organized to present information in a visually balanced and accessible layout. The package allows authors to define poster size, scaling, and layout themes directly from the preamble of the document.

To begin designing a poster, the document must first declare the `beamer` class as its base. The `beamerposter` package is then loaded with appropriate options for paper size and content scaling. These settings determine the dimensions of the final output and the relative size of the text, figures, and block structures on the page.

Basic Poster Setup

LaTeX Code:

```
\documentclass[final]{beamer}
\usepackage[size=a0,scale=1.4]
{beamerposter}
```

Explanation:
This configuration specifies an A0-sized poster and sets a scaling factor of 1.4, which increases text and layout proportions to suit large-format output. The `final` option ensures that the document is optimized for production, omitting any visual aids used during drafting.

The `size` option accepts predefined values such as `a0`, `a1`, or custom dimensions using syntax like `width=100,height=120` (in centimeters). The `scale` option adjusts the internal font and element sizing to ensure readability at a distance, typically between 1.2 and 1.5 for most poster formats.

Although the document uses the `beamer` class, the workflow and layout differ significantly from a slideshow. Content in a poster is modular, not linear. Each unit of information is placed inside a visual block, which is then manually positioned on the page. There is no concept of "slides" in the traditional sense. Instead, the layout resembles a grid, composed of multiple content boxes, each representing a logical unit of the poster.

3.2.2 Choosing a Theme

One of the defining features of the `beamerposter` package is its support for modular layout themes, which govern the spatial arrangement, background styles, header/footer structures, and the general visual identity of your poster. Selecting an appropriate theme ensures that your content is displayed clearly, professionally, and in a manner consistent with the purpose of your presentation, whether scientific, institutional, or informational.

To apply a layout theme, the command `\usetheme` is used in the preamble. Among the most widely used themes are `confposter`, which provides a balanced academic layout; `simple`, which offers a clean and minimalist design; and `tud`, used widely in technical institutions.

Applying a Layout Theme

LaTeX Code:

```
\usetheme{confposter}
```

Explanation:
This line activates the `confposter` layout, which divides the poster into well-proportioned header, footer, and column blocks. It is suitable for

conference-style posters with structured sections like Introduction, Methodology, Results, and References.

Beyond layout, the visual tone of the poster can be refined using color and font themes. These options enhance readability and branding and can be adapted to match institutional palettes or personal aesthetic preferences. For example, `seahorse` is a popular color theme with muted, professional tones, while `professionalfonts` invokes the base LaTeX font families, ensuring typographic consistency across platforms.

Customizing Color and Font Appearance

LaTeX Code:

```
\usecolortheme{seahorse}
\usefonttheme{professionalfonts}
```

Explanation:
These lines apply a warm, accessible color palette and a font setting that prioritizes clarity and compatibility. You may experiment with other color options like `dolphin`, `whale`, or `orchid` to find the best match for your poster content.

It is important to note that not all themes support every color or font variation. Some combinations may override or ignore certain settings based on the theme's predefined constraints. Therefore, it is advisable to review the theme's documentation or perform small tests to ensure compatibility. Additionally, because poster presentations are visual by nature, the clarity and contrast of text against the background should guide your aesthetic decisions more than personal taste alone.

3.2.3 Organizing Content with Blocks

In poster presentations created using the `beamerposter` package, information is typically divided into thematically grouped sections such as *Introduction*, *Objectives*, *Methodology*, *Results*, and *Conclusion*. Each of these segments is encapsulated within a `block` environment, which not only provides a visual boundary but also ensures consistent formatting across the poster.

The `block` environment works much like a LaTeX theorem or definition environment, visually boxing off its content with a title header and a defined area. Here is a basic usage example:

Defining a Poster Block

LaTeX Code:

```
\begin{block}{Introduction}
This section introduces the
research theme and the key
objectives of the study.
\end{block}
```

Explanation:
This block titled "Introduction" sets off the beginning of the poster content. It provides readers with orientation and purpose. Blocks like this are styled by the active theme and typically have a shaded title bar and a clean content body.

To construct a structured layout suitable for posters, multiple blocks are usually organized into vertical or horizontal columns. This is achieved using the `columns` environment in conjunction with individual `column` segments. This technique allows presenters to balance dense content areas with white space and maintain a visual rhythm across large-format paper sizes such as A0 or A1.

Below is a typical example showing how two blocks, Introduction and Methods, can be placed side by side in separate columns:

Using Columns to Arrange Blocks

LaTeX Code:

```
\begin{columns}

\begin{column}{0.48\textwidth}
\begin{block}{Introduction}
This section introduces the
research topic, goals, and
background.
\end{block}
\end{column}

\begin{column}{0.48\textwidth}
\begin{block}{Methodology}
This section describes the methods
and tools used to conduct the study.
\end{block}
\end{column}

\end{columns}
```

Explanation:
Two columns are created within the overall page canvas. Each column is about 48% of the total text width to allow for a small gap between them. The blocks remain internally independent but visually aligned, creating a structured reading experience.

In more complex posters, multiple columns can be used across different rows, or blocks may span across the entire width if the content requires more space, such as figures, charts, or summarized conclusions. The placement of blocks is flexible and can be adapted to suit both the theme's layout restrictions and the poster's informational hierarchy.

Care should be taken to maintain uniformity in column widths and spacing. Furthermore, blocks should not be overcrowded; concise language, bullet points, and visual aids like icons or mini-figures can be integrated within blocks to help distill key messages.

3.2.4 Inserting Logos and Images

One of the most distinguishing features of a conference poster is the inclusion of institutional or sponsor logos, often placed at the corners or header of the layout. In the `beamerposter` class, a logo can be added globally using the `\logo` command, which is typically placed in the preamble before `\begin{document}`. This ensures that the logo appears on every slide (or the single poster frame, as is usually the case).

A typical command for including a logo looks like this:

Adding a Logo to the Poster

LaTeX Code:

```
\logo{
\includegraphics
[height=4cm]
{university-logo.png}
}
```

Explanation:
This line sets a logo image (sized 4 cm in height) to appear globally, usually at the bottom or top corners of the poster, depending on the active theme.

Within the content blocks of the poster, standard figures and illustrations can be inserted using the `\includegraphics` command, provided by the `graphicx` package. These figures are often included within a `block` environment and can be centered or resized as needed. Since the layout is large format, care should be taken to adjust image dimensions for visual balance rather than scale alone.

3.2.5 Example: A Simple Poster Layout

The example below illustrates how all these components, theme settings, logos, authorship metadata, and columnar content blocks, come together to produce a clean, two-column academic poster. The `confposter` theme is used here in conjunction with the `seahorse` color palette. Blocks are organized into two columns and include the most common headings found in scientific posters.

Poster Layout with beamerposter (Code and Explanation)

LaTeX Code:

```
\documentclass[final]{beamer}
\usepackage[size=a0,scale=1.4]
{beamerposter}
\usepackage{graphicx}
\usetheme{confposter}
\usecolortheme{seahorse}
\logo{\includegraphics[height=4cm]
{logo.png}}
\title{A Poster on Poster-Making}
\author{Dr. LaTeX}
\institute{Department of TeXology,
LaTeX University}
\date{Conference on Poster Creation,
    2025}
\begin{document}
\begin{frame}[t]
```

```
\begin{columns}
\column{0.48\textwidth}
\begin{block}{Introduction}
This section introduces the purpose,
scope, and motivation of the project.
\end{block}
\begin{block}{Methodology}
A description of the approach, tools,
and techniques used to carry out the
research.
\end{block}
\column{0.48\textwidth}
\begin{block}{Results}
This section presents the findings
with graphs, charts, or textual
summaries.
\end{block}
\begin{block}{Conclusion}
Key takeaways and future directions
are outlined here.
\end{block}\end{columns}\end{frame}
\end{document}
```

Explanation:

This example poster employs a clear two-column structure. The left column contains the *Introduction* and *Methodology*, while the right column contains *Results* and *Conclusion*. The global logo is placed using the `\logo` command and the theme settings ensure that all blocks are consistently styled. Each block is titled and visually enclosed, contributing to readability and structural clarity.

The overall layout is well-balanced, providing a framework suitable for academic, scientific, or institutional presentation needs.

This structure can be further enhanced by adjusting color themes, fonts, or block spacing. In larger posters (e.g., A0 size), additional columns or wider blocks may be incorporated to accommodate figures, tables, or expanded discussion sections.

3.2.6 Output Illustration

The expected layout of the poster generated by the example above would appear as shown in the Fig. 3.1. The content is organized into two columns, with each section housed in a stylized block. The theme ensures consistent font usage and background color, while the header displays the title, author, and institutional logo.

Figure 3.1: Sample output of a poster using the `confposter` theme

3.2.7 Theme Comparison and Layout Guidance for `beamerposter`

Selecting the right visual theme is essential for designing an effective academic or professional poster using the `beamerposter` package. Themes in `beamerposter` govern the aesthetics of the poster, including the arrangement of headers, the visual hierarchy of blocks, and the overall color palette. A well-chosen theme can significantly improve readability and help draw attention to the most important elements of your content.

The `beamerposter` package includes several predefined themes such as `confposter`, `simple`, `tud`, and `Gemini`. Each theme presents a unique stylistic identity. For example, `confposter` is widely used in academic conferences for its strong header banner and well-defined colored blocks, while `simple` offers a minimalistic layout ideal for researchers who prefer an uncluttered design.

To activate a theme, use the command:

Setting a beamerposter Theme

LaTeX Code:

```
\usetheme{confposter}
```

Explanation:
The `\usetheme` command determines the structural layout of the poster. Replace `confposter` with other supported themes such as `simple` or `tud` as needed.

Additional appearance customization can be achieved by combining a layout theme with color and font themes. These are declared as follows:

Optional Style Themes

LaTeX Code:

```
\usecolortheme{seahorse}
\usefonttheme{professionalfonts}
```

Explanation:
Color and font themes refine the look of text and blocks. Here, the "seahorse" color palette and professional font settings are applied globally.

Visual Theme Comparison Table

The following table summarizes the visual characteristics and appropriate use cases for commonly used poster themes:

Theme	**Header style**	**Block appearance**	**Recommended use**
`confposter`	Full-width banner	Colored, boxed blocks	Standard conference posters
`simple`	Minimal text	Plain, unboxed sections	Lightweight, text-focused layouts
`tud`	Left-aligned header	Tabbed, shaded sections	Technical and institutional posters
`Gemini`	Elegant dual-row banner	Rounded, gradient blocks	Visually rich, formal settings

Block Layout and Structural Diagram

Most `beamerposter` layouts are designed using a multi-column format, often with two or three vertical columns filled with `block` environments. Each block typically corresponds to a logical section of the poster, such as "Introduction," "Methodology," "Results," and so on.

Here is a visual representation of a typical two-column poster layout:

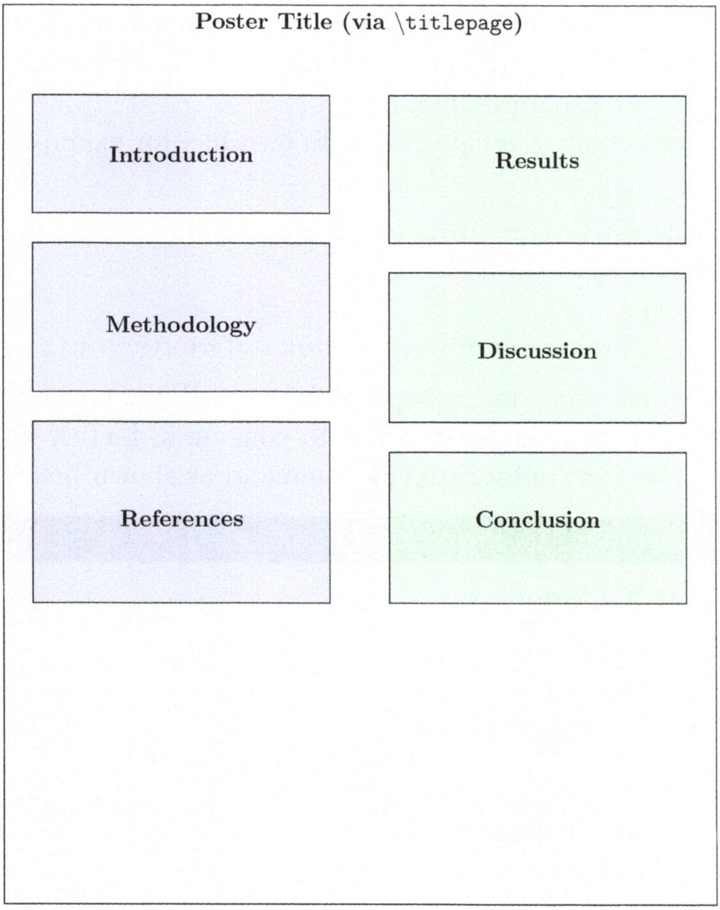

This format is easy to scan, ideal for visually summarizing work, and compatible with the most popular poster printing services. Blocks are well-contained, and the layout flows naturally from top to bottom, left to right.

Including a Poster Within a LaTeX Book

In cases where you are writing a book, dissertation, or thesis, it may be useful to include your poster (compiled separately using `beamerposter`) as a static figure within your main document. Since `beamerposter` requires a separate document class and layout settings, it is best practice to keep it in a separate `.tex` file.

First, create your poster in its own file, for example:

```
poster.tex
% contains the poster code using
% beamerposter
book.tex
% your main document (book, thesis, etc.)
```

Compile the poster separately to a PDF. Once it is generated, you can include it into your main LaTeX book using the `\includegraphics` command as shown below:

Embedding the Poster in a Book

LaTeX Code:

```
\begin{figure}[H]
\centering
\includegraphics[
width=0.95\textwidth]{poster.pdf}
\caption{Conference Poster:
A LaTeX-based Layout}
\end{figure}
```

Explanation:
This technique allows the static poster PDF to be included as a page or section of your book. It avoids

conflicts between document classes and keeps your project modular and clean.

This approach ensures that both your book and poster compile efficiently while maintaining design integrity across different formats. It also enables better collaboration when your poster is prepared as part of a team project or delivered independently for conference submission.

3.2.8 Adding Institutional Branding to a `beamerposter`

In academic and professional settings, it is often essential that posters conform to an institution's branding guidelines. Whether for internal consistency or for presenting at conferences, branding elements such as official logos, color schemes, and footer templates contribute significantly to the visual identity and credibility of a poster. The `beamerposter` class provides enough flexibility to incorporate these institutional features seamlessly.

One of the most visible elements of branding is the institutional logo. In the `beamerposter` framework, logos are typically included near the title area of the poster. This is achieved using the `\titlegraphic` command, which allows an image to be inserted adjacent to the poster title. For example:

Adding a Logo Beside the Poster Title

LaTeX Code:

```
\usepackage{graphicx}
\titlegraphic{
  \includegraphics[height=4cm]
  {university-logo.png}
```

```
}
```

Explanation: The logo file, ideally in high resolution (e.g., PNG, SVG converted to PDF), is displayed at the top of the poster next to the title and author information. Its positioning may depend on the theme used.

Beyond logos, many universities provide standardized color palettes that define their identity, often in RGB or hexadecimal format. These can be applied to block headers, backgrounds, and other poster elements by using the `xcolor` package. Colors can be declared using RGB values and then assigned to the desired poster components. Consider the following example:

Customizing Poster Color Scheme

LaTeX Code:

```
\usepackage{xcolor}
\definecolor{instblue}{RGB}{0,51,102}
\definecolor{instgold}{RGB}{255,204,0}

\setbeamercolor{block title}
{fg=white, bg=instblue}
\setbeamercolor{block body}
{bg=instgold!10!white}
```

Explanation: This setup uses the institution's official dark blue for the title bar of each content block, while a lightened version of the university's gold serves as the block background. This ensures visual consistency throughout the poster.

Institutional identity may also be reflected in a footer that provides the university name, contact email, or copyright details. To customize the footer in `beamerposter`, redefine the `footline` template using `\setbeamertemplate`. Here's an example of how to do this elegantly:

Modifying the Footer with Institutional Info

LaTeX Code:

```
\setbeamertemplate{footline}{
\leavevmode
\hbox{
\begin{beamercolorbox}
[wd=0.96\paperwidth,
ht=2.5ex,dp=1.125ex,
left]{author in head/foot}
\hspace*{1em}Department of TeXology,
University of Example
\hfill jane.doe@university.edu
\hspace*{1em}
\end{beamercolorbox}
  }
}
```

Explanation: This footer appears at the bottom of each slide or poster panel. It provides affiliation and contact information in a uniform format, reflecting institutional standards.

When applied together, these elements help unify the poster's visual and institutional identity. The use of an official logo alongside designated colors and footer formatting makes the poster not only informative but also representative of the presenter's academic or professional affiliation.

It is advisable to consult your university's branding manual for precise color codes and logo usage policies. Some institutions provide downloadable LaTeX templates or guidelines for integrating logos and color palettes that align with their graphic design standards.

3.3 Creating Posters with the baposter Class

While the `beamerposter` package extends Beamer for poster presentations, another elegant and powerful option is the `baposter` document class. This class is specifically designed for creating scientific and academic posters with visually appealing layouts, particularly suited for large-format printouts. Developed by Brian Amberg, `baposter` provides a flexible grid-based layout system, customizable headers for each block, and visually distinct columns and boxes.

To begin using `baposter`, your document must start with the appropriate document class declaration. Unlike most LaTeX documents, you do not use `article` or `beamer` as the base. Instead, you declare:

Poster Class Declaration

LaTeX Code:

```
\documentclass[a0,landscape]
{baposter}
```

Explanation:
This command sets the poster size to A0 in landscape orientation. Other options such as `a1`, `portrait`, or even custom dimensions can be passed as well.

After the document class, you begin the poster layout using the `baposter` environment. Within this environment, the poster content is divided into blocks using the `posterbox` command, where each block can have a title, content, background color, and frame settings.

Here is a minimal example of a complete poster using `baposter`:

Minimal Example of a baposter Poster

```
\documentclass[a0,landscape]{baposter}
\usepackage{graphicx}
\usepackage{lipsum} % For dummy text

\begin{document}
\begin{poster}{
    grid=false,
    columns=2,
    eyecatcher=false,
    background=none,
    headerborder=closed,
    colspacing=1em,
    bgColorOne=white,
    bgColorTwo=white,
    borderColor=black,
    headerColorOne=blue!50!black,
    headerColorTwo=blue!20,
    boxColorOne=white,
    boxColorTwo=white
}
% Title, authors, and logos
{\bfseries A Sample Poster with
\texttt{baposter}} % Title
{\textsc{Dr. LaTeX}} % Author
{\includegraphics[height=5cm]
{example-image}} % Right logo

% Introduction block
\headerbox{Introduction}
{name=intro,column=0,row=0}{
  \lipsum[1]
}
```

```
% Methods block
\headerbox{Methodology}
{name=method,column=1,row=0}{
  \lipsum[2]
}
\end{poster}
\end{document}
```

In this example, the poster contains two columns, each with one block: "Introduction" and "Methodology." You can define rows and columns for each `headerbox`, and their placement is automatically managed based on your configuration.

The `baposter` class offers:

- Precise placement of poster blocks using row/column logic
- Customizable color themes and borders
- Support for logos and institutional branding
- Good print-quality support for large dimensions

Unlike `beamerposter`, which relies on overlays and the Beamer structure, `baposter` treats each block as a visually isolated unit with consistent formatting, making it ideal for static, information-dense posters.

Finally, because `baposter` is a standalone document class, it is often used as a completely separate `.tex` file and compiled independently from your primary LaTeX project. This allows modular poster creation while maintaining consistency with your other documents by importing common packages and macros where needed.

3.3.1 Switching Between Columns in baposter

In the `baposter` class, poster layout is governed by a grid-like system of columns and rows. Unlike standard LaTeX environments where one might use a command such as `\columnbreak` to move from one column to another, in `baposter`, column placement is explicitly controlled by the `column=` option inside each `\headerbox` command.

Each content block on a poster is enclosed in a `\headerbox` environment, which accepts several key-value options, including `column=`, `row=`, and optionally, `below=` for stacking blocks. Column indexing starts at `0` for the leftmost column, so for a two-column layout, use `column=0` and `column=1`, and for a three-column layout, go up to `column=2`.

The following example demonstrates how to assign different blocks to different columns in a poster with three columns:

Assigning Blocks to Specific Columns in baposter

LaTeX Code:

```
\documentclass[a0paper,portrait]
{baposter}
\usepackage{graphicx}
\usepackage{color}

\begin{document}
\begin{poster}{
  columns=3,
  colspacing=1em,
  bgColorOne=white,
  bgColorTwo=white,
  borderColor=gray,
```

```
  headerColorOne=blue!70,
  headerColorTwo=blue!40
}{
  % Poster title and author
  \bfseries Poster Title}{
  Author Name}{
  Institution Name}{
  \includegraphics[height=4cm]{logo.png}
}

% Block in first column (column 0)
\headerbox{Introduction}{name=intro,
column=0,row=0}{This block is placed
in the leftmost column.
}

% Block in second column (column 1)
\headerbox{Methodology}
{name=method,column=1,row=0}{This
block appears in the center column.
}
% Block in third column (column 2)
\headerbox{Results}{name=results,
column=2,row=0}{This block is
placed in the rightmost column.
}
\end{poster}
\end{document}
```

Explanation

- The `column=` option is used to specify the exact column in which the `\headerbox` will appear.

- Columns are indexed starting from `0`, not `1`. Therefore, a three-column poster uses `column=0`, `column=1`, and `column=2`.
- The `row=0` argument places the block at the top of the column. You can place subsequent blocks using `row=1` or by referencing another block with `below=<block name>`.

This method allows precise control over where each content block appears and ensures a visually organized layout for multicolumn posters (Fig. 3.2).

Example: A Full Text Two-Column Poster

LaTeX Code:

```
\documentclass[a1paper,landscape]
{baposter}

\usepackage{graphicx}
\usepackage{color}

% Poster setup
\begin{document}

\begin{poster}
{
  grid=false,
  columns=2,
  colspacing=1em,
  bgColorOne=white,
  bgColorTwo=white,
  borderColor=black,
  headerColorOne=myblue,
  headerColorTwo=myblue,
  headerFontColor=white,
  boxColorOne=mygray,
```

```
  textborder=roundedleft,
  eyecatcher=true
}
% Eye catcher (logo)
{
 \includegraphics[height=2cm]
 {example-image}
  % Dummy logo placeholder
}
% Title
{
  \bfseries\LARGE LaTeX
  Poster Presentation
}
% Author block
{
\textbf{Dr. LaTeX} \\
Department of LaTeX,
University of Technology
}
% Event or right header content
%{
  %\textbf{Axioms, 2023, Volume 12,
  Issue 8, Article 865}
%}

% Title, authors, and logos
%{\bfseries A Sample Poster with
\texttt{baposter}} % Title
%{\textsc{John Doe}} % Author
%{\includegraphics[height=2cm]
{example-image}} % Right logo

% Introduction block
\headerbox{Abstract}{name=abstract,
```

```
column=0,row=0}{
\begin{itemize}
\item Allows sum of cubes of membership
and non-membership.
\item Introduces fairness-based
aggregation operators
(AOs):
\begin{itemize}
\item Fermatean Fuzzy Fairly Weighted
Average (FRF-FWA)
\item Fermatean Fuzzy Fairly Ordered
Weighted Average
(FRF-FOWA)
  \end{itemize}
\item Real-world green supplier case
study confirms efficacy.
\end{itemize}
}

% Introduction & Motivation
\headerbox{Introduction and Motivation}
{name=intro,column=0,below=abstract}{
\begin{itemize}
\item \textbf{Decision-making} is
essential in personal and professional
life, especially when navigating
multiple conflicting criteria.
\item In sustainable business practices,
\textbf{green supplier selection}
demands informed decisions based on
environmental responsibility.

\item Traditional models like
\textbf{Fuzzy Sets (FS)},
\textbf{Intuitionistic Fuzzy Sets
```

```
(IFS)},
and \textbf{Pythagorean Fuzzy
Sets (PFS)} help handle imprecision but
have limitations.
\end{itemize}
}
\end{poster}
\end{document}
```

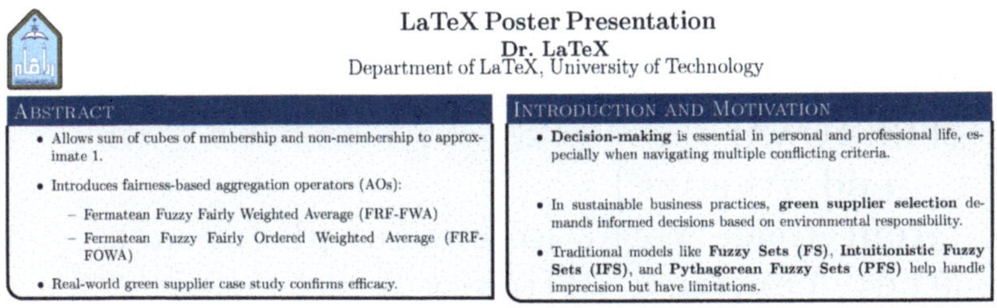

Figure 3.2: Sample output of a poster using the `abposter` in two columns

3.4 Comparison and Best Practices for Scientific Posters

3.4.1 Comparison of `beamerposter` and `baposter`

When it comes to creating professional academic posters in LaTeX, two major options stand out: the `beamerposter` package and the `baposter` class. Both are widely used in the scientific community for creating high-quality, large-format posters for conferences, seminars, and symposia. However, they differ significantly in their design philosophy, layout flexibility, learning curve, and customization capabilities.

Design Philosophy and Structure The `beamerposter` package builds on the familiar `beamer` presentation class, making it an intuitive choice for users already comfortable with creating slides using Beamer. Its internal logic mimics slide frames and block environments, extended with columns to adapt to a poster format.

In contrast, `baposter` is a dedicated document class specifically designed for posters. It does not depend on the Beamer ecosystem and instead uses an entirely separate layout model that relies on block positioning by rows and columns, with explicit header and block styling options. This independence makes `baposter` self-contained and suitable for users who need fine-grained control over every design element.

Customization and Layout One of the strengths of `baposter` lies in its ability to finely control each content block's position, dimensions, and appearance. Users can specify exact rows and columns for block placement; define gradients, rounded corners, background fills; and manage multiple block widths with ease.

`beamerposter`, while still flexible, leans on the constraints of the Beamer layout system. It is more suitable for posters that follow a strict columnar design, where content flows from top to bottom within each column. Complex grid arrangements are harder to manage without additional packages or manual tuning.

Learning Curve and Community Support Since `beamerposter` is a package that extends Beamer, it is easier to learn for those already familiar with Beamer slide creation. The transition from slides to posters can be relatively straightforward. In contrast, `baposter` requires learning its unique syntax and layout engine, but rewards the effort with unmatched visual control and design precision.

Side-by-Side Summary To offer a concise overview, the following table compares key aspects of the two poster creation tools:

Feature	`beamerposter`	`baposter`
Base structure	Beamer-based	Standalone document class
Ease of use	Easier for Beamer users	Steeper learning curve
Layout control	Column-based; top-down content flow	Grid-based; precise positioning using row/column
Block customization	Moderate; based on theme	High; gradient fills, borders, alignment
Theming	Inherits Beamer themes and color schemes	Custom themes or manual color specification
Logo placement	Via `\logo` or `\titlegraphic`	Typically in `\titlegraphic`
Suitable for	Academic users familiar with Beamer	Users needing more visual and spatial control
File type	Uses `.tex` with `beamerposter` package	Uses `.tex` with class `baposter`

Ultimately, both `beamerposter` and `baposter` are capable tools for creating stunning posters, and the choice between them depends on the user's familiarity with Beamer, desired layout complexity, and aesthetic requirements. For standard academic posters with a simple structure and minimal design customizations, `beamerposter` is likely sufficient. For posters requiring detailed styling, overlapping blocks, custom headers, or multicolumn footers, `baposter` provides the necessary flexibility.

3.4.2 Best Practices for Presentation

When preparing a Beamer presentation, following certain best practices can significantly enhance its effectiveness and the audience's engagement. Below are some key guidelines to keep in mind, each designed to improve both the visual clarity and pedagogical value of your slides:

1. **Limit Content per Slide:** Avoid overloading slides with information. Presenting a small, manageable amount of material on each slide allows your audience to focus better and helps reinforce key points without overwhelming them.

2. **Maintain Simplicity:** Simplicity is essential. Avoid unnecessary visual elements that may distract from the core message of your presentation. Clean layouts and minimalistic designs tend to be more effective and professional.

3. **Ensure Consistency:** Use a consistent style throughout your slides. Fonts, colors, layout, and alignment should be uniform to provide visual coherence. Consistency also helps establish a polished and deliberate presentation tone.

4. **Incorporate Visuals Thoughtfully:** Where appropriate, include relevant pictures, diagrams, or charts to support your content. Visuals can aid understanding, add interest, and help illustrate complex ideas more clearly than text alone.

5. **Use Lists Effectively:** Organizing information into numbered or itemized lists can enhance readability

and structure. Lists are useful for highlighting steps, summarizing concepts, or drawing comparisons.

6. **Include Examples:** Demonstrating concepts through examples makes abstract ideas more concrete and relatable. Examples also provide practical context, which can be especially valuable in technical or mathematical presentations.

7. **Reference Further Reading:** Always point your audience toward additional resources. Citing references, textbooks, or websites allows interested viewers to explore the topic further and adds academic credibility to your presentation.

Adhering to these practices not only makes your slides more accessible but also contributes to a more effective and engaging presentation experience.

Exercises for Chap. 3: Advanced Presentations and Posters

3.1 Animations and Overlays

1. **Overlays for Lists**: Create a `beamer` presentation where bullet points appear one by one using `\pause` and overlays. Use the `overlay` option to control when each point appears.

2. **Animating Content**: Write a slide where different sections of content appear with animations. Use `\only`, `\uncover`, or `\visible` to control the visibility of text and elements.

3. **Slide Transitions**: Experiment with different slide transitions in your `beamer` presentation. Use `\transwipe` or other transition commands to add effects between slides.

3.2 Creating Scientific Posters with `beamerposter`

1. **Basic Poster Layout**: Create a basic scientific poster using the `beamerposter` class. Choose a theme (e.g., `ConfPoster` or `Simple`) and divide the poster into at least four blocks (e.g., Introduction, Methods, Results, Conclusion).

2. **Column Arrangement**: Design a poster layout with three columns. Use `columns` and `column` environments to organize content such as figures, bullet lists, and charts.

3. **Adding Logos and Footers**: Add your institution's logo and a custom footer with your name and contact information. Use the `graphicx` package and header/footer commands from `beamerposter`.

4. **QR Code Integration**: Generate and include a QR code linking to a paper or website. Use the `qrcode` or `pst-barcode` package to embed the code in the poster.

3.3 Creating Posters with the `baposter` Class

1. **Poster Framework Setup**: Create a basic poster using the `baposter` class. Include a title, author block, and at least three content boxes using the `\headerbox` command.

2. **Visual Enhancements**: Customize box colors and fonts to improve visual appeal. Use options such as `boxColor`, `headerColorOne`, and font settings to personalize the style.

3. **Content Organization**: Arrange content into left, center, and right columns using the positioning options of `baposter`. Place figures and tables strategically for visual balance.

4. **Side-by-Side Comparison**: Use two different color schemes or layout configurations to create two versions of the same poster. Reflect on the readability and aesthetics of each version.

3.4 Comparison and Best Practices for Scientific Posters

1. **Poster Comparison Report**: Create one scientific poster using `beamerposter` and another using `baposter`. Compare them based on layout flexibility, ease of customization, and visual appeal. Write a short report summarizing your observations.

2. **Best Practices Checklist**: Develop a checklist of at least ten best practices for designing academic posters (e.g., font size, color contrast, minimal text, graphical balance). Use it to evaluate your own poster.

3. **Poster Review Activity**: Review two existing posters (from conferences or online repositories) and critique their strengths and weaknesses in design, clarity, and content organization. Suggest improvements based on LaTeX capabilities.

Chapter 4

Advanced LaTeX Topics

Contents

Md. Aquib, *Advanced LaTeX*, University Texts in the Mathematical Sciences,
https://doi.org/10.1007/978-981-96-9322-1_4

Abstract: As your familiarity with LaTeX grows, so does the desire to push its capabilities beyond the basics. This chapter explores a range of advanced features and techniques that allow for greater customization, automation, and control over your document's appearance and behavior. Whether you are typesetting a large thesis, writing a collaborative paper, or preparing a complex technical report, mastering these topics will significantly enhance your efficiency and output quality.

In this chapter, we explore sophisticated layout manipulation, including custom page styles, conditional formatting, and advanced document structuring. You will learn how to define and manage new environments, work with counters and lengths, and create professional-quality front matter and appendices. Special emphasis is placed on designing modular document, splitting large projects into manageable components, and optimizing your codebase for readability and reuse.

Additionally, we explore how to automate tasks within LaTeX, from creating custom loops and macros to integrating with external tools like `Makefile` or `lilypond-book`. For those interested in building reusable templates or creating class files for journals, institutions, or publishers, this chapter also provides foundational insight into defining your own document classes and packages.

By the end of this chapter, you will be equipped with the skills to craft highly tailored, professional documents and to leverage LaTeX as a full-fledged typesetting system capable of handling the most demanding publishing requirements.

Keywords: LaTeX algorithms, Custom environments, LaTeX macros, LaTeX books, LaTeX theses, Conditional commands

4.1 Writing Algorithms and Pseudocode

Algorithms are a fundamental aspect of computer science and mathematics, and LaTeX provides several ways to present algorithms in a clean and structured format. Whether you are writing pseudocode or formal algorithms, LaTeX packages like `algorithm2e`, `algpseudocode`, and `algorithmicx` make it easy to create well-structured algorithm presentations. In this section, we will explore how to write algorithms and pseudocode in LaTeX using the `algorithm2e` package, which is one of the most versatile and widely used packages for this purpose.

4.1.1 Using the `algorithm2e` Package

To present algorithms in a structured and visually appealing format, the `algorithm2e` package is one of the most versatile and widely adopted tools in the LaTeX ecosystem. It offers a high-level interface specifically designed for typesetting algorithms and pseudocode, making it a popular choice among researchers, educators, and students alike.

Unlike generic environments such as `verbatim` or `listings`, which are meant for source code, `algorithm2e` focuses on clarity of algorithmic structure. It includes predefined keywords for data declaration, input/output descriptions, control-flow elements (such as loops and conditionals), and line formatting. These features allow you to present procedural logic with a layout that mirrors real-world programming documentation or textbook-style pseudocode.

To use the package, include the following line in your document preamble:

```
\usepackage[ruled,vlined]{algorithm2e}
```

The options `ruled` and `vlined` enhance the visual structure of the algorithm. The `ruled` option adds horizontal lines above and below each algorithm block, clearly distinguishing it from the surrounding text, much like figures or tables. Meanwhile, the `vlined` option ensures that the control structures like `for` loops or `if` statements are vertically aligned and connected, making the flow of the algorithm easier to follow.

Once the package is included, the main environment provided is `algorithm`. Each algorithm is typeset using:

```
\begin{algorithm}[H]
  ...
\end{algorithm}
```

The optional `[H]` placement specifier (provided by the `float` package) ensures that the algorithm appears exactly at the point where it is written in the source code. This is useful when you want to control the algorithm's positioning, such as placing it adjacent to related text or discussion.

Internally, the package provides a rich set of commands to describe each step of the algorithm, such as:

- `\SetAlgoLined` for activating line-by-line formatting
- `\KwData` and `\KwResult` for specifying inputs and outputs
- `\For`, `\If`, and `\While` for loops and conditional blocks

These commands are designed to be intuitive and syntactically similar to modern programming languages, which makes the resulting output easy to interpret, even for readers with only a basic background in algorithms.

4.1.2 Writing a Simple Algorithm

Presenting algorithms in a clear and consistent format is crucial for conveying procedural logic effectively. In LaTeX, the `algorithm2e` package provides a high-level environment tailored to writing readable and professional-looking algorithms with minimal setup. It supports features like indentation, loops, conditional branches, and user-defined keywords, all essential components of structured pseudocode.

To get started, the package must be loaded in the document preamble with the following line:

```
\usepackage[ruled,vlined]{algorithm2e}
```

The options `ruled` and `vlined` enhance the visual presentation: the `ruled` option places horizontal lines above and below the algorithm block (mimicking typical figure captions), and `vlined` aligns block structures such as loops and conditionals vertically for improved readability.

Once loaded, the environment `algorithm` can be used to create your algorithm block. Here is a basic example that demonstrates a simple procedure with initialization, iteration, and a conditional statement.

Basic Algorithm in `algorithm2e`

LaTeX Code:

```
\begin{algorithm}[H]
    \SetAlgoLined
    \KwData{Input data}
    \KwResult{Processed output}
    Initialize variables\;
    \For{each element in the
    data}{Process the element\;
    }
    \If{condition is met}{
        Return result\;
    }
    \caption{Basic Algorithm}
\end{algorithm}
```

Output:
A boxed algorithm titled "Basic Algorithm" containing:

- A **Data** block stating the input
- A **Result** block indicating expected output
- A loop with a clear vertical brace connecting iterative steps

- A conditional with its block indented and visually distinct

In this example, the algorithm is written using clear pseudocode conventions. The `\KwData` and `\KwResult` commands define the expected input and output of the procedure. These appear at the top of the algorithm block, providing quick context for the reader. The actual steps are then laid out in sequential logic. The `\For` construct introduces a loop that iterates over each element, while the `\If` construct handles a decision-making branch.

Each line ends with a semicolon, which is standard in pseudocode style and helps separate operations cleanly. Indentation is automatically managed by the package, and the vertical bars generated by the `vlined` option provide additional structural clarity, especially in nested environments.

This structure ensures that algorithms are not only functional but also readable and accessible to a wide audience. As we move forward, we will explore how to further customize the visual style of these algorithm blocks and how to format more detailed pseudocode with additional constructs.

4.1.3 Customizing Algorithms

While the default settings of the `algorithm2e` package offer a clean and functional layout for algorithmic content, one of its most powerful features is the ability to customize how algorithms appear. This customization is especially useful when aligning the style of your algorithms with the rest of your document, be it for academic papers, dissertations, instructional material, or technical reports.

At the core of this flexibility is the ability to redefine keywords, control indentation, and introduce structured semantic elements like input, output, and user-defined procedures. These enhancements not only improve visual consistency but also make your algorithms more readable and expressive.

Let us examine a concrete example where we define custom keywords to represent named procedures and input/output declarations. This provides a more intuitive and modular structure, particularly helpful in longer or nested algorithms.

Customizing Keyword Appearance and Structure

LaTeX Code:

```
\documentclass{article}
\usepackage[ruled,vlined]{algorithm2e}

% Define custom keywords and functions
\SetKwFunction{FMain}{Main}
\SetKwFunction{FProcess}{Process}
\SetKwInOut{Input}{Input}
\SetKwInOut{Output}{Output}

\begin{document}

\begin{algorithm}[H]
  \SetAlgoLined
  \Input{A set of numbers}
  \Output{The sum of the numbers}
  \FMain{
    Initialize sum to 0\;
    \For{each number in the set}{
      \FProcess{number}\;
    }
    \Return sum\;
  }
  \FProcess{number}{
```

```
    Add the number to the sum\;
  }
  \caption{Sum of Numbers Algorithm}
\end{algorithm}

\end{document}
```

Output:

An algorithm titled "Sum of Numbers Algorithm" is displayed with:

- A clearly labeled **Input** and **Output** section
- A main block labeled `Main`, representing the primary algorithm
- A sub-block labeled `Process`, functioning like a subroutine
- Proper indentation, vertical structure, and automatic semicolon handling

In this example, two procedures are defined using `\SetKwFunction`: `\FMain` to represent the main routine and `\FProcess` for an inner function that handles each data element. This modular structure is typical of real-world algorithmic thinking and allows for natural decomposition of steps. Meanwhile, the `\SetKwInOut` command is used to define `\Input` and `\Output` keywords, providing a semantic summary of what the algorithm consumes and produces.

These customizations do not change the logic of the algorithm, but they greatly enhance clarity and typographic consistency. The resulting presentation is not only more legible but also easier to reference and explain, especially in educational or collaborative settings where procedural flow must be transparent to all readers.

By tailoring the language and structure of your algorithms, algorithm2e enables you to create algorithms that are both visually professional and logically expressive. This flexibility sets the foundation for further enhancements in the appearance and behavior of pseudocode, which we will explore in subsequent sections.

4.1.4 Displaying Pseudocode

While the algorithm2e package is fully capable of formatting structured, formal algorithms, it also adapts exceptionally well to presenting high-level pseudocode. In contrast to precise implementations tied to specific programming languages, pseudocode prioritizes clarity and intuition over syntax. Its primary role is to convey the logical steps of an algorithm in a way that is easy to read and understand, especially for general audiences, students, or interdisciplinary readers.

One of the reasons algorithm2e excels in this area is its flexibility. You can use the same environment and structural commands to compose pseudocode that omits language-specific keywords and focuses instead on descriptive actions. At the same time, you retain visual organization through indentation, line numbering, and vertical alignment of control structures.

The following example demonstrates how a common sorting routine, Bubble Sort, can be presented using plain-text, high-level instructions. The pseudocode describes the steps conceptually, without referring to data types, syntax, or explicit code constructs.

High-Level Pseudocode Using algorithm2e

LaTeX Code:

```
\documentclass{article}
```

```
\usepackage[ruled,vlined]{algorithm2e}

\begin{document}

\begin{algorithm}[H]
\SetAlgoLined
\KwData{A list of numbers}
\KwResult{Sorted list of numbers}
Initialize the list\;
\While{the list is not sorted}
{Swap adjacent elements if they
are in the wrong order\;
  }
\caption{Bubble Sort Pseudocode}
\end{algorithm}

\end{document}
```

Output:

An algorithm box labeled "Bubble Sort Pseudocode" that includes:

- A brief input/output description
- Simple, descriptive steps
- An intuitive `while` loop written in plain English

Here, the algorithm is introduced with the `\KwData` and `\KwResult` fields, which define the context of the input and expected output. These lines provide a quick conceptual overview. The main steps that follow describe initialization and iterative comparisons, using natural language rather than code-like syntax.

The loop structure is still indicated using `\While`, which maintains the visual cue of a repeated action, but the condition and step within the block are expressed in everyday terms: "the list is not sorted" and "Swap adjacent elements if they are in the wrong order." This results in a pseudocode block that is not only technically accurate but also pedagogically approachable.

One of the advantages of this method is that it maintains consistency with more formal algorithms elsewhere in the document. You can use the same environment and layout style whether you are teaching first-time programmers or documenting algorithms in a research paper. This uniformity makes your document easier to follow and avoids switching between formats or packages.

In general, `algorithm2e` allows authors to seamlessly move between formal algorithms and informal pseudocode without changing tools, making it one of the most flexible choices for algorithm presentation in LaTeX.

4.2 Customizing Theorem Styles

In LaTeX, theorems, lemmas, corollaries, and similar structures are often used in mathematical documents. LaTeX provides a powerful environment for writing such statements, and by customizing the appearance of theorem environments, you can give your document a more professional and polished look. In this section, we will explore how to define and customize theorem styles using the `amsthm` package.

4.2.1 The `amsthm` Package

Mathematical writing frequently relies on theorem-like statements, such as theorems, lemmas, propositions, and corollaries, not only to convey logical arguments but also to present them in a visually structured and recognizable format. LaTeX offers native support for such statements through its built-in `theorem` environment, but for more consistent typesetting and professional customization, the **amsthm** package is the preferred tool. Developed by the American Mathematical Society, **amsthm** is part of the AMS-LaTeX suite and provides robust tools for defining, numbering, and formatting mathematical theorems.

To begin using the package, it must be included in the document preamble:

```
\usepackage{amsthm}
```

Once loaded, **amsthm** provides the foundational command **\newtheorem**, which allows the authors to define new environments that behave like theorems. These environments are not limited to actual theorems; they can be used for lemmas, corollaries, definitions, remarks, and any other formally stated result or structure in a mathematical exposition.

At its core, the package distinguishes between two components: the logical structure of the theorem (e.g., where the label, number, and statement appear) and its visual presentation (e.g., whether it appears in italics or upright text). Although visual customization is covered in a later subsection, the initial value of **amsthm** lies in its ability to allow you to consistently create and refer to new theorem-like environments throughout your document.

The following example illustrates how loading the package sets the stage for future theorem definitions:

Loading amsthm for Theorem Support

LaTeX Code:

```
\documentclass{article}
\usepackage{amsthm}

\begin{document}

% At this point, we can define
  theorem environments
```

```
% using \newtheorem (covered later).

\end{document}
```

Output:
The document compiles normally with support for defining theorem environments. No theorems are visible yet—just the foundational setup.

It is important to understand that loading `amsthm` does not define any environment of theorems by itself. Instead, it equips the user with the tools to create them in a systematic and typographically correct way. This modular approach ensures flexibility: users can define exactly the environments they need, associate them with specific numbering schemes, and tailor their visual style to suit the tone of the document.

4.2.2 Defining Theorem Environments

After loading the `amsthm` package in your LaTeX document, the first essential step toward incorporating mathematical statements like theorems, lemmas, or corollaries is to define the corresponding environments. The core command used for this purpose is `\newtheorem`, which registers new theorem-like structures that LaTeX will then format and number automatically.

The syntax for defining a basic theorem environment is simple and elegant:

\newtheorem{theorem}{Theorem}

This command creates a new environment called `theorem`. When used in the document, it will print the label "Theorem" followed by an incrementing number (e.g., "Theorem 1," "Theorem 2," etc.) and typeset the contents accordingly. Importantly, this number is automatically managed by LaTeX and requires no manual tracking.

The following example illustrates how such a theorem can be defined and then used in the document body. This is the most fundamental use of the `amsthm` package and serves as the basis for all further customizations.

Defining and Using a Theorem Environment

LaTeX Code:

```
\documentclass{article}
\usepackage{amsthm}
\newtheorem{theorem}{Theorem}
\begin{document}
\begin{theorem}
If \( a + b = c \), then
    \( c - b = a \).
\end{theorem}
\end{document}
```

Output:

Theorem 1. If $a+b=c$, then $c-b=a$.

This environment is now available throughout the document. Each time `\begin{theorem}...\end{theorem}` is used, a new consecutively numbered theorem will appear. By default, the content is italicized and the theorem heading (e.g., "Theorem 1") is set in bold, producing a well-balanced and typographically distinct block of mathematical text.

The key benefit of defining such environments upfront is consistency. Theorems across an entire document or across multiple documents sharing a template will follow the same style and numbering system. This is particularly valuable in textbooks, lecture notes, theses, or academic papers, where clarity and structure are paramount.

4.2.3 Creating Other Theorem-Like Environments

In mathematical writing, it is common to encounter a variety of theorem-like structures beyond the primary `theorem` environment. These may include lemmas, corollaries, propositions, definitions, and remarks, each serving a unique rhetorical or logical purpose within a document. Fortunately, the `amsthm` package makes it easy to define any number of such environments using the same mechanism as for theorems.

The command `\newtheorem` is versatile: by changing the name and label provided, you can create multiple related environments, each with its own title and internal counter. For instance, a lemma is typically a supporting result used in proving a larger theorem, whereas a corollary is a statement that follows as an immediate consequence of a previously proven result.

The following example demonstrates how to define two additional environments, `lemma` and `corollary`, alongside their usage in a document. These environments are structurally identical to the default `theorem` but are given distinct labels for clarity and semantic meaning.

Defining Lemma and Corollary Environments

LaTeX Code:

```
\documentclass{article}
\usepackage{amsthm}
\newtheorem{lemma}{Lemma}
\newtheorem{corollary}{Corollary}

\begin{document}

\begin{lemma}
For any two real numbers \( x \)
```

```
and \( y \), \( x + y = y + x \).
\end{lemma}

\begin{corollary}
If \( x + y = y + x \), then the sum of
two numbers is independent of their
order.
\end{corollary}

\end{document}
```

Output:

Lemma 1. For any two real numbers x and y, $x + y = y + x$.

Corollary 2. If $x + y = y + x$, then the sum of two numbers is independent of their order.

As shown, once the environments are defined in the preamble using `\newtheorem`, they can be invoked in the document body using the familiar `\begin{...}...` `\end{...}` syntax. LaTeX handles the numbering automatically, ensuring that each environment type is tracked separately, unless otherwise configured to share counters, which we will discuss in later sections on numbering customization.

This modularity allows authors to use precise labels for different types of mathematical content, improving clarity and making the document easier to follow for readers. Each environment can carry its own weight in the logical structure of a proof or argument, helping to visually separate main results from intermediate or derived conclusions.

In subsequent sections, we will explore how to control the numbering of these environments, whether sequential, section-based, or shared across types, as well as how to tailor their visual appearance to match the tone and style of your document.

4.2.4 Customizing Theorem Numbering

In mathematical writing, clarity often benefits from a structured and hierarchical numbering scheme, especially in long or multipart documents. By default, theorem environments defined with the `amsthm` package are numbered sequentially throughout the document. That is, each theorem, lemma, or corollary receives a unique number in the order they appear, such as "Theorem 1," "Lemma 2," "Corollary 3," and so on.

While this flat numbering may suffice in shorter papers, it quickly becomes inadequate in documents with multiple sections or chapters. In such cases, it is more useful to number theorems within the context of their section (e.g., "Theorem 2.1," "Theorem 2.2") or chapter (e.g., "Theorem 3.1.1" in a book document class). This helps readers locate and reference results more easily, and it enhances the semantic organization of the content.

To customize theorem numbering by section, the `\newtheorem` command accepts an optional argument that links the environment to the current sectional counter. For example, to number theorems within each section, the following definition is used.

```
\newtheorem{theorem}{Theorem}[section]
```

This tells LaTeX to reset the theorem number every time a new section begins and to prefix the theorem number with the current section number. So, if this definition appears in a document where a theorem is placed in Section 2, the first theorem in that section will be numbered as "Theorem 2.1."

The following example illustrates this approach in a working document:

Theorem Numbering by Section

LaTeX Code:

```
\documentclass{article}
\usepackage{amsthm}
\newtheorem{theorem}{Theorem}[section]
\begin{document}
\section{Basic Properties}
\begin{theorem}
If \( a + b = c \), then
    \( c - b = a \).
\end{theorem}
\section{Commutativity}
\begin{theorem}
For any \( x, y \in \mathbb{R} \),
\( x + y = y + x \).
\end{theorem}

\end{document}
```

Output:

Theorem 1.1. If $a+b = c$, then $c-b = a$.

Theorem 2.1. For any $x, y \in \mathbb{R}$, $x + y = y + x$.

This kind of sectional numbering not only keeps the presentation tidy but also makes cross-referencing more meaningful. For instance, a reader can immediately infer the section in which a theorem appears based solely on its number. This is particularly advantageous in documents with a formal structure, such as theses, research papers, or textbooks.

Note that this logic can be extended further: in the `book` document class, for instance, it is common to number theorems by chapter instead. In that case, you would substitute `[chapter]` instead of `[section]` in the `\newtheorem` command. These adjustments integrate seamlessly with LaTeX's internal counter system, offering consistency without manual tracking.

4.2.5 Customizing Theorem Styles

The `amsthm` package does more than define and number theorems; it also gives authors control over the stylistic presentation of these environments. While logical structure and consistency are essential in mathematical exposition, the visual distinction between types of statements (like theorems, definitions, and remarks) also plays a critical role in guiding the reader's attention and understanding.

To support this, `amsthm` introduces the command `\theoremstyle`, which sets the typographic style for all theorem-like environments defined after it. This command allows you to switch between several predefined styles, each tailored to a different communicative purpose.

There are three primary theorem styles available:

- The `plain` style is the default and is used for mathematically significant results like theorems, lemmas, and propositions. It sets the heading in bold and the body text in italics to emphasize formal structure.

- The `definition` style is designed for definitions and similar explanatory content. It uses bold headings but retains upright body text, reflecting a neutral tone suited for conceptual clarification.

- The `remark` style is used for informal observations or commentary. Both the heading and the body text are set in upright (roman) font, creating a lighter, conversational tone.

The following example demonstrates how to define different environments using each of these styles:

Customizing Theorem Appearance with \theoremstyle

LaTeX Code:

```
\documentclass{article}
\usepackage{amsthm}

\theoremstyle{definition}
\newtheorem{definition}{Definition}
\theoremstyle{remark}
\newtheorem{remark}{Remark}

\theoremstyle{plain}
\newtheorem{proposition}{Proposition}
\begin{document}

\begin{definition}
A prime number is a natural number
greater than 1 that has no positive
divisors other than 1 and itself.
\end{definition}

\begin{remark}
2 is the only even prime number.
\end{remark}

\begin{proposition}
If \( p\) is a prime and \( p \mid ab\),
then \( p \mid a \) or \( p \mid b \).
\end{proposition}

\end{document}
```

Output:

- The **definition** heading appears in bold, and its content is typeset in upright (non-italic) font.
- Both the **remark** heading and text are upright, creating an informal tone.
- The **proposition** heading is bold and the content is italicized, emphasizing its formal role.

The placement of the `\theoremstyle` command is crucial. It must appear before the corresponding `\newtheorem` command. Once a style is set, it remains in effect until it is changed by another `\theoremstyle` declaration. This means you can switch between styles multiple times in a document, depending on your needs.

Using this feature allows you to establish a consistent typographic vocabulary for different types of mathematical discourse. Readers quickly learn to associate visual cues, like italicized content or upright text, with specific types of information. This improves both readability and retention.

4.2.6 Theorem Customization with `thmtools`

While the `amsthm` package provides a solid foundation for defining and styling theorem environments, there are times when greater flexibility is required, particularly for large documents or publications with strict formatting requirements. This is where the `thmtools` package becomes invaluable. Built as an extension of `amsthm`, `thmtools` enables advanced customization of theorem environments, including modular styling, inline referencing, and the ability to create boxed or shaded theorems.

To use `thmtools`, you must first include it in the document preamble:

```
\usepackage{thmtools}
```

Although it builds upon `amsthm`, `thmtools` does not replace it; the two packages work in tandem. In fact, many of the theorem environments you define using `amsthm` can be further enhanced with the functionality provided by `thmtools`.

A particularly striking visual effect is achieved by placing theorems inside colored boxes. This can be done by combining `thmtools` with the `mdframed` package. The command `\mdtheorem` provided by `thmtools` allows for both the definition and customization of such boxed theorems. For instance, the following example demonstrates how to define a boxed theorem with a colored border:

Defining a Boxed Theorem with thmtools

LaTeX Code:

```
\documentclass{article}
\usepackage{amsthm}
\usepackage{mdframed}
\usepackage{thmtools}

\mdtheorem[linecolor=blue,
linewidth=2pt]{thmbox}{Theorem}

\begin{document}

\begin{thmbox}
If \( f \) is continuous on a closed
interval, then it is bounded.
\end{thmbox}

\end{document}
```

Output:

A theorem box titled "Theorem" with:

- A blue border
- 2pt line thickness
- Clear visual emphasis

The `\mdtheorem` command is a core feature that combines the structure of theorem environments with the aesthetic versatility of the `mdframed` package. In this example, we created a custom theorem environment named `thmbox` with a blue frame. The parameters `linecolor` and `linewidth` control the color and thickness of the frame respectively.

This customization proves especially useful in teaching materials, conference presentations, or online notes, where visual emphasis helps readers quickly locate and digest core mathematical content. Unlike traditional plain-theorem environments, boxed theorems stand out, making the document more visually engaging.

The power of `thmtools` lies not only in aesthetics but also in logical control. It integrates smoothly with LaTeX's referencing and numbering system and allows you to reuse and redefine styles without rewriting environments. This becomes particularly helpful in longer texts where consistency is critical.

4.3 Defining New Environments

In LaTeX, environments are used to encapsulate content that should follow a specific format or behavior. Some environments are predefined, such as `itemize`, `align`, and `figure`, but you can also define your own custom environments to structure your document in unique ways. Custom environments can help improve the organization of your La-

TeX code and allow for more flexible formatting. In this section, we will explore how to define new environments using the `\newenvironment` command.

4.3.1 Basic Syntax of \newenvironment

In LaTeX, environments provide a consistent way to apply formatting to structured blocks of content. While common environments like `itemize`, `align`, and `table` are predefined, users often benefit from creating their own custom environments to maintain cleaner code and encapsulate reusable formatting patterns. This is where the command `\newenvironment` becomes essential.

The command `\newenvironment` defines a new environment by specifying a name and the formatting code to be applied both at the beginning and at the end of the environment's usage. Its general syntax is:

```
\newenvironment{name}[num]{begin-code}
{end-code}
```

Each part of this command plays a crucial role:

- `name`: This is the identifier for your new environment. It must follow LaTeX's naming rules for commands and must not conflict with existing environment names.

- `[num]`: This optional argument specifies the number of arguments the environment will accept. If omitted, the environment accepts no arguments. Since this section focuses on basic environments, we assume this to be zero.

- `begin-code`: This block contains the LaTeX code that will be executed as soon as the environment begins. It typically starts a set of formatting instructions or a display structure.

- `end-code`: This block defines what should happen when the environment ends. It usually includes closing any opened formatting commands or restoring layout structure.

To make this concept concrete, let us consider a simple example: defining an environment that places content inside a centered, boxed layout. This is achieved by combining LaTeX's centering and tabular features within the environment definition.

Custom Boxed Environment Using `\newenvironment`

LaTeX Code:

```
\documentclass{article}

\newenvironment{myenv}
  {\begin{center}
   \begin{tabular}{|p{10cm}|} \hline}
  {\\ \hline
   \end{tabular}
   \end{center}}

\begin{document}

\begin{myenv}
This is a custom environment that
displays text in a centered box.
\end{myenv}

\end{document}
```

Output:

A single-column table appears centered on the page, containing the message:

This is a custom environment that displays text in a centered box.

This definition works as follows: when `\begin{myenv}` is called, LaTeX executes the code in the "begin" block, which starts centering and creates a one-column table with a visible border. When `\end{myenv}` is encountered, the "end" block is run, completing the table and ending the centering context. Together, this forms a reusable, cleanly defined environment for boxed text.

By abstracting formatting into environments like this, authors can improve both the visual structure and the maintainability of their LaTeX documents. More importantly, once defined, such environments can be reused consistently across chapters, papers, or entire books.

In subsequent subsections, we will explore how to define environments that accept arguments, how to safely nest environments, and how to design more sophisticated structures using counters and optional customization.

4.3.2 Custom Environments with Arguments

In LaTeX, the ability to define custom environments gives authors a powerful mechanism for organizing and reusing layout patterns. When these environments are extended to accept arguments, they become even more flexible. An environment with arguments allows you to vary certain parts of its output each time it is used, much like a command with parameters.

The syntax for creating such an environment builds upon the standard `\newenvironment` command. In this extended form, you specify the number of arguments the environment accepts using an optional bracketed value immediately after the environment name. These arguments can then be accessed using `#1`, `#2`, and so on within the opening and closing parts of the environment. This method allows you to create formatting templates that respond to custom inputs at each usage point.

To illustrate this concept, consider a scenario in which you want to display a block of content inside a centered box with a title at the top. Rather than hard-coding the title each time, you can design the environment to accept the title as an argument. The following example shows how to do this using a table-based layout for the visual appearance:

Boxed Environment with a Title Argument

LaTeX Code:

```
\documentclass{article}

\newenvironment{boxtitle}[1]
  {\begin{center}
   \begin{tabular}{|p{10cm}|} \hline
   \textbf{#1} \\ \hline}
  {\\ \hline
   \end{tabular}
   \end{center}}

\begin{document}

\begin{boxtitle}{Important Note}
This is a custom environment
with a title in the box.
\end{boxtitle}

\end{document}
```

Output:

A centered box appears, formatted as:

Important Note
This is a custom environment with a title in the box.

In this example, the environment named `boxtitle` takes one argument, which is used to display a bold heading within the box. The content that follows is placed underneath this title, formatted within a bordered table that spans a fixed width of 10 centimeters. The argument `#1` appears in the top line of the table, and the remaining content flows naturally beneath it.

The elegance of this setup is that the structure of the box remains consistent regardless of the heading used. By simply changing the argument in the environment call, the same layout can be reused to highlight different types of content. For example, one could use it to display tips, notes, or warnings by changing only the argument text.

This technique forms the foundation for more advanced LaTeX environments that can handle multiple arguments or even provide defaults. Those features will be explored in the following subsections, but this example offers a practical first step into dynamic and customizable formatting with environments.

4.3.3 Advanced Environments

While simple environments in LaTeX serve well for basic formatting needs, there are occasions when more sophisticated behavior is required, such as automatic numbering, labeling, and conditional formatting. Fortunately, LaTeX offers a mechanism for this through user-defined counters, which can be combined with `\newenvironment` to produce custom, theorem-like structures with their own numbering schemes and titles.

To construct such an environment, you first need to define a new counter using the `\newcounter` command. This counter keeps track of how many times the environment has been invoked and allows you to reference or format its value. Once the counter is in place, the `\newenvironment` command can be used to create an environment that not only wraps content but also attaches a numbered label and formatting rules to it.

Consider the following example, which defines a custom environment called `mytheorem`. This environment creates a label such as "Theorem 1:" and formats its content in italics. Additionally, it allows the user to customize the label (e.g., "Proposition" or "Observation") by supplying an optional argument.

Custom Theorem-Like Environment with Counter and Argument

LaTeX Code:

```
\documentclass{article}
\newcounter{mythm}
\newenvironment{mytheorem}[1][Theorem]
{\refstepcounter{mythm}\
textbf{#1 \themythm:} \itshape}{\par}
\begin{document}
\begin{mytheorem}
If \( a + b = c \), then
    \( c - b = a \).
\end{mytheorem}
\begin{mytheorem}[Proposition]
The sum of two even numbers is
always even.
\end{mytheorem}
\end{document}
```

Output:

Theorem 1: *If* $a + b = c$, *then* $c - b = a$.
Proposition 2: *The sum of two even numbers is always even.*

This definition begins by introducing a new counter named `mythm`. Each time the environment is used, the counter is incremented using `\refstepcounter`, which not only updates the count but also allows the result to be referenced via cross-referencing commands elsewhere in the document.

The environment accepts an optional argument, defaulting to the label "Theorem." If the user provides a different label, such as "Proposition" or "Observation," it replaces the default text in the heading. The heading is typeset in bold, followed by the current number (e.g., "Theorem 1" or "Proposition 2"), and the content of the environment is rendered in italics to distinguish it from the surrounding text.

This technique is particularly useful for documents that require multiple styles of labeled statements but where the overhead of defining entirely separate environments (with `\newtheorem`) may be too rigid or inflexible. It is also useful in nonmathematical documents where similar labeling behaviors are desirable—for example, boxed warnings, questions, or structured dialogue annotations.

By controlling counters directly, authors can build precise and professional-looking environments tailored to their document's needs. The flexibility of this approach makes it a foundational technique for developing more advanced LaTeX macros and layout features.

4.3.4 Nesting Environments

A common and powerful technique in LaTeX is the nesting of environments, placing one environment within another. This is especially useful when composing structured mathematical documents where statements like theorems, lemmas, and definitions are immediately followed by corresponding proofs or explanations. Nesting not only reinforces logical grouping but also enhances the visual flow of the document.

LaTeX allows environments to be nested as long as each environment is opened and closed correctly. This capability enables authors to define outer structures like a theorem or proposition and, within it, include a related proof, boxed result, or even figures and itemized lists.

To understand this in practice, let us revisit the custom `mytheorem` environment previously introduced and define a matching `proof` environment to pair with it. The `proof` environment will display a bold label at the start, followed by italicized content, and will conclude with the QED symbol, commonly typeset as a hollow square, signaling the end of the logical argument.

The following example illustrates how to define such an environment and how to nest it within a theorem.

Nesting a Proof Inside a Custom Theorem

LaTeX Code:

```
\documentclass{article}

\newcounter{mythm}
\newenvironment{mytheorem}[1][Theorem]
{\refstepcounter{mythm}
\textbf{#1 \themythm:} \itshape}{\par}

\newenvironment{proof}{\textbf{Proof: }
\itshape}{\hfill $\square$}

\begin{document}

\begin{mytheorem}
Let \( x \) be a real number.
Then \( x^2 \geq 0 \).
\end{mytheorem}
```

```
\begin{proof}
If \( x > 0 \), then \( x^2 > 0 \).
If \( x = 0 \), then \( x^2 = 0 \).
In either case, \( x^2 \geq 0 \).
\end{proof}

\end{document}
```

Output:
Theorem 1: *Let x be a real number. Then $x^2 \geq 0$.*

Proof: *If $x > 0$, then $x^2 > 0$. If $x = 0$, then $x^2 = 0$. In either case, $x^2 \geq 0$.*$\square$

This example demonstrates how the environments `mytheorem` and `proof` can be used together. The custom `mytheorem` environment displays the statement with a numbered label and italic formatting, while the `proof` environment provides a clear visual cue that a logical explanation follows. The conclusion of the proof is marked by the QED symbol, automatically inserted at the end.

Nesting environments like this is not limited to theorem-proof structures. It can also be applied to pair figures with captions, examples with exercises, or explanatory notes with boxed highlights. The only requirement is that LaTeX must be able to parse the environments without ambiguity, so it is important to ensure that each `\begin` has a matching `\end` and that they are not accidentally overlapped.

This capability contributes greatly to both the logical organization and visual polish of a LaTeX document. In complex mathematical writing, where layered reasoning and explanatory detail are essential, nested environments help maintain clarity and structure without sacrificing style or modularity.

4.4 Handling Large Documents (Books, Theses)

Writing large documents such as books or theses in LaTeX requires careful organization and use of LaTeX's powerful tools for structuring content, managing references, and creating a polished final output. In this section, we will explore how to efficiently handle large LaTeX documents, focusing on splitting content into smaller files, managing references, creating tables of contents, and managing complex structures like bibliographies and appendices.

4.4.1 Using the `book` and `report` Document Classes

When composing lengthy documents such as books, theses, or dissertations, choosing the appropriate LaTeX document class is essential for maintaining structure, typographic consistency, and clarity. LaTeX offers two primary document classes suited for large-scale projects: "book" and "report."

The `book` class is designed specifically for publishing long-form documents that follow a traditional chapter-based structure. It supports elements like front matter, main matter, and back matter, a terminology that reflects the typesetting practices of printed books. The `report` class, while similar, omits some of the more elaborate front-matter structures and is often used for technical reports, shorter theses, or manuscripts that require chapters but do not demand book-like formatting.

To illustrate how the `book` class works, consider the following minimal working example. This sample demonstrates how to introduce a title page, a preface, and the first chapter of the main content using appropriate structural commands.

Book Class with Structured Sections

LaTeX Code:

```
\documentclass{book}

\begin{document}

\title{My Book}
\author{Author Name}
\date{\today}
\maketitle

\frontmatter
\chapter{Preface}
This is the preface of the book.

\mainmatter
\chapter{Introduction}
This is the introduction.

\end{document}
```

Output Overview:
The document begins with a centered title page that displays the title, author, and date. Following the title page, the preface appears as Chapter 1 but uses Roman numerals (I, II, ...) since it is part of the front matter. After `\mainmatter`, the chapter numbering switches to Arabic numerals, and the introduction is labeled as Chapter 1.

The command `\frontmatter` marks the beginning of introductory content. It disables chapter numbering in the table of contents and switches the numbering scheme from Arabic to Roman numerals, commonly used for prefaces, abstracts, and acknowledgments. Once the introductory material is complete, the `\mainmatter` command is used to resume conventional Arabic numbering for the main chapters of the book.

The `report` class follows a similar structure but omits the use of front and main matter divisions. This makes it more suitable for simpler documents that require chapters but not a formal preface or dedication section. Because both classes support chapters, sections, figures, tables, and appendices, the choice between them depends primarily on the desired formality and length of the document.

Choosing the correct document class early in the writing process helps establish a solid structural foundation. It also ensures compatibility with LaTeX packages and features that are commonly required in academic writing, such as cross-referencing chapters, generating lists of figures, or integrating bibliographies and appendices, all of which will be discussed in later subsections.

4.4.2 Splitting Content into Separate Files

As a LaTeX document grows in length, managing the entire source code in a single file becomes increasingly inefficient. Editing, proofreading, and navigating large blocks of code can be tedious and error-prone. To make the writing process more organized and modular, LaTeX provides mechanisms to split content into smaller, manageable files. This is particularly beneficial in books, theses, or lengthy reports, where each chapter or section can be stored in its own source file.

The most straightforward approach to splitting content is to use the `\input` command. This command inserts the contents of another file as if it were typed directly into the main document. It requires no special packages and works seamlessly across all standard LaTeX classes.

To illustrate, imagine a book project where each chapter is saved in its own file, named `chapter1.tex`, chapter2.tex, and so on. The main file, typically named main.tex, acts as the master document that compiles everything together.

Splitting a Book into Separate Chapter Files

Main File: main.tex

```
\documentclass{book}

\begin{document}

\title{Modular Book Project}
\author{Author Name}
\date{\today}
\maketitle

\tableofcontents

\input{chapter1}
\input{chapter2}
\input{chapter3}

\end{document}
```

Chapter File: chapter1.tex

```
\chapter{Introduction}
This is the first chapter of the book.
```

Output Overview:

The output begins with a title page generated from the metadata in the main file. A table of contents follows, listing each chapter's title. The chapters themselves appear one after the other, with their content automatically inserted in the order specified by the \input commands.

In this example, "Introduction" is the title of Chapter 1, and it is defined entirely within the `chapter1.tex` file.

The modularity of this structure offers several benefits. It allows multiple contributors to work on different chapters simultaneously without interfering with the core structure of the document. It also reduces compile-time errors that arise from large files and enables authors to focus their attention on a single logical section at a time. Furthermore, editing, spell-checking, and version control become much more efficient.

It is important to note that the `\input` command does not introduce a new page or alter formatting on its own; it merely includes the contents of the specified file inline. Therefore, each included file should contain complete structural commands such as `\chapter` or `\section`, as appropriate for its role in the document.

This technique lays the foundation for even more advanced workflows, such as conditional compilation or selective chapter inclusion, which are supported through packages like `subfiles`, a topic that will be discussed in a later section.

4.4.3 Managing Bibliographies and Citations

In any large document, especially academic works such as theses or technical books, citing references accurately and consistently is essential. LaTeX offers several tools to manage bibliographic data, but one of the most modern and flexible is the `biblatex` package. It replaces older tools like `natbib` and `bibtex`, offering greater control over citation styles, sorting schemes, and multilingual support.

To use `biblatex`, you begin by adding the package to the preamble and specifying `biber` as the backend, which is responsible for compiling the bibliography data. The actual bibliographic entries are stored in a separate file with a `.bib` extension, where you list each reference using standard BibTeX entry types such as `@book`, `@article`, or `@misc`.

Let us consider a basic example that demonstrates this workflow. The reference data is stored in a file named `references.bib`, and it is cited and printed in the main LaTeX document using `biblatex`.

Bibliography File: `references.bib`

Bibliography File: `references.bib`

```
@book{latexcompanion,
author= {Frank Mittelbach and Michel
               Goossens},
title= {The LaTeX Companion},
year = {2004},
publisher = {Addison-Wesley},
}
```

Main File: `main.tex`

Bibliography File: `references.bib` **Main File:** `main.tex`

```
\documentclass{book}
\usepackage[backend=biber]{biblatex}
\addbibresource{references.bib}
\begin{document}
\chapter{Introduction}According
to \cite{latexcompanion}, LaTeX
is a powerful tool for large
```

```
documents.
\printbibliography
\end{document}
```

Output Overview:
Inside the main text, the command [**?**] generates an in-text citation formatted according to the chosen style (the default is numeric or author-year, depending on the style options used).
At the end of the document, the command `\printbibliography` prints a formatted list of all works cited in the document. The entry will appear as:
Frank Mittelbach and Michel Goossens, *The LaTeX Companion*, Addison-Wesley, 2004.

The division between bibliographic content and document content makes this system particularly powerful. You can build a shared `.bib` file that is reused across multiple documents, reducing redundancy and ensuring consistency in how references are handled. This is especially valuable for collaborative projects or institutional writing that follows a prescribed citation format.

To compile documents that use `biblatex` with `biber`, the process involves running `pdflatex`, followed by `biber`, and then `pdflatex` again twice. Many LaTeX editors (such as Overleaf, TeXstudio, or TeXShop) automate this sequence.

If you wish to change the appearance of your citations or bibliography, `biblatex` supports a wide range of styles such as `authoryear`, `numeric`, or `alphabetic`, all of which can be declared via an optional `style` argument in the package options. For example, setting `style=authoryear` formats citations using the author-year convention common in the humanities and social sciences.

This modular system of bibliography management enhances the clarity and professionalism of large documents, ensuring that references remain accurate, readable, and stylistically consistent throughout the manuscript.

4.4.4 Creating a Table of Contents, List of Figures, and List of Tables

In large documents such as books, theses, and technical reports, readers rely on navigational aids to locate information quickly. LaTeX supports this requirement by automatically generating a table of contents (TOC), as well as lists of figures and tables. These features are not only easy to implement, but they also update automatically as the document grows, ensuring accuracy and consistency.

To create these elements, you simply place the relevant commands in your document at the appropriate location—typically after the title page and before the first chapter. LaTeX will scan the entire document and build these lists based on your use of sectional commands and floating environments like `figure` and `table`.

The three essential commands are:

- `\tableofcontents`: Inserts the table of contents
- `\listoffigures`: Generates a list of all figures with captions and page numbers
- `\listoftables`: Creates a list of tables with corresponding captions and page numbers

The following example shows how to include all three in a document using the “book” class.

Generating TOC, List of Figures, and List of Tables, Sharp Corners

LaTeX Code:

```
\documentclass{book}

\begin{document}

\title{A Sample Book}
\author{Author Name}
\date{\today}
\maketitle

\tableofcontents
\listoffigures
\listoftables

\chapter{Introduction}

\begin{figure}[h]
\centering
\rule{5cm}{3cm}
\caption{Example Figure}
\end{figure}

\begin{table}[h]
\centering
\begin{tabular}{|c|c|}
\hline A & B \\
\hline 1 & 2 \\
\hline
\end{tabular}
\caption{Example Table}
\end{table}

\end{document}
```

Output Overview:
Upon compiling this document (twice), LaTeX automatically generates:

1. A table of contents listing the "Introduction" chapter with its page number
2. A list of figures with the caption "Example Figure" and its page location
3. A list of tables showing "Example Table" and its corresponding page

These lists appear in the document in the order in which the commands were placed.

Each entry in these lists is populated using information from the document structure itself. For the table of contents, entries are generated from commands like `\chapter`, `\section`, and `\subsection`. For the figure and table lists, captions provided via `\caption{...}` are used.

To ensure these lists are fully populated, the document must be compiled at least twice. The first pass collects the necessary data, while the second uses it to generate the output. Most modern LaTeX editors perform these multiple compilation steps automatically.

You may also customize the title of these lists or suppress them in certain chapters, but such tasks are discussed later when we explore advanced formatting techniques. For now, this basic setup provides everything necessary to offer your readers clear navigation through a complex document.

With these components in place, the structure of your book or thesis becomes much easier to follow, both for your readers and for yourself as you revise and expand the document over time.

4.4.5 Managing Appendices

Appendices are a vital part of academic and technical documents. They allow authors to include supplemental content, such as additional data, extended proofs, background material, or raw experimental results, without interrupting the flow of the main text. LaTeX provides built-in support for appendices through the `\appendix` command, which transitions the document from regular chapter or section numbering to alphabetic appendix labels such as "Appendix A," "Appendix B," and so on.

Using appendices in LaTeX is straightforward. Once you insert the `\appendix` command into your document, all subsequent chapters (or sections, depending on your document class) will be numbered using capital letters. The formatting of the title also changes to reflect that it belongs to an appendix.

To demonstrate this feature, consider a simple document that consists of an introduction, a conclusion, and a single appendix chapter.

Using \appendix in a Book

LaTeX Code:

```
\documentclass{book}

\begin{document}

\chapter{Conclusion}
This is the conclusion of the book.

\appendix
\chapter{Additional Data}
This appendix contains supplementary
material not included in the main
chapters.
```

```
\end{document}
```

Output Overview:
After chapter "Conclusion," the `\appendix` command switches the numbering to alphabetical mode. The next chapter appears as "Appendix A" with the title "Additional Data." LaTeX also adjusts the formatting in the table of contents (if used), reflecting the new label format for appendices.

It is important to place the `\appendix` command at the point in the document where the main content ends and the appendices begin. This command does not take any arguments and does not itself create a chapter or section. Instead, it changes the internal numbering scheme for subsequent chapters or sections based on your document class.

To tie all structural elements together in one complete example, including title pages, TOC, bibliography, and an appendix, you might write a document like the following:

Full Document with Appendix and Bibliography

```
\documentclass{book}
\usepackage[backend=biber]{biblatex}
\usepackage[a4paper,margin=1in]
    {geometry}
\addbibresource{references.bib}

\begin{document}

\maketitle
\tableofcontents
\listoffigures
```

```
\listoftables

\chapter{Introduction}
According to \cite{latexcompanion},
LaTeX is ideal for managing large
documents.

\chapter{Conclusion}
This is the conclusion.

\appendix
\chapter{Additional Data}
This appendix contains supplemental
information relevant to earlier
chapters.

\printbibliography

\end{document}
```

This setup allows authors to manage both core content and supplementary materials in a clean, well-organized manner. The `\appendix` command not only ensures professional document structure but also enhances readability by clearly signaling a transition to secondary material.

Exercises for Chap. 4: Advanced LaTeX Topics

4.1 Writing Algorithms and Pseudocode

1. **Basic Algorithm in LaTeX**: Write a LaTeX document that uses the `algorithm2e` or `algorithmic` package to present a simple algorithm (e.g., finding

the maximum element in an array). Add comments and labels for each step of the algorithm.

2. **Using Pseudocode**: Create a LaTeX document where you write pseudocode for any mathematical or programming problem. Use the `algorithmic` package to structure your pseudocode clearly.

3. **Complex Algorithm with Loops and Conditions**: Write a LaTeX document that contains a more complex algorithm involving loops and conditional statements. Use either `algorithmic` or `algorithm2e` and explain how each part of the algorithm works.

4.2 Customizing Theorem Styles

1. **Basic Theorem Style**: Write a LaTeX document that defines a new theorem environment using the `amsthm` package. Create a simple theorem and prove it, making sure to use your custom environment.

2. **Customizing Theorem Appearance**: Customize the appearance of your theorem environment. Change the font style and color of the theorem title and body text. Create another theorem to test your customization.

3. **Defining Multiple Theorem Types**: Define multiple types of theorems in LaTeX, such as `proposition`, `lemma`, and `corollary`. Write examples of each in your document and explain the differences.

4.3 Defining New Environments

1. **Creating a Custom Environment**: Define a new environment in LaTeX that creates a boxed paragraph for highlighting important information. Write a LaTeX document where you use your custom environment to display a note or important statement.

2. **Parameterizing Custom Environments**: Define a custom environment that accepts parameters. For example, create an environment for adding a colored box with user-defined colors. Write a LaTeX document that demonstrates the use of this environment with different color options.

3. **Modifying Existing Environments**: Modify an existing environment (such as `quote` or `verbatim`) to change its appearance or behavior. Write a LaTeX document to test your modifications.

4.4 Handling Large Documents (Books, Theses)

1. **Creating a Book Structure**: Write a LaTeX document that uses the `book` document class to create a basic structure for a book. Include chapters, sections, and subsections, and generate a table of contents.

2. **Handling Bibliography and Indexes**: Create a large document (e.g., a thesis or book) with a bibliography and an index. Use the `biblatex` package for managing references and the `makeidx` package for generating an index.

3. **Customizing Chapter Titles and Headers**: Customize the appearance of chapter titles and section headers in a book or thesis document. Use the `titlesec` or `fancyhdr` package to modify how the headers appear.

Chapter 5

Multilingual and Global Typesetting

Contents

Md. Aquib, *Advanced LaTeX*, University Texts in the Mathematical Sciences,
https://doi.org/10.1007/978-981-96-9322-1_5

Abstract: As LaTeX continues to serve a diverse global community of scholars, researchers, and professionals, the need for multilingual document preparation has grown significantly. Whether you are typesetting Arabic mathematical texts, Chinese research articles, or bilingual conference proceedings, LaTeX offers robust support for a wide range of scripts, writing systems, and language-specific typographic conventions. This chapter explores the essential tools and packages required for producing documents in non-Latin alphabets and multiple languages. We cover foundational concepts such as input encoding, font selection, and language switching, along with specialized packages like `babel`, `polyglossia`, `CJKutf8`, and `arabtex`. Additionally, we examine best practices for integrating multilingual content in both traditional and modern compilation workflows, including PDFLaTeX, XeLaTeX, and LuaLaTeX. By the end of this chapter, readers will be equipped to create polished, linguistically accurate documents that meet international publishing standards.

Keywords: Multilingual typesetting, Babel package, Polyglossia package, Right-to-left text, CJK characters, Non-Latin scripts

5.1 Changing Languages in LaTeX

One of the powerful features of LaTeX is its multilingual support. Whether you are preparing a document in French, German, Arabic, or any other language, LaTeX provides tools to typeset content with correct hyphenation rules, punctuation conventions, and language-specific typographic details. This section explains how to change the document language in LaTeX, either globally or locally, and outlines two principal methods: using the `babel` package with pdflatex and using the polyglossia package with xelatex or lualatex.

5.1.1 Using the babel Package

For documents compiled with pdflatex, the standard way to introduce multilingual support is by using the babel package. This package allows you to adapt your document to a variety of languages by enabling proper hyphenation patterns, punctuation conventions, localized captions (like "Chapter" or "Table of Contents"), and date formatting. It is particularly effective for documents written in Latin-script languages such as English, French, German, or Spanish.

The language you specify with babel becomes the primary language of your document and influences how the text is rendered throughout.

Setting the Document Language with babel

LaTeX Code:

```
\documentclass{article}
\usepackage[english]{babel}

\begin{document}
This document is in English.
\end{document}
```

Output:

This document is in English.

In the example above, the language is explicitly set to English. You can substitute english with other options like french, german, or spanish, depending on your needs. This change will affect the entire document unless you override it locally.

One of the most useful features of babel is its ability to switch languages inline. This feature is particularly important in multilingual texts, such as comparative linguistic studies or international publications, where multiple languages may appear on the same page.

Switching Languages Inline with babel

LaTeX Code:

```
\documentclass{article}
\usepackage[english,french]{babel}

\begin{document}

\selectlanguage{french}
Bonjour tout le monde.

\selectlanguage{english}
Hello, world.

\end{document}
```

Output:

Bonjour tout le monde.
Hello, world.

Note that when switching between languages, the \selectlanguage command is used. This command ensures that the typographic rules, hyphenation, and punctuation spacing adapt to the target language. For instance, in French, non-breaking spaces are automatically inserted before colons and exclamation marks, which follow French typesetting conventions.

If you need to switch languages temporarily within a sentence rather than for an entire paragraph or section, you can also use \foreignlanguage:

Short-Term Language Switching with \foreignlanguage

LaTeX Code:

```
\documentclass{article}
\usepackage[english,french]{babel}

\begin{document}
She said, \foreignlanguage{french}
{« Bonjour »}, and smiled.
\end{document}
```

Output:

She said, Bonjour , and smiled.

This method is ideal when quoting phrases, greetings, or proper nouns in a different language without changing the main flow of the document.

5.1.2 Using the polyglossia Package

The `polyglossia` package is a modern multilingual solution for LaTeX documents that require support for non-Latin scripts, complex directionality, or Unicode font handling. Unlike `babel`, which works primarily with `pdflatex`, `polyglossia` is designed for use with `xelatex` or `lualatex`, both of which support full Unicode rendering and fontspec-based font selection. This makes `polyglossia` an excellent choice when working with languages such as Arabic, Hebrew, Hindi, Russian, or Chinese, where correct text shaping and font rendering are essential.

To begin, one must load the `fontspec` and `polyglossia` packages in the preamble. The main language of the document is set using `\setmainlanguage`, and additional languages can be declared with

`\setotherlanguage`. For languages that use non-Latin scripts, such as Arabic, a suitable Unicode font must be specified with `\newfontfamily`, ensuring proper display and typographic features such as ligatures and contextual alternates.

Below is a minimal working example demonstrating how to write a multilingual document with English and Arabic using `polyglossia` and `xelatex`:

Multilingual Document with Arabic and English

LaTeX Code:

```
\documentclass{article}
\usepackage{fontspec}
\usepackage{polyglossia}

\setmainlanguage{english}
\setotherlanguage{arabic}
\newfontfamily\arabicfont
  [Script=Arabic]{Amiri}
\begin{document}
This is English text.
\begin{arabic}
هذا نص باللغة العربية.
\end{arabic}
\end{document}
```

The output will show English text followed by Arabic text rendered right to left using the Amiri font. The direction and shaping of Arabic text are handled automatically.

This setup ensures that each language is rendered with typographically appropriate fonts and layout behaviors. Arabic, for instance, is rendered from right to left, with proper ligature shaping and contextual character selection, a process handled seamlessly by `xelatex` and `polyglossia`.

In addition to `\begin{arabic}...\end{arabic}`, short Arabic snippets can also be inserted inline using `\textarabic{...}`, which is especially useful for parenthetical usage within English prose. Fonts for other supported languages can be similarly configured by defining new font families using the same mechanism.

It is important to note that `polyglossia` should always be compiled with `xelatex` or `lualatex`. Attempts to compile such documents using `pdflatex` will either fail or yield improper rendering, as `pdflatex` lacks support for complex script layout and Unicode fonts.

5.1.3 Choosing Between babel and polyglossia

When selecting a language-handling package in LaTeX, the choice between `babel` and `polyglossia` largely depends on the typesetting engine being used, the languages involved in the document, and the level of typographic sophistication required.

The `babel` package is a well-established and robust solution for multilingual typesetting when using `pdflatex`. It provides excellent support for a wide range of Latin-based languages such as English, Spanish, French, German, and Italian. It automatically adjusts hyphenation patterns, date formats, and predefined words such as "Chapter" or "Figure" based on the selected language. For many users working exclusively with Western European scripts, `babel` offers a lightweight and reliable solution.

However, when your document involves non-Latin scripts, such as Arabic, Hebrew, Hindi, or Chinese, or when precise font control and Unicode support are required, `polyglossia` becomes the more appropriate choice. Designed as a modern multilingual interface, `polyglossia` works only with Unicode-capable engines like `xelatex` and `lualatex`. It not only handles the typographic conventions of complex scripts but also supports directionality settings (left to right and right to left) and integrates smoothly with the `fontspec` package to allow direct access to system-installed OpenType fonts.

To illustrate this distinction, consider the following example. If you are preparing a document in English and French using `pdflatex`, the following setup with `babel` is efficient and sufficient:

Babel with Western Languages

LaTeX Code:

```
\documentclass{article}
\usepackage[english,french]{babel}
\begin{document}

\selectlanguage{english}
This is in English.

\selectlanguage{french}
```

Ceci est en français.

```
\end{document}
```

Output:

English and French text appear in appropriate formatting, and automatic translation of predefined terms such as "Table of Contents" will occur.

Now, suppose you are working with Arabic or any non-Latin script. The following configuration with `polyglossia` and `xelatex` would be recommended:

Polyglossia with Right-to-Left Languages

LaTeX Code:

```
\documentclass{article}
\usepackage{fontspec}
\usepackage{polyglossia}
\setmainlanguage{english}
\setotherlanguage{arabic}
\newfontfamily\arabicfont
  [Script=Arabic]{Amiri}
\begin{document}
This is in English.
\begin{arabic}
هذا نص باللغة العربية.
\end{arabic}
\end{document}
```

Output:
This document will typeset Arabic text with correct right-to-left direction, ligatures, and shaping. The Amiri font provides a beautiful and scholarly Arabic script.

5.1.4 Supported Languages

Both `babel` and `polyglossia` support dozens of languages. Some common language keys include:

Language	babel key	polyglossia key
English	english	english
French	french	french
German	german	german
Spanish	spanish	spanish
Arabic	arabic (with extras)	arabic
Russian	russian	russian
Hindi	hindi (via `polyglossia`)	hindi

Refer to the package documentation for a full list of supported languages and their specific options.

5.1.5 Compiling Multilingual Documents

When preparing multilingual documents, especially those that incorporate non-Latin scripts like Arabic, Chinese, or Devanagari, choosing the right compiler is critical to ensuring that fonts, character encoding, and typesetting direction are handled correctly.

For documents that use the `babel` package, which primarily supports Latin-based languages, the recommended compiler is:

```
pdflatex
```

This engine is suitable for Western European languages but is not designed to handle Unicode fonts or right-to-left (RTL) scripts such as Arabic or Hebrew.

In contrast, documents that use the `polyglossia` package, specifically intended for Unicode and RTL support, must be compiled using either of the following engines:

```
xelatex
lualatex
```

These compilers provide native support for Unicode and work seamlessly with the `fontspec` package, which allows access to system-installed OpenType or TrueType fonts. This capability is essential when working with complex scripts like Arabic, as it ensures proper glyph shaping, bidirectional text, and ligature handling.

Arabic Font Support

To correctly render Arabic text using `polyglossia`, it is important to specify an Arabic font that supports full shaping and contextual forms. Commonly used fonts include:

- **Amiri**: A classical Arabic font based on traditional typesetting
- **Scheherazade**: A Unicode-compliant font from SIL designed for readability and elegance
- **Lateef**: Another SIL font designed for extended Arabic script, including complex diacritics

If you are compiling the document on a local system, you should ensure that these fonts are installed. On Linux, fonts can typically be installed using the system package manager or manually placed in the .fonts or /usr/share/-fonts directory. On Windows or macOS, installing the font involves double-clicking the `.ttf` file and selecting "Install."

For users working on Overleaf, the Amiri font is preinstalled and available without any additional configuration. If you wish to use a custom font (such as Scheherazade), you can upload the `.ttf` file to your Overleaf project directory and then load it using:

```
\newfontfamily\arabicfont[Script=Arabic]
{Scheherazade-Regular.ttf}
```

Editor and Compiler Configuration
Modern LaTeX editors such as Overleaf, TeXstudio, and TeXworks allow you to select the compiler engine from a dropdown menu or configuration panel. When compiling Arabic or any multilingual document using `polyglossia`, it is essential to use either `xelatex` or `lualatex`; otherwise, the font rendering and RTL directionality may not function as expected.

By combining `polyglossia`, `fontspec`, and a suitable compiler, LaTeX users can create elegant, typographically accurate documents in Arabic and many other world languages.

5.2 Typesetting Arabic with `arabtex`

Arabic typesetting in LaTeX can be achieved using a variety of tools, but one of the earliest and most flexible packages is `arabtex`. Developed to support right-to-left typesetting and Arabic script through transliteration, it provides a traditional alternative to modern Unicode-based systems like `polyglossia`. This section discusses how to set up and use the `arabtex` package, illustrates both transliteration and UTF-8 input, and explains how it can work in conjunction with the `babel` package to improve multilingual support.

The `arabtex` package has long served as a traditional solution for rendering Arabic script in LaTeX documents, using transliterated input mapped to internally defined fonts. While this approach is suitable for many academic and archival workflows, it is important to recognize the underlying limitations of the `pdfTeX` engine, which powers `pdfLaTeX`. Specifically, `pdfTeX` offers limited native support for complex-script languages such as Arabic, Hebrew, Devanagari, or Malayalam. These scripts require advanced typographic features including contextual shaping, bidirectional text handling, and OpenType font support—features not fully available in the `pdfLaTeX` environment.

For users whose publication pipelines mandate `pdfLaTeX`, `arabtex` remains a viable tool, particularly due to its robustness and long-standing integration with ASCII transliteration. However, authors who have the flexibility to choose their compiler are strongly encouraged to consider more modern engines such as `XeLaTeX` (built on the `XeTeX` engine) or `LuaLaTeX` (based on the `LuaHBTeX` engine). These compilers offer full Unicode support, access to system fonts, and advanced capabilities for right-to-left and complex-script typesetting. Among them, `LuaLaTeX`, with its HarfBuzz integration, delivers the most comprehensive solution for professional-quality Arabic typography in LaTeX documents.

In the following sections, we will examine both traditional and modern techniques for typesetting Arabic, beginning with `arabtex` and then contrasting its capabilities with those of `polyglossia` and Unicode-based compilers.

5.2.1 Notes on the arabtex Package

The `arabtex` package was originally developed by Klaus Lagally beginning in 1991, conceived initially as a personal research and typesetting project. According to Appendix B of the package documentation, `arabtex` was created in a pre-Unicode, pre-TEX engines like `pdfTeX`, `LuaHBTeX`, and `XeTeX` era. In fact, its earliest iterations predate the release of `pdfTeX` by nearly five years and the introduction of Unicode-aware TeX engines by more than a decade.

At its core, `arabtex` represents a significant technical achievement in the domain of macro-level TEX programming. It provides the means to render Arabic script using a custom transliteration scheme and a series of highly specialized font encodings designed for the TEX system. Given the limited typesetting capabilities available at the time, especially with respect to right-to-left scripts and contextual shaping, the package employed ingenious workarounds that are still operational today.

However, it is important to note that much of `arabtex`'s internal codebase, including core support files and font definitions, dates back to the early 2000s, with many components last updated around 2003. This means that despite its continued utility, the package may exhibit compatibility issues when used with modern LaTeX distributions or recent versions of packages with which it was never originally tested. Moreover, since `arabtex` does not natively support Unicode input or OpenType font rendering, it is somewhat constrained compared to newer tools built for modern typesetting engines.

Nonetheless, `arabtex` remains a valuable tool for archival workflows, especially when Unicode support is not required or when working within legacy publishing environments where `pdfLaTeX` is mandated. The following sections will demonstrate how to use `arabtex` effectively and how it compares to Unicode-based solutions using engines like `XeLaTeX` and `LuaLaTeX`.

Here is a minimal document that uses `arabtex` to typeset a simple Arabic phrase:

Input Using `arabtex`

```
\documentclass[a4paper,10pt]{article}
\usepackage{arabtex}
\usepackage{utf8}
\setcode{utf8}

\begin{document}
The word assalamu alaykum is written in Arabic: \<السلام عليكم>.
You can also use the command \verb|\RL{arabic text}| as: \RL{السلام عليكم}.

\end{document}
```

This will render the output:

The word **assalamu alaykum** written in Arabic as: السلام عليكم. You can also use the command `\RL{arabic text}` like: السلام عليكم.

5.2.2 arabtex: Transliteration or UTF-8 Input

The `arabtex` package offers a distinctive approach to typesetting Arabic text by utilizing a specialized transliteration system. Instead of writing Arabic in its native script, users represent Arabic words using an extended form of the Latin alphabet. This transliterated input is then automatically processed and converted into properly shaped Arabic glyphs during compilation.

This transliteration-based workflow is a fundamental design choice of `arabtex`, particularly suited to the pre-Unicode era in which the package was developed. It allows authors unfamiliar with Arabic keyboards or lacking right-to-left input tools to type Arabic content using only standard ASCII characters.

Below is a small example illustrating how transliterated Latin script is interpreted and rendered as Arabic text:

Basic Example with Transliteration

```
\documentclass[12pt]{article}
\usepackage{arabtex}
\usepackage{utf8}
% For compatibility with Unicode editors
\begin{document}
\setarab       % use Arabic conventions
\vocalize      % include short vowels
%\transtrue %if you want
%transliteration,
```

```
                uncomment this
\arabtrue
% enable Arabic script rendering
\centerline{\RL{qAlat 'ummu Zayd:
yA waladI, hal faraghta min
wA.zifataka?}}
\begin{RLtext}
faqAla Zayd: na`am yA 'ummI, ra.tabtu
kutubI, wa-'a`dattu .darsI, wa-ghasaltu
'asnAnI.qAlat 'ummu Zayd:.hasanan yA
waladI, 'antaka waladun mujtahidun.
\end{RLtext}
\end{document}
```

This arabtex example will produce right-aligned Arabic script with full vocalization (i.e., short vowels), simulating a dialogue between a boy named Zayd and his mother. The Arabic text will appear properly shaped, connected, and formatted from right to left as:

قَالَت أُمُّ ■َيد: يَا وَلَدِي، هَل فَرَگهتَ مِن وَاظِفَتَكَ؟

فَقَالَ ■َيد:

نَعَم يَا أُمِّي، رَطَبتُ كُتُبِي، وَأَعدَتُّ ضَرسِي، وَگهَسَلتُ أَسنَانِي.

قَالَت أُمُّ ■َيد:

حَسَنَن يَا وَلَدِي، أَنتَكَ وَلَدُن مُجتَهِدُن.

While recent engines such as `XeLaTeX` and `LuaLaTeX` allow direct UTF-8 input of Arabic characters, `arabtex` remains an option for workflows requiring transliteration or where Unicode is not fully supported. In addition, the transliteration system may aid beginners in understanding Arabic phonetics and structure before transitioning to native-script input.

It is worth noting that although `arabtex` does support UTF-8 input to some degree, it is primarily designed for transliterated input and may exhibit inconsistent behavior with direct Arabic script unless carefully configured. For full UTF-8 input support and advanced font rendering, modern alternatives like `polyglossia` with `XeLaTeX` are strongly recommended.

5.2.3 An arabtex Using babel

To enable better integration in multilingual documents, `arabtex` can be combined with the `babel` package.

Combining arabtex with babel

```
\documentclass[12pt]{article}
\usepackage[arabic,english]{babel}
\usepackage{arabtex}
\usepackage[utf8]{inputenc}
\begin{document}

\selectlanguage{arabic}
\setarab
\transtrue

\RL{al-hamdu li-llaahi rabbi
al-caalaamiiin}

\selectlanguage{english}
\textbf{Translation:} Praise be to God,
Lord of the Worlds.

\end{document}
```

5.2.4 Encoding and Language Configuration for Arabic in `arabtex` with `babel`

Typesetting Arabic with the `arabtex` package often involves additional configuration to ensure that input encoding, language-specific document elements, and font rendering are correctly handled. Although `arabtex` uses its own transliteration system, integration with the `babel` package can enhance the document's multilingual functionality, especially when paired with appropriate encoding support.

Input Encoding. Historically, LaTeX documents compiled with `pdfLaTeX` required explicit declaration of the input encoding to correctly interpret text files stored in different character encodings. For UTF-8 encoded files, a common format for modern editors and operating systems, this was traditionally done by adding the following line in the document preamble:

```
\usepackage[utf8]{inputenc}
```

However, since the release of TeX Live 2018, UTF-8 has become the default input encoding for LaTeX. Therefore, it is no longer necessary to explicitly load the `inputenc` package for documents using UTF-8, provided your TeX distribution is up to date. That said, for compatibility or clarity, some users still prefer to include it explicitly in legacy projects or when working with older systems.

Language-Specific Document Elements. When integrating `arabtex` with the `babel` package, one can benefit from improved handling of Arabic-specific typesetting features, such as directionality and localized document elements (e.g., date formats and section titles). The basic setup looks like this:

```
\usepackage[arabic]{babel}
```

This configuration provides Arabic names for standard document elements and supports bidirectional text rendering. If Latin script is needed within an Arabic environment, it can be inserted using the `\textLR{...}` command:

```
\textLR{This is a Latin phrase.}
```

This tells `babel` to temporarily switch to left-to-right mode, preserving the correct layout of multilingual documents.

Font Encoding. Finally, successful Arabic typesetting depends on having access to fonts that include the necessary Arabic glyphs. The output encoding must be matched with appropriate fonts to correctly render Arabic characters. In traditional LaTeX with `arabtex`, font handling is somewhat limited, as it relies on older font encodings compatible with `pdfLaTeX`. Modern engines such as `XeLaTeX` or `LuaLaTeX` offer better support for Arabic by enabling direct access to Unicode and OpenType fonts, but with `arabtex` under `pdfLaTeX`, users must ensure that the required fonts and format definitions are preinstalled and correctly referenced.

5.3 Typesetting Chinese

Typesetting Chinese in LaTeX poses unique challenges compared to Latin-based languages. Chinese is a logographic writing system that does not use alphabetic characters or word spacing, and its character set spans tens of thousands of glyphs. As such, successful typesetting of Chinese content in LaTeX requires appropriate support for Unicode input, as well as fonts capable of rendering Chinese characters accurately. To meet these requirements, modern LaTeX engines such as `XeLaTeX` and `LuaLaTeX` have become essential tools. Both compilers provide native support for UTF-8 encoding and are capable of working with system-installed OpenType and TrueType fonts, making them ideal choices for Chinese document preparation.

To simplify Chinese typesetting in LaTeX, the `ctex` bundle offers a set of document classes and packages tailored to Chinese users. Among these, the `ctexart` class is the most commonly used, particularly for articles or smaller documents. When compiled with `XeLaTeX`, the `ctexart` class automatically configures the document for Chinese typesetting: it loads appropriate fonts, enables bidirectional support for mixing Chinese and Latin scripts, and localizes document elements such as the abstract and table of contents.

The following example illustrates a minimal LaTeX document written using the `ctexart` class. It includes simplified and traditional Chinese text, alongside English sentences and mathematical expressions, demonstrating the ease with which multilingual content can be typeset using modern tools:

Example: Chinese Typesetting with ctexart

LaTeX Code:

```
\documentclass{ctexart}
\begin{document}
\tableofcontents
\begin{abstract}
本文展示了如何在同一份文档中混合使用中文、英文与数学公式。
\end{abstract}
\section{引言}
欢迎阅读本文件。本章节主要介绍中文排版与英文混排的基础内容。
\section{数学与多语言混排}
我们可以很自然地将数学公式与不同语言的文本结合在一起，例如：
\[
E = mc^2
\]
在这里，中文、英文 (English)、以及数学表达式同时出现在一段内容中。
\section{繁體中文示範}
這裡是一些繁體中文的示例文字，適合展示不同中文字符集的兼容性。
\end{document}
```

This will render the output:

目录

摘要

本文展示了如何在同一份文档中混合使用中文、英文与数学公式。

1 引言

欢迎阅读本文件。本章节主要介绍中文排版与英文混排的基础内容。

2 数学与多语言混排

我们可以很自然地将数学公式与不同语言的文本结合在一起，例如：

$$E = mc^2$$

在这里，中文、英文 (English)、以及数学表达式同时出现在一段内容中。

3 繁體中文示範

這[F]是一些繁體中文的示例文字，適合展示不同中文字符集的兼容性。

This example demonstrates several key features of the `ctexart` class. First, it confirms that Chinese characters can be typed directly into the source file using UTF-8 encoding. No additional packages such as `inputenc` are necessary, and there is no need for environment wrappers such as `CJK` or `RLtext` for right-to-left alignment. The engine takes care of font selection and layout. Second, both simplified Chinese and traditional Chinese render properly within the same document, provided that the selected fonts support both writing systems. Finally, Latin text and mathematical expressions can be freely mixed with Chinese characters, allowing seamless multilingual and technical typesetting.

The flexibility of this setup makes it especially useful for international academic writing, educational documents, and technical reports that require the integration of Chinese text with formal mathematical notation. For longer projects such as books or theses, this approach ensures professional formatting while maintaining compatibility with international typesetting standards.

Subsequent sections will explore more specific tools and packages for Chinese typesetting, including the use of `xeCJK` with `XeLaTeX`, the `CJKutf8` package with `pdfLaTeX`, and customization strategies for fonts and layout using the `ctex` suite.

5.3.1 The ctex Classes

Chinese typesetting in LaTeX is significantly simplified through the use of the `ctex` bundle, which provides a robust and modern solution for documents written in simplified or traditional Chinese. Unlike older tools that required manual configuration of fonts, input encodings, and language settings, the `ctex` package streamlines these processes by offering a set of document classes tailored specifically for Chinese content. These include `ctexart`, `ctexrep`, `ctexbook`, and `ctexbeamer`, which are functionally parallel to the standard LaTeX classes `article`, `report`, `book`, and `beamer`, respectively.

To begin using one of these classes, a user simply needs to declare it at the top of the document using the standard `\documentclass` syntax. For example, writing `\documentclass{ctexart}` in the preamble activates the class with Chinese localization already configured. Once loaded, this class automatically takes care of several localization tasks. Section headings like "Abstract" and "Table of Contents" are translated; Chinese date formats are applied; and fonts are assigned appropriately for Chinese scripts, all without the need for manual setup.

A key advantage of the ctex classes lies in their integration with modern compilers such as XeLaTeX and LuaLaTeX. These engines provide native support for UTF-8 encoding and system fonts, eliminating the need for 8-bit encodings or virtual font setups. Users can easily specify fonts with the \setCJKmainfont command. For instance:

Font Configuration

LaTeX Code:

```
\documentclass{ctexart}
\usepackage{fontspec}
\setCJKmainfont{BabelStone Han}
\begin{document}
(....your message in Chinese....)
\end{document}
```

Expected Output:
A document rendered with the message "(...Chinese output...)" displayed in the BabelStone Han font, assuming the font is available on the system or uploaded to Overleaf

Beyond the main body font, the ctex package also allows users to assign specific fonts for different font families. The commands \setCJKsansfont and \setCJKmonofont enable customization of sans-serif and monospaced text, which is especially useful when working with structured layouts, tables, or code listings.

Although the ctex classes are primarily configured for simplified Chinese, they are also compatible with traditional Chinese characters, as long as the selected font includes the necessary glyphs. For example, the default Fandol font supports both variants, enabling the seamless use of both writing systems within a single document. However, if the chosen font lacks glyphs for traditional Chinese, characters may be rendered as blank boxes or result in compilation errors. Thus, font selection remains a critical step for ensuring proper display across dialects.

For more advanced scenarios, such as using a custom document class, perhaps a thesis class provided by an academic institution, it is still possible to incorporate `ctex`'s functionality without changing the base class. By loading the `ctex` package manually in the preamble, users can access Chinese typesetting features while retaining the structure and styling defined by the original class. For instance:

Using `ctex` with Custom Classes

```
\documentclass{UniThesis}
\usepackage{ctex}
```

This approach preserves compatibility with institutional templates while adding robust Chinese language support, including proper hyphenation, punctuation spacing, and date formatting.

In conclusion, the `ctex` classes and package offer an accessible, powerful framework for producing Chinese-language documents. They provide localization, font management, and structural conventions with minimal configuration, making them the preferred choice for users seeking high-quality Chinese typesetting in LaTeX. Future sections will explore additional tools such as `xeCJK` for more lightweight customization, or the use of `CJKutf8` for `pdfLaTeX`-based workflows.

5.3.2 Using `xeCJK` with XeLaTeX

While the `ctex` classes offer comprehensive support for Chinese documents, there are cases where a lightweight approach is preferred, especially when working with custom document classes or when full localization is unnecessary. In such situations, the `xeCJK` package provides a flexible and efficient solution for typesetting Chinese characters. This package is designed to work with the XeLaTeX compiler and leverages Unicode support and OpenType font capabilities to render Chinese text accurately.

The `xeCJK` package allows direct input of UTF-8 encoded Chinese characters, which is particularly convenient for bilingual or multilingual documents that require mixing Latin and CJK (Chinese, Japanese, Korean) scripts. Additionally, it supports both simplified and traditional Chinese through proper font configuration.

Basic Example Using `xeCJK`

Below is a simple LaTeX document that demonstrates the use of `xeCJK` to include Chinese sections in a document. Note that this must be compiled with XeLaTeX:

Chinese Typesetting with `xeCJK`

LaTeX Code:

```
\documentclass{article}
\usepackage{xeCJK}
\setCJKmainfont{FandolSong-Regular} % or another installed Chinese font

\begin{document}
\section{前言}
这是一些文字。

\section{关于数学部分}
数学、中英文皆可以混排。You can intersperse math,
Chinese and English (Latin script) without adding
extra environments.

這是繁體中文。
\end{document}
```

This will render the output:

1 前言

这是一些文字。

2 关于数学部分

数学、中英文皆可以混排。You can intersperse math, Chinese and English (Latin script) without adding extra environments.

這是繁體中文。

In this example, the `\setCJKmainfont` command is used to select a Chinese font already available in the system, such as `FandolSong-Regular`. You can replace this with other fonts like `SimSun`, `KaiTi`, or any custom OpenType font depending on your platform.

This approach provides a clean and minimal configuration for documents that do not require the full localization features offered by `ctex`. It also works seamlessly for inserting Chinese snippets into primarily English documents or vice versa.

Remark 5.3.1 *You must use XeLaTeX to compile documents that use `xeCJK`. Attempting to compile with `pdfLaTeX` or `LuaLaTeX` will result in errors.*

5.3.3 Using `xeCJK` with XeLaTeX

Although the `ctex` bundle provides a rich, localized environment for producing full Chinese-language documents, there are many cases where users may not need such a comprehensive setup. When the primary requirement is simply to include Chinese text, either in short passages or intermixed with English, the `xeCJK` package becomes an elegant and lightweight alternative. Unlike `ctex`, which modifies many aspects of document structure and localization, `xeCJK` focuses solely on enabling proper font rendering and spacing for Chinese, Japanese, and Korean (CJK) characters. This makes it ideal for multilingual or academic documents where English is dominant and Chinese is used sparingly.

The `xeCJK` package requires the XeLaTeX engine, which offers native support for UTF-8 encoding and OpenType font technologies. This makes it possible to write Chinese text directly in the source file using modern fonts available on your system or through Overleaf's font set. Because `xeCJK` does not assume any localization or document class requirements, it integrates easily with standard LaTeX classes such as `article`, `report`, or even custom templates.

To illustrate how `xeCJK` works in practice, consider the following minimal example. It shows how to include a small amount of Chinese text, seamlessly embedded within an otherwise English document. The document must be compiled with XeLaTeX:

Example: Minimal Chinese Typesetting Using xeCJK

LaTeX Code:

```
\documentclass{article}
\usepackage{xeCJK}
\setCJKmainfont{FandolSong-Regular} % or another installed Chinese font

\begin{document}
\section{前言}
这是一些文字。

\section{关于数学部分}
数学、中英文皆可以混排。You can intersperse math,
Chinese and English (Latin script) without adding
extra environments.

這是繁體中文。
\end{document}
```

This will render the output:

1 前言

这是一些文字。

2 关于数学部分

数学、中英文皆可以混排。You can intersperse math, Chinese and English (Latin script) without adding extra environments.

這是繁體中文。

In this example, the key command `\setCJKmainfont` sets the primary font for Chinese text. The font name must refer to an installed OpenType or TrueType font that supports Chinese characters. The `FandolSong-Regular` font is widely available and works well as a default choice, but users can substitute other fonts such as `SimSun`, `Noto Serif CJK`, or `KaiTi` if desired. Overleaf users should ensure the font they specify is either supported by the platform or uploaded manually as part of the project files.

One of the great strengths of `xeCJK` is its unobtrusive behavior: it enables proper line breaking, kerning, and inter-script spacing without altering other aspects of your document. For example, mathematical expressions, tables, or code listings remain unaffected. This makes the package ideal for scientific papers, instructional material, or technical documentation in which Chinese and English content coexist naturally.

It is important to note that `xeCJK` is only compatible with the XeLaTeX compiler. Attempting to use it with `pdfLaTeX` or `LuaLaTeX` will result in compilation errors. For LuaLaTeX users, the analogous package is `luaCJK`, though its ecosystem is less mature.

Remark 5.3.2 *Always compile **`xeCJK`**-based documents with XeLaTeX. Neither **`pdfLaTeX`** nor **`LuaLaTeX`** supports the font commands or CJK spacing mechanisms used by this package.*

5.3.4 Typesetting Chinese with `CJKutf8` and `pdfLaTeX`

Although modern LaTeX compilers such as XeLaTeX and LuaLaTeX offer robust support for multilingual typesetting, including Chinese, there are still scenarios in which users may prefer or be required to use the traditional `pdfLaTeX` engine. In such cases, the `CJKutf8` package provides a workable solution for including Chinese (and other CJK) text in LaTeX documents. However, due to the inherent limitations of `pdfLaTeX` in handling Unicode and OpenType fonts, the process requires specific environments and font encodings to render non-Latin scripts correctly.

The `CJKutf8` package enables UTF-8 input for Chinese, Japanese, and Korean scripts when used with `pdfLaTeX`. Unlike XeLaTeX or LuaLaTeX, which can typeset UTF-8 characters directly, `pdfLaTeX` relies on legacy font encodings. Therefore, Chinese text must be enclosed within a special environment called `CJK*`, which activates the CJK typesetting mode while suppressing intercharacter spacing that might otherwise appear between glyphs.

To illustrate how this works, consider the following example:

Example: Using CJKutf8 with pdfLaTeX

LaTeX Code:

```
\documentclass{article}
\usepackage{CJKutf8}
\begin{document}
\begin{CJK*}{UTF8}{gbsn}
\section{介绍}
欢迎来到这篇文档。在这里我们将展示如何使用 LaTeX 排版中文内容。
\section{混合排版示例}
你可以轻松地将数学符号与文字混合，例如：$\int_0^1 x^2 \, dx = \frac{1}{3}$。
此外，还可以插入英语单词，如 \textit{integration}。
\end{CJK*}
Now continuing in English only.
\begin{CJK*}{UTF8}{bsmi}
這是一段展示如何使用繁體中文的簡單例子。排版效果應該是正確的。
\end{CJK*}
\end{document}
```

This will render the output:

1 介绍

欢迎来到这篇文档。在这里我们将展示如何使用LaTeX 排版中文内容。

2 混合排版示例

你可以轻松地将数学符号与文字混合，例如：$\int_0^1 x^2\,dx = \frac{1}{3}$。此外，还可以插入英语单词，如*integration*。

Now continuing in English only.

這是一段展示如何使用繁體中文的簡單例子。排版效果應該是正確的。

This document will compile successfully with `pdfLaTeX`, and the Chinese text will render correctly, assuming your TeX distribution includes the appropriate font files for the `gbsn` and `bsmi` encodings. In this example, the simplified Chinese portion is enclosed within a `CJK*` environment using the `gbsn` font encoding, while the traditional Chinese portion uses the `bsmi` encoding.

The first argument of the `CJK*` environment (`UTF8`) specifies the input encoding of the source file; UTF-8 is the most commonly used encoding today and is natively supported in modern editors and platforms like Overleaf. The second argument refers to the font encoding scheme. Common values include:

- `gbsn` for simplified Chinese (using fonts like `gbsn00lp.ttf`)
- `bsmi` for traditional Chinese
- `min`, `mj`, `sjis` for Japanese
- `ks` for Korean

These font encodings map character codes to legacy bitmap or Type 1 fonts that are bundled with distributions like TeX Live or MiKTeX. While these fonts may not be visually comparable to modern OpenType fonts, they remain functional for many academic or archival use cases.

It is worth noting that the `CJKutf8` package is particularly useful in documents that are primarily written in a Western language, such as English, but require occasional inclusion of CJK text. In these contexts, wrapping CJK phrases or sections within a `CJK*` environment avoids switching compilers and ensures compatibility with existing `pdfLaTeX`-based workflows. However, for documents written predominantly in Chinese or those requiring high typographic quality, full Unicode font support, and more advanced formatting, it is advisable to use XeLaTeX or LuaLaTeX with the `ctex` or `xeCJK` packages instead.

Remark 5.3.3 *Unlike XeLaTeX or LuaLaTeX, which can render Chinese text directly using system-installed fonts, `pdfLaTeX` cannot use arbitrary TrueType or OpenType fonts. The CJK font encodings used with `CJKutf8` are fixed and generally non-extensible.*

5.4 Typesetting French, German, and Spanish

5.4.1 Typesetting French

French is one of the most widely used languages in international publications, academic writing, and formal documentation. When typesetting French in LaTeX, it is important not only to support accented characters such as â, ê, î, ô, û but also to ensure that language-specific rules, such as proper hyphenation, spacing before punctuation marks, and translated interface elements (like "Table des matières" instead of "Table of Contents"), are correctly applied.

This section explores the best practices for typesetting French in LaTeX, including configuration using packages such as `babel` and `polyglossia`, depending on your compiler. We will focus on both monolingual French documents and multilingual documents that combine French with other languages, such as English.

Whether you are preparing a thesis, article, letter, or poster, the goal is to make sure that your document adheres to typographic standards of the French language while leveraging the typesetting power of LaTeX.

Transliterated Input Using `arabtex`

```
\documentclass{article}
% UTF-8 input assumed as default
(since 2018)

% Set the font (output) encoding
\usepackage[T1]{fontenc}
% Not needed by LuaLaTeX or XeLaTeX

% German-specific commands
```

```
\usepackage[ngerman]{babel}
\usepackage[autolanguage]{numprint}
% For the \numprint and \nombre commands

% Hyphenation rules
\usepackage{hyphenat}
\hyphenation{In-for-ma-tik Algo-rith-mus
Da-ten-ver-ar-bei-tung}
\begin{document}
\tableofcontents
\vspace{2cm} % Add vertical space
\begin{abstract}
Dies ist eine kurze Zusammenfassung des
Inhalts dieses Dokuments, das in
deutscher Sprache verfasst wurde.

\end{abstract}

\section{Einleitung}
Dies ist der erste Abschnitt, der einige
typische Merkmale der deutschen Sprache
demonstriert. Wörter werden korrekt
getrennt, und Sonderzeichen wie Umlaute
oder das werden automatisch unterstützt.

\section{
Beispiel für Listen und Mathematik}

Dieser Abschnitt demonstriert die
Verwendung von Listen und
mathematischen Ausdrücken in einem
deutschsprachigen Dokument.
\begin{itemize}
    \item Erstes Element
```

```
    \item Zweites Element
\end{itemize}
Hier ist eine mathematische Formel mit
eingebetteter Zahl:

\[
\lim_{n \to \infty}
f(n) = \nombre{103476.21}
\]
\end{document}
```

Understanding Text Encoding in LaTeX Environments

At its core, a text file, such as a LaTeX source file with the extension `.tex`, is a sequence of integers that correspond to character representations. These integers are not characters themselves, but codes that refer to specific symbols, letters, or control instructions. Therefore, processing any text file inherently involves interpreting these numeric codes into readable characters based on a predetermined set of rules known as a text encoding scheme.

The critical question becomes: what do those integers actually stand for? The answer lies in the encoding system that was used when the file was written. Encoding schemes such as ASCII, Latin-1, or UTF-8 define mappings between integers and characters, determining how a computer interprets the raw numeric data in a text file.

Text files can be created in countless environments around the world, utilizing diverse operating systems, input tools, and regional language settings. The encoding used to save a text file may depend on the local conventions of the originating system. Although such text files may display correctly within their native ecosystem, issues can arise when these files are opened on a different system that assumes a different encoding. This often results in garbled or unreadable characters, commonly referred to as "mojibake."

For seamless exchange and interpretation of text files, both the producing and consuming systems must share a common understanding of the encoding used. If not, the result is likely to be misinterpretation of the character data. Furthermore, correct interpretation of characters alone is not sufficient; appropriate fonts must also be available on the system to visually render the characters as recognizable symbols or glyphs.

In the context of LaTeX, particularly when working with non-ASCII content or multilingual documents, understanding text encoding is essential. Choosing the right encoding and ensuring proper font support plays a critical role in producing accurate and aesthetically correct documents.

Understanding Input and Output Encodings in LaTeX

When working with multilingual or accented text in LaTeX, it is essential to understand how characters are interpreted during both the input and output stages of document compilation. This involves two related but distinct concerns: input encoding, which affects how characters in your source file are read, and output encoding, which governs how characters are represented and typeset in the resulting document.

Input Encoding: `inputenc`, UTF-8, and the 2018 Change

Historically, a wide variety of 8-bit encoding schemes—such as Latin-1, Windows-1252, and others, were used for text files across different platforms. To ensure compatibility between files created with different encodings, the LaTeX community developed the `inputenc` package. This package allowed authors to specify which encoding was used in their source file, enabling the correct interpretation of non-ASCII characters.

Over time, however, the computing world moved toward a unified character encoding system, Unicode, and in particular its popular variant, UTF-8. UTF-8 became the standard for encoding text files, enabling support for virtually every character in use today, including those from non-Latin alphabets.

Before 2018, it was standard practice to include the following line in the preamble of any UTF-8 encoded LaTeX document:

```
\usepackage[utf8]{inputenc}
```

This directive informed LaTeX to interpret the input file as being encoded in UTF-8. However, with the release of TEX Live 2018, a major change was introduced: UTF-8 became the default input encoding for all LaTeX documents. As a result, it is no longer necessary to explicitly load the `inputenc` package when using UTF-8, although doing so remains harmless. For example, all text files created on Overleaf are UTF-8 encoded by default, and documents compiled using `pdfLaTeX` will correctly process them without requiring additional configuration.

Output Encoding: The `fontenc` Package

While input encoding tells LaTeX how to interpret the source file, output encoding is concerned with how characters are typeset, i.e., how they are mapped to glyphs in the fonts used by the document. This process is handled by the `fontenc` package.

By default, LaTeX uses the OT1 encoding, which is a 7-bit font encoding capable of representing only 128 characters. It does not include precomposed accented characters (e.g., é, ñ, ü), so LaTeX must simulate them by combining a base letter with a separate accent mark. This method of constructing accented characters not only affects hyphenation but also causes issues with copy-pasting text from generated PDFs, accents may be lost or misinterpreted.

To improve output quality and functionality, it is strongly recommended to switch to the T1 encoding by including the following line in your preamble:

```
\usepackage[T1]{fontenc}
```

Using T1 encoding allows access to prebuilt glyphs for accented characters and improves hyphenation patterns for many European languages. It also ensures that copying and pasting from the resulting PDF preserves the correct characters, which is especially important for digital documents.

Using `babel` and `numprint` for French Language Support

To support the unique typographic and grammatical features of specific languages, LaTeX provides a number of language-aware packages. When working with French documents, one of the most essential packages is `babel`, which facilitates not only proper hyphenation rules but also translates common document elements, such as section headings, the title of the abstract, and the table of contents, into French.

To enable this functionality, the `babel` package should be loaded with the appropriate language option in the document preamble:

```
\usepackage[french]{babel}
```

Once this is done, LaTeX automatically adjusts many elements of the document. For instance, the word "Abstract" will be rendered as "Résumé," and "Contents" will appear as "Table des matières." These translations are handled internally by `babel` based on the selected language and require no further intervention from the user.

In addition to `babel`, other language-sensitive packages may also be used to enhance formatting behavior. One such example is the `numprint` package, which is particularly helpful when dealing with numerical data. To ensure that numbers are formatted according to French typographic conventions, such as using a comma as the decimal separator and inserting non-breaking spaces for digit grouping, you can load `numprint` as follows:

```
\usepackage[autolanguage]{numprint}
```

This configuration allows the package to detect the current language setting automatically and adjust the formatting of numbers accordingly. For instance, using the command `\nombre{12345.67}` will print the number as "12345,67" in French typesetting, applying correct spacing and punctuation norms.

Together, `babel` and `numprint` provide a solid foundation for producing documents that are not only linguistically accurate but also typographically appropriate for the French language.

5.4.2 Typesetting German

German is one of the most widely supported Western European languages in LaTeX. It requires proper handling of special characters such as umlauts (ä, ö, ü), the eszett (ß), as well as specific hyphenation rules. In this section, we demonstrate how to typeset German text with correct localization of document elements like headings, captions, and number formatting.

Understanding Text Encoding and Character Representation

Every LaTeX source file, or any plain text file, is ultimately a sequence of numerical codes. These codes are integer values, and each one corresponds to a specific character through a predefined system called a text encoding. The encoding scheme determines how those numerical values should be interpreted: for example, does the number 97 refer to the Latin lowercase letter "a," or does it represent a different symbol in another language?

This concept becomes particularly important when files are created and shared across different systems and locales. A text file produced on one operating system, in a specific language environment, may assume an encoding that is not recognized by another system reading the file. Since most text files do not explicitly declare their encoding, confusion may arise when a sequence of numbers is interpreted using the wrong mapping scheme, resulting in garbled or unreadable output.

To avoid such mismatches, it is crucial that both the producer and the consumer of a LaTeX document or any text-based data agree on the character encoding being used. This agreement ensures that the numbers stored in the file accurately correspond to the intended characters, whether they are Latin letters, accented characters, or scripts like Arabic or Devanagari.

Moreover, once characters are correctly identified, they still require a suitable font for visual representation. The chosen font must include the necessary glyphs, the graphical shapes of the characters to render them on screen or in print. Without such a font, even correctly decoded characters may appear as blank boxes or question marks.

In modern LaTeX workflows, UTF-8 has become the standard encoding format, supporting virtually all human languages through a unified set of mappings. Still, understanding the underlying principles of text encoding remains essential for resolving errors and ensuring multilingual documents render properly across all platforms.

Input and Output Encodings in LaTeX

The ability to represent and typeset characters accurately in LaTeX documents depends fundamentally on two encoding mechanisms: input encoding, which interprets the characters in the source file, and output encoding, which determines how those characters are rendered using fonts.

Historically, LaTeX was designed to work with a variety of 8-bit input encodings, which differed widely across platforms and languages. To accommodate this diversity, the `inputenc` package was introduced, allowing users to specify the character encoding of their input files explicitly. For instance, one could write `\usepackage[utf8]{inputenc}` in the preamble to indicate that the source file was encoded using UTF-8. Prior to 2018, this declaration was essential for enabling proper interpretation of multilingual or accented characters in documents processed with `pdfLaTeX`.

However, the landscape of text encoding evolved with the widespread adoption of Unicode and its UTF-8 encoding standard, which became the default across most computing environments. Recognizing this shift, the LaTeX development team made a significant change in 2018: they designated UTF-8 as the default input encoding. Consequently, users no longer need to specify `\usepackage[utf8]{inputenc}` explicitly in documents created with modern LaTeX distributions such as TeX Live 2018 and later. Nevertheless, including the package does no harm and may still be useful for backward compatibility or clarity. Additional details on this transition can be found in the April 2018 issue of *LaTeX News* and the Overleaf blog post titled "TeX Live upgrade, September 2019."

While input encoding determines how characters are read, output encoding is responsible for how they are displayed. In LaTeX, this task is managed by the `fontenc` package, which maps character codes to specific glyphs in the font. By default, LaTeX uses the 7-bit OT1 encoding, which does not include precomposed glyphs for many accented characters. As a result, it often constructs these characters from a base letter and an overlaid accent, a method that can interfere with proper hyphenation and copy-pasting from PDFs.

To address these limitations, users are encouraged to include `\usepackage[T1]{fontenc}` in their document preambles. The T1 encoding expands the character set to include most Latin-based glyphs used in European languages, enabling better hyphenation and ensuring that accented characters are correctly typeset as single, unified symbols. This change improves both the appearance of the document and its accessibility for digital consumption.

Together, the `inputenc` and `fontenc` packages have historically played a vital role in supporting multilingual typesetting in LaTeX. Although their roles have diminished slightly in XeLaTeX and LuaLaTeX workflows, which handle Unicode natively and allow direct font specification—they remain essential tools in documents compiled with `pdfLaTeX`.

Enabling German Language Features with `babel`

To support German language conventions in LaTeX documents, including hyphenation, localized document elements, and typographical standards, the `babel` package offers robust functionality. When writing in modern German, it is advisable to load the package with the `ngerman` option:

```
\usepackage[ngerman]{babel}
```

This command activates contemporary German spelling rules, adhering to the reforms ratified in 1998, and ensures that LaTeX uses appropriate translations for structural elements of your document. For instance, section titles such as "Abstract" and "Contents" will automatically appear as "Zusammenfassung" and "Inhaltsverzeichnis," respectively.

It is important to distinguish between the two available options for German: `german` and `ngerman`. The former adheres to the pre-1998 orthography, while the latter implements the updated spelling conventions now widely accepted in Germany, Austria, and Switzerland. Choosing `ngerman` is therefore essential for documents that aim to comply with current linguistic standards in official, academic, or publishing contexts.

Using `babel` with German also enables support for typographical conventions specific to the language, such as proper quotation marks and date formatting. When combined with other packages like `inputenc`, `fontenc`, or `csquotes`, this setup ensures accurate and polished German-language typesetting with minimal additional configuration.

5.4.3 Typesetting Spanish

Spanish is one of the most widely spoken languages in the world and is well-supported in LaTeX. Typesetting Spanish documents requires careful handling of accented characters such as á, é, í, ó, ú, and the letter ñ, as well as appropriate language-specific typographic rules. In this section, we explore how to create Spanish-language documents in LaTeX that are linguistically accurate and typographically correct.

Understanding Text Encoding and Character Representation

Just like any LaTeX source file, a Spanish-language document is fundamentally a sequence of numbers, integer values that encode specific characters based on a chosen encoding scheme. This numerical representation allows LaTeX to map values in the text file to readable characters. For instance, the number 241 may represent the Spanish letter ñ in UTF-8, but it might refer to a completely different character in another encoding.

Because text files are created and read across diverse operating systems, locales, and applications, encoding mismatches can occur if the originating and receiving environments do not agree on how the numerical data should be interpreted. When such discrepancies arise, special characters (including accented letters and punctuation) may display as corrupted glyphs or not at all.

Ensuring consistent character rendering in a Spanish LaTeX document therefore involves both selecting a universal encoding, such as UTF-8, and ensuring that a proper font with support for Spanish characters is available. The font must contain the necessary glyphs for accented vowels, the inverted question and exclamation marks (¿, ¡), and other orthographic features unique to Spanish.

Today, UTF-8 has become the dominant encoding standard across platforms. When used in conjunction with a properly configured LaTeX environment, UTF-8 ensures that Spanish text is interpreted and displayed correctly, regardless of the system on which it is compiled.

5.4.4 Input and Output Encodings in LaTeX

Accurate representation of Spanish characters in a LaTeX document requires proper handling of both input and output encoding. Input encoding determines how the characters typed into the LaTeX source file are interpreted by the compiler, while output encoding governs how those characters are rendered on the page using the appropriate font glyphs.

Historically, LaTeX relied on various 8-bit encodings, which varied by region and platform. To address this fragmentation, the `inputenc` package was developed to allow users to specify the input encoding explicitly. The UTF-8 encoding became a preferred standard for its broad character support, and documents using `pdfLaTeX` would often begin with the line:

```
\usepackage[utf8]{inputenc}
```

However, since 2018, LaTeX distributions such as TeX Live and MiKTeX default to UTF-8 input encoding, eliminating the need to declare it manually. Including the `inputenc` package is still harmless and may be helpful for legacy support or clarity in document headers.

Output encoding is equally essential. By default, LaTeX uses the OT1 encoding, which lacks many of the precomposed glyphs required for Spanish. This can lead to inaccurate hyphenation and poor copy-paste behavior from generated PDFs. To fix this, use the `fontenc` package with the T1 encoding:

```
\usepackage[T1]{fontenc}
```

The T1 encoding supports a wide range of Latin-script characters, enabling LaTeX to access properly formed glyphs for Spanish accents, punctuation, and ligatures. This improves both the visual presentation of the text and its interaction with digital tools like screen readers and PDF viewers.

Together, `inputenc` and `fontenc` form the backbone of reliable Spanish typesetting in `pdfLaTeX`. If you use `xelatex` or `lualatex`, these encodings are handled automatically, and font selection can be managed directly through the `fontspec` package.

Enabling Spanish Language Features with babel

To activate Spanish typographic conventions in a LaTeX document, the recommended approach is to load the `babel` package with the `spanish` option:

```
\usepackage[spanish]{babel}
```

This command enables localized document elements (e.g., replacing "Abstract" with "Resumen" and "Contents" with "Índice"), supports Spanish-style punctuation and spacing, and applies appropriate hyphenation patterns. For documents targeting audiences in Spain or Latin America, these adjustments are essential for linguistic accuracy and stylistic correctness.

Using `babel` with Spanish also ensures correct behavior of quotation marks, date formatting, and decimal symbols, aligning with the typographic standards followed by Spanish-language publications.

As with German, `babel` for Spanish integrates seamlessly with other key LaTeX packages and works in conjunction with `inputenc`, `fontenc`, and `csquotes` to produce high-quality, professionally typeset documents. For multilingual texts, `babel` also allows on-the-fly language switching using commands such as `\foreignlanguage{spanish}{...}` or `\selectlanguage{spanish}`.

By combining the right encoding setup with language-specific customization provided by `babel`, LaTeX becomes a powerful tool for writing Spanish content in both academic and professional contexts.

5.5 Typesetting Russian

Russian, written in Cyrillic script, presents unique challenges in LaTeX due to its non-Latin character set. To typeset Russian accurately and elegantly, users must consider character encoding, font selection, and language-specific typographic rules. This section explains how to create Russian-language LaTeX documents using modern and legacy methods.

5.5.1 Understanding Cyrillic Text Encoding and Rendering

Unlike languages using the Latin script, Russian relies on a different writing system that requires fonts and encodings specifically tailored to the Cyrillic alphabet. As with any LaTeX input file, the characters typed into the document are stored as a series of numeric codes. These codes must be interpreted using an appropriate text encoding (such as UTF-8) to map each number to a meaningful Cyrillic character.

Given the widespread use of Unicode and the UTF-8 encoding standard, most LaTeX editors and distributions now support Russian text seamlessly, provided the correct packages and compilers are used. However, compatibility issues may arise when switching between systems or using outdated workflows. Therefore, it is essential to ensure the document encoding, compiler, and font all support Cyrillic text.

In addition to correct character interpretation, Russian documents require fonts that contain the glyphs for Cyrillic letters. Without appropriate font support, the output may contain missing symbols or misrendered characters, especially when using `pdfLaTeX` and the default OT1 encoding.

5.5.2 Input and Output Encodings for Russian

To create Russian documents using `pdfLaTeX`, two key packages are required: `inputenc` for specifying the input encoding and `fontenc` for controlling the output glyphs.

Input Encoding with `inputenc`: Before 2018, it was necessary to explicitly include the following line in the preamble to inform LaTeX that the input text uses UTF-8 encoding:

```
\usepackage[utf8]{inputenc}
```

Since 2018, UTF-8 is the default encoding in most LaTeX distributions (such as TeX Live and Overleaf), and the `inputenc` line is often optional. However, including it does no harm and may help with backward compatibility or clarity when sharing your source files.

Output Encoding with `fontenc`: To properly render Cyrillic characters in the output, you should load the `fontenc` package with the `T2A` encoding, which supports Cyrillic glyphs:

```
\usepackage[T2A]{fontenc}
```

Without this, LaTeX may fall back on encodings that are not designed for Cyrillic, resulting in poor typesetting or unreadable characters.

5.5.3 Language Support with `babel` and `polyglossia`

To activate Russian language conventions such as proper hyphenation, translation of document elements, and punctuation styles, the `babel` package can be used with the `russian` option:

```
\usepackage[russian]{babel}
```

If you are using `XeLaTeX` or `LuaLaTeX`, the recommended alternative is `polyglossia`, a modern multilingual typesetting package that is Unicode-aware. Here is a minimal setup:

```
\usepackage{fontspec}
\usepackage{polyglossia}

\setmainlanguage{russian}
\newfontfamily\russianfont{FreeSerif}
```

You can replace `FreeSerif` with any other system-installed font that supports Cyrillic script, such as `DejaVu Serif`, `CMU Serif`, or `Times New Roman`.

5.5.4 Minimal Working Example: Russian with babel and pdfLaTeX

Basic Russian Document (pdfLaTeX)

LaTeX Code:

```
\documentclass{article}
\usepackage[utf8]{inputenc}
\usepackage[T2A]{fontenc}
\usepackage[russian]{babel}
\title{Пример документа}
\author{Доктор ЛаТех}
\date{\today}

\begin{document}
\maketitle
\section{Введение}
Это пример документа на русском языке,
с использованием кириллического алфавита
и русской локализации.

\end{document}
```

This will render the output:

Пример документа

Доктор ЛаТех

25 апреля 2025 г.

1 Введение

Это пример документа на русском языке, с использованием кириллического алфавита и русской локализации.

5.5.5 Minimal Working Example: Russian with polyglossia and XeLaTeX

Basic Russian Document (XeLaTeX)

LaTeX Code:

```
\documentclass{article}
\usepackage{fontspec}
\usepackage{polyglossia}
\setmainlanguage{russian}
\newfontfamily\russianfont{DejaVu Serif}
\title{Пример документа}
\author{Доктор ЛаТех}
\date{\today}

\begin{document}
\maketitle
\section{Введение}
Это пример текста на русском языке,
с правильной кодировкой и шрифтом.
\end{document}
```

This will render the output:

Пример документа

Доктор ЛаТех

25 апреля 2025 г.

1. Введение

Это пример текста на русском языке, с правильной кодировкой и шрифтом.

Typesetting Russian in LaTeX is straightforward with proper configuration. For legacy workflows using pdfLaTeX, make sure to load inputenc, fontenc with T2A, and babel with the russian option. For modern documents using Unicode and OpenType fonts, XeLaTeX or LuaLaTeX with polyglossia and fontspec provide superior results. Regardless of the approach, ensuring consistent encoding and font support is key to producing high-quality Russian documents in LaTeX.

Exercises for Chap. 5: Multilingual and Global Typesetting

5.1 Changing Languages with `babel` and `polyglossia`

1. **Language Switching with `babel`**: Create a short LaTeX document using the `babel` package to switch between English and French. Include one paragraph in each language and demonstrate proper hyphenation and quotation marks.

2. **Using `polyglossia` with XeLaTeX**: Compile a document using `polyglossia` and XeLaTeX with English as the main language and Russian as the secondary language. Include sample text in both languages and ensure proper font rendering.

3. **Right-to-Left vs. Left-to-Right Layout**: Use `polyglossia` to create a document with both Hebrew and English. Ensure the correct text direction and alignment are achieved in each section.

5.2 Typesetting Arabic

1. **Basic Arabic Document**: Write a paragraph in Arabic using either `arabtex` with pdfLaTeX or `polyglossia` with XeLaTeX. Ensure correct script direction and character joining.

2. **Mixed Language Paragraphs**: Create a document with alternating paragraphs in English and Arabic. Highlight how to control text direction using commands such as `\begin{RTL}` and `\begin{LTR}`.

3. **Arabic Font Selection**: Experiment with different Arabic fonts using the `fontspec` package. Write a short paragraph in Arabic and apply two different fonts to compare the visual impact.

5.3 Typesetting Chinese

1. **UTF-8 Chinese Text with `CJKutf8`**: Write a basic Chinese paragraph using `CJKutf8` and pdfLaTeX. Make sure to set the document encoding and wrap the Chinese text in the `CJK*` environment.

2. **Using XeLaTeX with Chinese Fonts**: Create a document using XeLaTeX and `fontspec` to typeset Chinese characters. Select a traditional Chinese font and write a short introduction in Mandarin.

3. **Mixed Chinese-English Document**: Compose a bilingual paragraph that includes both Chinese and English sentences. Maintain appropriate spacing and font consistency for both scripts.

5.4 Typesetting French, German, and Spanish

1. **Diacritics and Special Characters**: Create a LaTeX document with short paragraphs in French, German, and Spanish. Use `babel` to switch languages and demonstrate proper use of diacritics and punctuation (e.g., ñ, ü, ç, ß, ¿, ¡).

2. **Quotations and Hyphenation**: Write one paragraph in each of the three languages using language-specific quotation styles and observe hyphenation rules. Use quotation commands such as `\og ... \fg` (French) and `"‘..."’` (German).

3. **Language-Dependent Typographic Settings**: Experiment with list formatting and date styles under different language settings using `babel` or `polyglossia`.

5.5 Typesetting Russian

1. **Russian Cyrillic with `babel`**: Create a document using the `babel` package with the `russian` option. Type a simple Russian paragraph using Cyrillic characters in UTF-8 encoding.

2. **Russian with `polyglossia` and XeLaTeX**: Reproduce the same content using `polyglossia`. Compare typographic quality and font control with `babel`.

3. **Combining Russian and English**: Create a mixed-language document with headings in English and body text in Russian. Ensure correct font and direction settings are preserved in each section.

Chapter 6

Troubleshooting and Best Practices

Contents

Md. Aquib, *Advanced LaTeX*, University Texts in the Mathematical Sciences, https://doi.org/10.1007/978-981-96-9322-1_6

Abstract: As powerful as LaTeX is, users, especially beginners, often encounter a variety of errors, unexpected behaviors, and formatting inconsistencies. These issues can range from minor typographical quirks to compilation failures that prevent document output entirely. Understanding how to diagnose and resolve such problems is essential to using LaTeX effectively and efficiently.

This chapter is designed to guide you through the most common challenges faced while working with LaTeX, including missing packages, undefined commands, compilation errors, and layout inconsistencies. It provides practical strategies for debugging documents, reading and interpreting log files, and narrowing down the source of an error through systematic isolation.

In addition to troubleshooting, this chapter emphasizes best practices that can help prevent many issues before they arise. Topics include organizing source files, using version control, commenting and structuring code, choosing reliable packages, and writing modular and reusable content. By adopting these habits, you can significantly improve the maintainability, scalability, and clarity of your LaTeX projects.

Whether you are working on a short article or a full-length dissertation, mastering these troubleshooting techniques and incorporating best practices will enhance both your workflow and your final output. This chapter serves as a reference you can return to whenever you encounter obstacles or seek to refine your LaTeX development process.

Keywords: Error handling, Debugging documents, Compilation issues, Git and overleaf, Code optimization, Troubleshooting techniques

6.1 Optimizing Compilation Speed

As your LaTeX project evolves into a longer document with multiple chapters, references, figures, and appendices, you may begin to notice a slowdown in compilation performance. This is especially common in theses, books, or technical reports. To maintain an efficient writing workflow, it is important to adopt strategies that optimize compilation speed during the drafting phase while still ensuring accuracy and document integrity in the final version.

One of the first decisions that impacts performance is the choice of LaTeX engine. The traditional `pdfLaTeX` engine is often the fastest and most compatible option for general use. It converts LaTeX source directly into a PDF, making it ideal for documents that do not require specialized typography, Unicode support, or advanced font features. If your document does require these advanced capabilities, such as custom OpenType fonts or direct system font access, you may consider using `XeLaTeX` or `LuaLaTeX`, both of which offer superior typographic control but at the cost of slower compilation. For most general use cases, however, `pdfLaTeX` remains the most efficient choice.

Another highly effective strategy is to suppress the rendering of images during development. High-resolution figures and graphics are a common bottleneck in LaTeX. By using the `draft` option in the document class, you can instruct LaTeX to skip image rendering entirely and instead display an empty box placeholder. This reduces the processing burden considerably during iterative editing.

Using Draft Mode to Speed Up Compilation

LaTeX Code:

```
\documentclass[draft]{article}
\usepackage{graphicx}

\begin{document}

\includegraphics[width=\textwidth]
  {large_image.png}

\end{document}
```

Output Overview:
Instead of loading and displaying `large_image.png`, LaTeX inserts an empty box showing the image dimensions. This change can dramatically decrease compile time when many images are used.

If only specific images are problematic, you can apply `draft` mode selectively at the image level:

```
\includegraphics[draft]{large_figure.png}
```

For even more fine-tuned control over large projects, it is common to break the document into modular components. Instead of keeping the entire content in a single `.tex` file, each chapter or section can be stored in a separate file and inserted using `\input`. This practice not only makes the source code easier to manage but also allows selective compilation. You can focus on a single chapter without waiting for the entire document to recompile.

To streamline this process even further, the `subfiles` package provides the ability to compile individual sub-documents independently while maintaining compatibility with the full document structure.

Working on Isolated Chapters with `subfiles`

Chapter File: `chapter1.tex`

```
\documentclass[../main.tex]{subfiles}

\begin{document}
\chapter{Introduction}
This chapter introduces the topic.
\end{document}
```

Output Overview:
You can compile `chapter1.tex` by itself for quick iteration or include it in the main file using `\subfile{chapter1}` to build the full document. This modular structure enhances performance and organization.

Another often-overlooked source of delay is the automatic generation of the bibliography. While citation systems such as `biblatex` are indispensable in the final document, compiling bibliographies using `biber` or `BibTeX` can be time-consuming during drafts. In such cases, it is helpful to temporarily disable citation processing using the `\nocite{*}` command or by commenting out bibliography generation lines entirely. This allows you to focus on editing content without triggering bibliography compilation during every build.

Finally, you can dramatically improve compilation efficiency by using an automated build tool such as `latexmk`. This utility only recompiles parts of the document that have changed and handles multiple passes, bibliographies, and indexes intelligently.

Automating Efficient Compilation with `latexmk`

Shell Command:

```
latexmk -pdf main.tex
```

Effect:
Runs `pdflatex` only when necessary. It also detects changes in references, citations, and indexes, automatically invoking `biber` or `makeindex` when needed. This avoids unnecessary full recompilation and reduces errors due to forgotten passes.

Together, these strategies provide a powerful workflow for writing and managing large LaTeX documents efficiently. By deferring heavy tasks like image rendering and bibliography compilation until the final stages and by embracing modular design and smart automation, authors can focus more on content and less on waiting for builds to complete.

6.2 Debugging LaTeX Errors Efficiently

As with any programming or typesetting system, debugging is an essential part of working with LaTeX. When errors occur, whether due to missing packages, mistyped commands, or conflicting definitions, it is important to know how to diagnose and resolve them efficiently. This subsection introduces some of the most effective strategies for identifying and fixing problems in your LaTeX documents.

A useful first step in debugging any issue is to consult the `.log` file generated during compilation. Every time you run LaTeX, it produces a detailed log that records errors, warnings, overfull boxes, and package conflicts. Although some errors appear directly in your console or editor output, the log file often provides deeper context. For example, it can point to a specific line number or indicate which package triggered an error. Opening the `.log` file is as simple as navigating to your project folder and opening the file with a text editor, or accessing it directly through your LaTeX editor.

When the source of an error is unclear, creating a minimal working example (MWE) is often the most effective approach. An MWE is a stripped-down version of your document that includes only the necessary content to reproduce the problem. This technique helps isolate the issue from the rest of your codebase and allows you to test potential fixes quickly.

Creating a Minimal Working Example (MWE)

LaTeX Code:

```
\documentclass{article}
\usepackage{amsmath}
```

```
\begin{document}

\section{Problematic Math}
Here is an equation:
\begin{equation}
    \frac{x}{y}
\end{equation}

\end{document}
```

Explanation:
This minimal file isolates a problematic equation. If the error was due to missing packages, incorrect syntax, or improper nesting, it becomes immediately apparent in this reduced form.

Another common cause of errors is the package conflict. Since LaTeX relies on many third-party packages to extend its core functionality, it is possible for two packages to interfere with each other. If you suspect a conflict, comment out the packages in question one at a time and recompile. You may also find clues in the log file, which will often state which command is being redefined or which symbol is missing. In cases where a package has changed behavior in a new version, reverting to a previous version or updating your TeX distribution might resolve the issue.

Two packages that can be particularly helpful for document-level debugging are `showlabels` and `todonotes`. The `showlabels` package reveals all LaTeX labels in the document directly in the margin, which is especially helpful when managing references and cross-references.

Using showlabels and todonotes

LaTeX Code:

```
\usepackage[inline]{showlabels}
\usepackage{todonotes}

\begin{document}

\section{Introduction}
\label{sec:intro}
\todo{Check cross-references here.}
See Section~\ref{sec:intro}.

\end{document}
```

Output:
The label `sec:intro` appears in the margin beside the section title, and a visible to-do note appears in the margin reminding you to check the reference. This is an excellent way to track issues during editing.

By combining these strategies, consulting the log file, isolating problems with an MWE, testing package interactions, and using visual debugging aids, you can resolve most LaTeX issues quickly and with minimal frustration. As your documents grow in complexity, these skills will become increasingly valuable for maintaining a smooth and productive writing process.

6.2.1 Compiling for Different Output Formats

When working on complex documents in LaTeX, it is sometimes necessary to compile to different output formats depending on the distribution method, image types, or typographic requirements. Fortunately, LaTeX supports multiple compilation workflows, each optimized for specific output needs such as PDF, DVI, or even HTML via intermediate tools. Understanding these workflows not only helps in choosing the right toolchain for your document but also ensures compatibility and efficient typesetting.

The most common and modern approach is to compile directly to PDF using `pdfLaTeX`, which is both fast and reliable for most types of documents. This compiler supports standard text typesetting, figures in PNG, JPEG, and PDF formats, and integrates well with packages like **`graphicx`**, **`amsmath`**, and **`biblatex`**. Unless your project has specific font or encoding needs, `pdfLaTeX` is the best default choice.

In contrast, some workflows, especially legacy ones, prefer the use of the classic LaTeX-to-DVI-to-PDF pipeline. This process first compiles the document into a DVI (DeVice Independent) file using the standard `latex` engine, and then converts the DVI to PDF using `dvipdf` or `dvips` followed by `ps2pdf`. This route is especially useful if your document includes EPS (Encapsulated PostScript) graphics, which are not natively supported by `pdfLaTeX`.

Lastly, `XeLaTeX` and `LuaLaTeX` are two advanced compilers that support modern typesetting features such as Unicode text, OpenType fonts, and native system fonts. These engines are ideal for multilingual documents, or when precise font control is required for aesthetic or accessibility reasons. Although slightly slower to compile, they provide a high degree of typographic flexibility.

The following example illustrates the setup of a document where the compilation path can influence the output:

Comparison of Compilation Modes

LaTeX Code:

```
\documentclass[draft]{article}
\usepackage{graphicx}
```

```
\usepackage{fontspec}
% For XeLaTeX/LuaLaTeX
\usepackage{showlabels}
\usepackage{todonotes}
\usepackage{polyglossia}
% For multilingual support

\setmainlanguage{english}
\setmainfont{Georgia}
% Requires XeLaTeX/LuaLaTeX

\begin{document}
\title{Optimizing Compilation
 in LaTeX}
\author{Author Name}
\date{\today}
\maketitle
\section{Figures}
\includegraphics[width=\textwidth]
 {figure.png}

\section{Notes}
\todo{Ensure font renders properly
in PDF.}

\end{document}
```

The choice of compiler should be informed by the features that your document requires. For general use, `pdfLaTeX` remains the best starting point. For advanced font management, `XeLaTeX` and `LuaLaTeX` offer superior capabilities. Meanwhile, DVI workflows can be considered when backward compatibility or EPS support is necessary. It is good practice to test your project with the appropriate compiler early in the writing process to avoid major format issues later.

6.3 Best Practices for LaTeX Code

Writing clean and efficient LaTeX code is essential for producing high-quality documents and maintaining readability, especially in large projects. In this section, we will explore the best practices for writing LaTeX code that is well organized, easy to debug, and flexible for future modifications.

6.3.1 Organize Your Document into Sections and Subsections

A well-structured document is one of the hallmarks of clean and professional LaTeX code. When working on any written project, be it an article, a thesis, or a book, it is important to divide the content into logical units. LaTeX provides a straightforward system of sectional commands that help authors maintain a hierarchical and readable structure. These commands not only improve the visual layout of the text but also allow automatic generation of the table of contents and facilitate navigation during editing.

The basic sectional commands available in LaTeX are `\section`, `\subsection`, and `\subsubsection`. These commands are hierarchical in nature. A `\subsection` belongs within a `\section`, and a `\subsubsection` belongs within a `\subsection`. For documents such as books or reports that use chapters, `\chapter` is available as a higher-level division, provided you use a document class like `book` or `report`.

Let us examine how to organize content using these commands. The following example illustrates how different sectional units are defined in a typical document:

Example: Sectional Structure

LaTeX Code:

```
\documentclass{article}

\begin{document}

\section{Introduction}
This is the main introduction.

\subsection{Background}
A deeper look into the context.

\subsubsection{Historical Context}
Here we discuss past developments.

\end{document}
```

Expected Output:

Introduction

This is the main introduction.

Background

A deeper look into the context.

Historical Context

Here we discuss past developments.

Organizing your content this way ensures clarity both for the reader and for you as the author. Each section represents a self-contained unit of thought, and sublevels allow you to expand ideas without overwhelming the reader with long, unstructured text.

Additionally, when you use these sectional commands, LaTeX automatically tracks them for inclusion in the table of contents. You don't need to manually number or format headings, nor do you need to worry about consistency. For large projects, this automation becomes especially valuable.

When structuring a long document, it is advisable to begin with a general outline and then assign each major concept to a section or chapter. Subsections and subsubsections can be added as your content grows. This top-down planning approach will help you write and revise more efficiently over time.

6.3.2 Keep the Preamble Clean and Minimal

In any LaTeX document, the preamble, the portion before the `\begin{document}` command, serves as the control center for defining the behavior, appearance, and functionality of your project. While it may be tempting to copy and paste long lists of packages from other documents or templates, a clean and minimal preamble is not only more efficient but also easier to maintain and less prone to errors or package conflicts.

The first rule of managing the preamble is to include only the packages you actually need. Loading a dozen packages "just in case" introduces unnecessary overhead, and some may even conflict with each other depending on your compiler or document class. For instance, if you are not using graphics or custom fonts, including packages like `graphicx` or `fontspec` is redundant.

The following example illustrates a clean and focused preamble setup:

Example: A Clean and Organized Preamble

LaTeX Code:

```
% Document class
\documentclass{article}

% Layout and mathematics
\usepackage{geometry}
\usepackage{amsmath, amssymb}

% Graphics and figures
\usepackage{graphicx}

% Font support
(only if needed)
% \usepackage{fontspec}
% For XeLaTeX or LuaLaTeX only
```

Explanation:
This preamble is minimal yet functional for many academic or technical documents. Packages are grouped by purpose:

- `geometry` controls page layout.
- `amsmath` and `amssymb` support mathematical symbols and environments.
- `graphicx` allows you to include images.

`fontspec` is commented out unless you plan to use `XeLaTeX` or `LuaLaTeX`.

Another helpful practice is to group related packages and define custom macros in separate blocks, using comments to indicate their purpose. This improves readability and allows quick navigation when adjustments are needed.

For larger documents, you may even move preamble definitions into a separate file (e.g., `preamble.tex`) and include it using the `\input` command. This makes the main file cleaner and modular.

Additionally, avoid redefining core LaTeX commands directly in the preamble unless you understand their consequences. Redefinitions should be tested thoroughly in isolated examples, as they can affect global formatting and cause compatibility issues with packages.

6.3.3 Use Comments for Documentation

Good documentation is as important in LaTeX as it is in any programming or markup language, especially when working on large projects such as theses, research papers, or books. One of the most effective ways to document your LaTeX source is by using comments. In LaTeX, the percent symbol (%) is used to introduce a comment. Anything following a percent sign on a line is ignored by the compiler and does not appear in the output.

Comments serve multiple purposes. At the most basic level, they allow you to annotate the purpose of a specific section or block of code. This is particularly useful when returning to your document after a long break, or when sharing it with collaborators who are unfamiliar with the structure or reasoning behind your formatting choices.

Consider the following example, where a comment is used to label the purpose of a section:

Example: Annotating Sections with Comments

LaTeX Code:

```
% This section introduces
the background of the topic
\section{Background}
The study of nonlinear
```

```
systems began in the 19th
century...
```

Explanation:
The comment above the `\section` command helps the author (or collaborators) quickly understand the role of this section, even without reading the full content that follows.

In addition to documentation, comments are often used as a temporary tool for disabling parts of the document during development or revision. This allows you to experiment with different formatting options or suppress certain content without deleting it permanently. For instance, you may want to disable an image while testing layout flow:

Example: Temporarily Disabling Code

LaTeX Code:

```
%\includegraphics[width=
\textwidth]{large_image.png}
```

Explanation:
The image will be skipped entirely, but the code remains available for restoration when needed; simply remove the percent sign.

While comments are invisible in the final output, they form a visible trail for future editing and debugging. If you are collaborating with others, it is a good practice to prepend your initials to each comment you add, which makes it easier to track who added what.

Over time, consistent commenting builds a readable and maintainable source file. The key is to strike a balance: comment just enough to clarify your intentions, but avoid cluttering the file with unnecessary or overly verbose remarks. For large projects, especially those using version control systems like Git, a well-commented LaTeX source can save hours of confusion and make the revision process more manageable.

6.3.4 Use Macros to Simplify Repetitive Code

One of LaTeX's greatest strengths is its ability to define custom macros that encapsulate frequently used commands. This feature is particularly helpful in large documents, where certain formatting or expressions recur throughout the text. By defining your own macros, you not only make the code cleaner and easier to read but also simplify future revisions: if you ever decide to change how something is formatted, you only need to update the macro definition rather than hunt through the entire document.

To define a macro, the standard approach is to use the `\newcommand` directive. A typical example is to define a macro that emphasizes certain text in bold. Instead of repeatedly typing `\textbf{...}`, you can define your own semantic wrapper, such as:

Defining a Macro

LaTeX Code:

```
\newcommand{\important}[1]
 {\textbf{#1}}

% Usage
\important{This is important
  text.}
```

Explanation:

This macro takes one argument and wraps it in bold text. Using `\important` makes it clear that the formatting has semantic meaning, not just visual styling.

Beyond visual styling, macros are particularly powerful for mathematical documents. Suppose you refer to a specific variable combination like Δt repeatedly and wish to ensure consistent formatting and spacing. You can create a macro such as `\deltat` and define it once:

Macro for Consistent Math Notation

LaTeX Code:

```
\newcommand{\deltat}
{\ensuremath
{\Delta t}}

% Usage
The time step is
denoted by \deltat.
```

Explanation:

This ensures that every instance of `\deltat` appears in math mode and with consistent formatting, regardless of whether it is used in inline or display math.

As your document grows, you may also define macros for frequently cited references, commonly used figure dimensions, or special typesetting commands. Keeping such definitions near the beginning of the document (or in a separate preamble file) ensures they are easy to locate and modify.

Overall, the judicious use of macros encourages clarity, maintainability, and scalability in LaTeX documents. By abstracting the formatting from the content, you reduce duplication and lay the groundwork for a more flexible and professional typesetting workflow.

6.3.5 Handle Figures, Tables, and Equations Efficiently

Managing figures, tables, and equations is central to technical and academic documents in LaTeX. While LaTeX's automatic handling of floats and math environments is powerful, it requires thoughtful structure to avoid common pitfalls and to maintain clarity and consistency throughout the document.

When working with figures and tables, always include a caption and a label. The caption provides context for readers, while the label enables cross-referencing elsewhere in the text. These two components are essential for navigability and for ensuring your document remains coherent, especially in longer works like theses or reports.

Here is an example of a properly constructed figure environment:

Example: Figure with Caption and Label

LaTeX Code:

```
\begin{figure}[h]
  \centering
  \includegraphics[width=0.7
  \textwidth]{image.png}
  \caption{A sample image}
  \label{fig:sampleimage}
\end{figure}
```

Usage:
As seen in Figure `\ref{fig:sampleimage}`, the results were significant.

This method ensures that the figure is not only clearly presented but also referenced dynamically. If the figure number changes due to document restructuring, LaTeX updates the reference automatically, preventing manual errors.

The same principle applies to tables. Encapsulate each table with the `table` environment, use `\caption` to describe it, and `\label` for referencing. Proper table formatting also includes alignment, clear column headings, and minimal but consistent use of vertical and horizontal rules.

Mathematical expressions, particularly lengthy or multi-step derivations, benefit from the `align` environment provided by the `amsmath` package. This environment not only improves readability but also gives you full control over line alignment, numbering, and spacing. Here is an example:

Example: Aligned Equations

LaTeX Code:

```
\usepackage{amsmath}
\begin{align}
f(x)
&= x^2 + 3x + 2 \\
&= (x+1)(x+2)
\end{align}
```

Output:

$$
\begin{aligned}
f(x) &= x^2 + 3x + 2 \\
&= (x+1)(x+2)
\end{aligned}
$$

Using `align` not only improves the structure of your mathematical reasoning but also avoids the overuse of `$$...$$`, which is discouraged in modern LaTeX documents.

Another useful tip when managing figures and tables is to group related elements closely in the source code to prevent floating problems. While LaTeX's float placement algorithms generally do a good job, authors should avoid scattering figures throughout unrelated sections. If more control is needed, packages like `float`, `placeins`, or `caption` can enhance float behavior and customization.

By applying these best practices, consistent labeling, smart use of math environments, and careful float placement, you can ensure that your LaTeX document is not only technically sound but also clear, polished, and easy to follow for your readers.

6.3.6 Avoid Hardcoding Layout Settings

When working with LaTeX, it can be tempting to manually adjust spacing, margins, or font sizes directly in the document using commands like `\vspace`, `\hspace`, or `\fontsize`. While such approaches may offer short-term fixes, they often lead to inconsistencies and maintenance issues in large documents. A better practice is to manage layout settings globally and semantically through dedicated LaTeX packages, which not only ensure uniformity but also make it easier to adapt your document to new formatting requirements later.

One of the most fundamental tools for layout customization is the `geometry` package. This package allows you to define page dimensions such as margins, paper size, and orientation in a clean and consistent way. For instance, rather than manually adding horizontal spaces or redefining margins locally, you can set the entire document's margins in the preamble with a single command:

Example: Setting Margins with `geometry`

LaTeX Code:

```
\documentclass{article}
\usepackage[a4paper,margin=1in]
{geometry}
\begin{document}
This document uses consistent
1-inch margins on A4 paper.
\end{document}
```

Effect:
The document now has uniform margins on all sides, making it easier to meet formatting requirements, such as for academic submissions or publishing standards.

Beyond page layout, line spacing is another element frequently manipulated with hardcoded `\vspace` or `\\[Xpt]` commands. These can disrupt the vertical rhythm of your document and complicate line breaks. A cleaner solution is to use the `setspace` package, which provides commands like `\singlespacing`, `\onehalfspacing`, and `\doublespacing` to apply spacing rules document-wide or within specific environments.

Likewise, rather than hardcoding font sizes with commands like `\fontsize{12}{14}\selectfont` scattered throughout the file, consider using document class options (e.g., `\documentclass[12pt]{article}`) or use packages such as `titlesec` to manage heading sizes and spacing in a centralized, readable way.

Hardcoding should also be avoided in header and footer placement. The `fancyhdr` package, for instance, provides a structured and consistent method for creating custom headers and footers across the entire document without ad hoc layout tweaks.

Ultimately, treating the layout as a semantic layer, separate from the content itself, not only improves the quality of your output but also simplifies the revision process. When the layout parameters change (for example, switching from A4 to US Letter or submitting to a different journal), using packages to handle formatting means you will not have to touch the body content at all.

By defining global layout settings up front and relying on LaTeX's package ecosystem for layout control, you keep your document scalable, professional, and easier to debug and maintain over time.

6.3.7 Use Logical File Structure for Large Projects

When working on large-scale LaTeX projects, such as books, theses, technical manuals, or dissertations, maintaining a clean and modular file structure becomes essential. As the length and complexity of your document grow, a single monolithic `.tex` file can quickly become difficult to navigate, maintain, or debug. LaTeX offers built-in support for modularization by allowing you to split your content into smaller files and include them within a master document. This not only improves clarity but also helps reduce compilation time when working on specific sections.

A typical project structure might look like this:

Example Directory Structure

```
main.tex               % Main file with preamble
                         and structure
chapters/
  chapter1.tex         % First chapter
  chapter2.tex         % Second chapter
figures/
  fig1.png             % Figure files
  diagram.pdf
references.bib         % Bibliography database
```

The `main.tex` file serves as the central document that ties everything together. This file typically contains the document class declaration, package imports, front matter, and `\input` or `\include` commands that pull in the actual content from external files.

Here is a minimal example of how such a master file might be constructed:

Master Document (`main.tex`)

LaTeX Code:

```
\documentclass{book}
\usepackage{graphicx}
\usepackage{amsmath}
\begin{document}
\maketitle
\tableofcontents
\input{chapters/chapter1}
\input{chapters/chapter2}
\end{document}
```

Effect:
LaTeX will read in and typeset the content of `chapter1.tex` and `chapter2.tex` at the locations of the `\input` commands. The entire document remains well structured and maintainable.

Each chapter file, such as `chapter1.tex`, should contain only the content relevant to that section. It should not include a `\documentclass`, `\usepackage`, or `\begin{document}` command. Here is an example of what `chapter1.tex` might look like:

Sample Chapter File (`chapters/chapter1.tex`)

```
\chapter{Introduction}
This is the introduction to the book.
 It outlines the motivation, scope, and
 structure of the content that follows.
```

Using this modular approach provides numerous advantages: it reduces cognitive load, allows for quicker iteration, and makes collaboration easier since multiple people can work on different files independently. Moreover, in long documents, it becomes much easier to isolate and debug specific parts without reprocessing the entire project.

If you wish to compile individual parts of the document separately (e.g., for testing or proofreading), consider using the `subfiles` package, which enables individual files to act both as standalone documents and as components of the full project. This further enhances flexibility without sacrificing consistency.

6.3.8 Consistent Naming Conventions

Maintaining consistent naming conventions throughout your LaTeX project is a fundamental best practice that significantly improves the clarity, maintainability, and scalability of your documents. This becomes especially important in large or collaborative projects, where multiple figures, tables, equations, custom commands, and cross-references are scattered across several files and sections.

A consistent scheme for naming ensures that all parts of your document can be easily referenced, updated, and understood both by yourself and others, even long after the document was first written. For instance, when labeling structural elements like figures and tables, it is useful to adopt a prefix-based system that clearly indicates the type of element being referred to.

Suppose you are labeling a figure and a table in your document. Instead of generic or inconsistent labels like `\label{fig1}` or `\label{mytable}`, it is better to use meaningful, type-specific identifiers that describe the content or purpose of the element:

Consistent Labeling Example

LaTeX Code:

```
\begin{figure}[ht]
```

```
  \centering
  \includegraphics[width=0.6\textwidth]
  {setup.png}
  \caption{Experimental setup for phase
  alignment}
  \label{fig:experiment-setup}
\end{figure}

\begin{table}[ht]
  \centering
  \begin{tabular}{cc}
    \hline
    Time (s) & Amplitude \\
    \hline
    0.1      & 3.5       \\
    0.2      & 3.6       \\
    \hline
  \end{tabular}
\caption{Results of amplitude over time}
  \label{tab:amplitude-results}
\end{table}
```

Result Overview:
Each item is labeled in a way that makes its role and content self-evident. This aids both referencing and maintenance:

- `\texttt{fig:experiment-setup}`clearly refers to a figure.
- `\texttt{tab:amplitude-results}`clearly refers to a table.

The use of prefixes such as `fig:`, `tab:`, `sec:`, and `eq:` for figures, tables, sections, and equations, respectively, is widely considered a best practice. Similarly, macros should be given names that indicate their function or output. Avoid cryptic names or abbreviations unless their

meaning is obvious from context. For example,
`\newcommand{\vect}[1]{\boldsymbol{#1}}`
is more descriptive than something like
`\newcommand{\v}[1]{\boldsymbol{#1}}`,
which might lead to confusion or naming collisions.

Consistency in naming also extends to file and folder names in your project directory. For instance, files named `chapter1.tex`, `chapter2.tex`, and `conclusion.tex` follow a predictable and intuitive scheme. In contrast, files named `first.tex`, `finaldraft.tex`, or `thing.tex` introduce ambiguity and hamper readability, especially when collaborating with others or revisiting the project after some time.

By adhering to clear and consistent naming conventions, you ensure that your LaTeX code remains organized, professional, and scalable, regardless of the size or complexity of your document. This habit not only saves time during the writing and editing process but also reduces the likelihood of errors and confusion when working across multiple files or with coauthors.

6.3.9 Regularly Check for Errors and Warnings

Maintaining high-quality LaTeX documents requires more than writing syntactically correct code; it involves continuously monitoring the health of your project through compilation messages. As your document grows, errors and warnings may begin to accumulate, and although LaTeX will often continue compiling despite them, ignoring such messages can compromise the document's appearance and reliability.

A common warning that writers often overlook is the overfull or underfull `hbox`. This warning indicates that a line of text or math extends beyond the allowed margin, which may result in awkward visual output or clipped content. For example, a long equation without appropriate line breaks can trigger an overfull box warning:

Overfull hbox Example

Problematic Code:

```
\documentclass{article}
\begin{document}
A very long sentence that
goes on and on without
any breaks and stretches
way beyond the margin
limits of the document.
\end{document}
```

Likely Result:
A warning in the log such as:
`Overfull \\ \hbox (5.12345pt too wide)`
`in paragraph`

The appropriate fix in this case would be to adjust the text manually, introduce line breaks, or use hyphenation commands to ensure LaTeX formats it within the allowed width.

Another common warning is the presence of unresolved references. If you refer to a figure, section, or equation that has not been defined or labeled properly, LaTeX will mark the reference with a placeholder like "??" and generate a warning. These should be resolved immediately, as they can undermine the professionalism of your output.

To assist in catching and addressing such issues early, it is highly recommended to inspect the `.log` file after each compilation. This file contains all error messages, line numbers, and detailed warnings generated during the LaTeX run. While some LaTeX editors display a simplified version of these messages, opening the log directly often reveals more specific context.

Automated tools like `latexmk` are invaluable in this regard. When invoked with the `-pvc` (preview continuously) or `-interaction=nonstopmode` flags, `latexmk` can compile your project and report errors without requiring manual recompilation. Many LaTeX editors (such as Overleaf, TeXstudio, and TeXmaker) integrate similar continuous compilation and error inspection features.

In addition to manual inspection, writing clean and logical LaTeX code helps reduce the likelihood of such problems appearing in the first place. When an error does occur, isolate the issue by commenting out surrounding code or by constructing a minimal working example (MWE) that captures just the problematic portion of the document.

To reinforce the importance of error checking and clean output, consider the following complete LaTeX example that includes figure labeling, captioning, and clear structure:

Full Example with Labels and Clean Output

LaTeX Code:

```
\documentclass{article}
\usepackage{graphicx}
\usepackage[a4paper,margin=1in]
{geometry}

\newcommand{\important}[1]{\textbf{#1}}

\begin{document}

\title{Best Practices for LaTeX Code}
\author{Author Name}
\date{\today}
\maketitle

\section{Introduction}
```

```
This document outlines the
best practices for writing
clean and efficient LaTeX code.

\section{Figures and Tables}
\begin{figure}[h]
  \centering
  \includegraphics[width=0.7
    \textwidth]{example.png}
  \caption{A sample figure}
  \label{fig:samplefigure}
\end{figure}

As seen in
Figure~\ref{fig:samplefigure},
figures should always have labels and
captions.

\section{Conclusion}
Following best practices makes
your LaTeX code more
maintainable and professional.

\end{document}
```

Expected Output:
A well-structured article with:

- Proper title and author info
- Clearly labeled and referenced figure
- No overfull boxes or reference errors

No warnings will appear in the .log file if everything is defined properly.

By making a habit of compiling frequently, inspecting warnings, and resolving issues as they arise, you ensure a polished and technically sound final document. This not only improves the quality of your typeset material but also saves time in the long run by avoiding the accumulation of hard-to-track errors later in the writing process.

6.4 Collaborating with Git and Overleaf

Collaboration is an important aspect of working on LaTeX documents, especially for academic projects, research papers, or team reports. Effective collaboration ensures that multiple authors can work on the same document without conflicting changes or losing important edits. This section will cover two popular tools for collaborating on LaTeX documents: Git and Overleaf.

6.4.1 Using Git for LaTeX Collaboration

In collaborative writing, version control is not just helpful, but also essential. Especially for LaTeX documents, where structure, formatting, and modular files make the project resemble software more than simple text, version control systems like Git offer a structured and reliable way to manage multiple authors, track revisions, and avoid losing work.

Git is a distributed version control system that records the history of changes made to a project, allowing authors to review, revert, or merge content as needed. It is ideal for academic collaborations, especially in writing books, theses, or multiauthor papers. In this context, Git ensures that contributors can work concurrently without overwriting each other's efforts while preserving a detailed and traceable history of all edits.

To begin using Git with a LaTeX project, you first need to install Git from the official website at https://git-scm.

com/. Once installed, navigate to the root directory of your LaTeX project and initialize a Git repository using the following command:

```
git init
```

This will create a hidden `.git` directory that stores all the versioning data. At this point, Git is ready to track your files, but LaTeX generates many auxiliary files that do not need to be versioned. These include files such as `.aux`, `.log`, `.out`, and others. To exclude these from version control, you should create a `.gitignore` file with entries like:

```
*.aux
*.log
*.out
*.toc
*.pdf
```

This ensures that only meaningful content, like your `.tex` files, bibliography files, and images, is committed to the repository. Once the ignore rules are in place, you can add your files and create the first commit:

```
git add .
git commit -m "Initial commit"
```

As multiple authors contribute to a document, Git's branching system becomes highly beneficial. Rather than working directly on the main branch (often named `main`), contributors can create branches to isolate their changes. For example, if you are working on a new section, you can create a branch named `section-editing` as follows:

```
git checkout -b section-editing
```

On this branch, you can freely modify the relevant files, and once your edits are complete and tested, you can stage and commit the changes:

```
git add section2.tex
git commit -m "Updated Section 2 content and
formatting"
```

To integrate your work into the main branch, simply switch back to it and use Git's merge feature:

```
git checkout main
git merge section-editing
```

This process enables smooth integration of individual contributions, even when multiple authors are working in parallel. If conflicting edits occur, such as two authors modifying the same line, Git will flag the conflict and allow the authors to resolve it manually before proceeding.

Collaboration becomes even more powerful when Git is paired with remote repositories on platforms like GitHub or GitLab. These services provide a central online repository where contributors can push their changes, pull updates, and even review each other's edits. To link your local project to a GitHub repository, first create a new repository on GitHub, and then run the following command to set the remote:

```
git remote add origin
https://github.com/username/repository.git
```

After configuring the remote, push your local content with:

```
git push -u origin main
```

From this point forward, all collaborators can clone the repository, create their own branches, contribute edits, and push changes back to GitHub. This distributed workflow allows the team to work asynchronously, reviewing pull requests and resolving conflicts in a centralized and transparent way.

6.4.2 Using Overleaf for Real-Time Collaboration

Overleaf is an intuitive and widely used cloud-based LaTeX editor designed specifically for collaborative academic writing. Unlike traditional LaTeX editors that rely on local file storage and manual synchronization, Overleaf enables real-time editing from any device with a Web browser. This makes it an excellent tool for researchers, students, and professionals who work in teams or wish to collaborate on documents such as research articles, theses, reports, and presentations.

To begin working with Overleaf, a user first needs to create an account at https://www.overleaf.com/. Once registered, the user can start a new project either by choosing from a variety of templates or by uploading an existing LaTeX project. Overleaf supports a full project structure, including folders, subfiles, bibliographies, and image assets, making it suitable for small articles as well as large-scale books or dissertations.

Sharing an Overleaf project with collaborators is a seamless process. From the main project interface, clicking the "Share" button allows the user to invite collaborators by email or generate a secure link with edit or read-only permissions. Once collaborators join the project, they can begin editing simultaneously. All changes are reflected in real time, so team members can work together without the need to exchange files manually or worry about version mismatches.

Beyond simultaneous editing, Overleaf includes several other features designed specifically for effective collaboration. One such feature is version history, which automatically stores incremental snapshots of the document. This allows authors to revisit and restore earlier states of the project, offering a reliable way to recover from accidental deletions or explore how a section evolved over time. Additionally, Overleaf offers a track-changes mode similar to that found in word processors, highlighting additions, deletions, and modifications along with the names of the contributors. This is particularly useful when reviewing or editing collaborative drafts.

Collaborators can also use the built-in commenting system, which lets them leave inline comments attached to specific lines or sections of the document. These comments act as annotations or conversation threads, allowing discussions about particular equations, formatting decisions, or paragraph structures, without modifying the core content of the text.

For users who are comfortable working with Git and prefer version control via command-line tools or GitHub repositories, Overleaf provides a powerful integration. Linking an Overleaf project to a GitHub repository allows changes to be synchronized between the two platforms. This dual workflow caters both to users who prefer working directly in the Overleaf interface and to those who manage their projects locally and use Git for tracking and collaboration. To enable GitHub synchronization, one must first authorize Overleaf to access their GitHub account. After that, the user can select the desired repository and configure Overleaf to push or pull changes. This is particularly helpful in interdisciplinary teams where some collaborators use Overleaf, while others prefer to write offline using their own LaTeX editors and Git clients.

In addition to GitHub, Overleaf also provides access via direct Git cloning. Each Overleaf project is assigned a unique Git URL, allowing users to clone the project locally, make changes, and push updates, just as they would with any Git-based repository. This flexibility ensures that Overleaf supports both graphical and command-line workflows, adapting to the technical comfort level of its users.

Altogether, Overleaf offers a unified platform that combines the convenience of online editing with the power of real-time collaboration. Its ease of use, strong document management features, and compatibility with Git-based workflows make it a compelling choice for individuals and teams who value accessibility, structure, and control over their LaTeX documents.

6.4.3 Best Practices for Collaboration

Effective collaboration on LaTeX documents, especially in academic or technical projects, involves more than just sharing files or editing content. To ensure a seamless workflow and avoid common pitfalls like conflicting edits, lost data, or formatting inconsistencies, it is crucial to follow a structured set of practices that support both productivity and clarity.

One of the first steps in collaborative writing is to clearly define the roles and responsibilities of each team member. For example, one person might be responsible for writing the introduction, another for typesetting mathematical content, while someone else handles bibliography management or formatting. By assigning sections or tasks in advance, collaborators can work in parallel without the risk of overlapping contributions. This division of labor is especially important when using version control systems like Git, where simultaneous editing of the same lines of code may result in merge conflicts.

Equally important is establishing a regular communication rhythm. Whether collaboration is conducted through the Overleaf's built-in commenting and chat system, Git commit messages, or external tools like Slack or email, it is helpful to document what changes have been made and why. For instance, including informative commit messages such as "restructured Sect. 6.3 for clarity" or "updated table formatting in Chap. 5" helps the team stay informed and makes it easier to review progress over time.

When using Git as your version control system, conflicts may occasionally arise, especially when two collaborators edit the same line or section. In such cases, it is best to resolve these merge conflicts promptly before moving forward with new edits. Leaving unresolved conflicts can cause more complicated issues later, especially in large projects with many dependencies or cross-references. Many LaTeX editors and Git interfaces (such as VS Code or GitKraken) offer visual tools for resolving conflicts, which can help clarify differences and streamline the reconciliation process.

Regardless of the platform, regular backups are another key safeguard in collaborative workflows. While Overleaf offers automatic version control and project history, it is still advisable to periodically download your project as a ZIP file or link it to a remote GitHub repository. If you are using a local Git-based system, regularly pushing your commits to a shared remote repository ensures that all contributors have access to the latest version and protects your work against loss due to local machine failure.

Finally, it is helpful to document the collaboration rules at the beginning of a project. For instance, agreeing on naming conventions for labels and files, or deciding how often to pull updates from the remote repository, can prevent confusion and make the process more efficient. In a Git-based project, contributors might follow a workflow in which they always create branches for new edits and submit pull requests or merge requests once their work is ready to be reviewed and integrated.

By combining thoughtful role assignment, open communication, prompt conflict resolution, and robust backup strategies, teams can maintain both momentum and document integrity throughout the writing process. These practices, when adopted consistently, turn collaborative LaTeX writing from a technical hurdle into a smooth and rewarding experience.

Exercises for Chap. 6: Troubleshooting and Best Practices

6.1 Optimizing Compilation Speed

1. **Using Draft Mode**: Compile a large LaTeX document with many figures and graphics in both normal and `draft` mode. Measure the compilation time in each case. Write a summary of the benefits and limitations of using draft mode during editing.

2. **Splitting Content Using `\input` and `\include`**: Create a multi-section document by splitting it into separate files using `\input` or `\include`. Observe the difference in incremental compilation when only one section is modified.

3. **Selective Compilation with `standalone`**: Use the `standalone` package to isolate and compile individual figures or diagrams. Describe how this approach can save time during large project development.

4. **Minimizing Unused Packages**: Compare the compilation time of a document with a minimal set of required packages versus one with unnecessary or redundant packages loaded. Explain how unused packages impact performance.

6.2 Debugging LaTeX Errors

1. **Identifying Missing Packages**: Deliberately attempt to use a command from a package (e.g., `\includegraphics`) without loading the necessary package (e.g., `graphicx`). Observe the compiler error and document how you resolved it.

2. **Mismatched Braces and Environments**: Write a small document with an unclosed environment or mismatched braces. Use the error message to trace and correct the mistake. Describe how LaTeX helps identify structural issues.

3. **Using Log Files for Diagnosis**: Create a document with multiple errors (e.g., undefined commands, missing references). Use the `.log` file and compiler messages to find and fix the issues. Write a summary of the debugging process.

4. **Testing with Minimal Working Example (MWE)**: Create a complex document with an error and isolate it by reducing the document to a minimal working example (MWE). Submit the MWE to an online LaTeX help forum (e.g., TeX StackExchange) or explain how this practice aids in efficient debugging.

6.3 Best Practices for LaTeX Code

1. **Organizing Your Preamble**: Write a LaTeX document and organize the preamble efficiently. Include package imports, custom commands, and any document-specific configurations. Explain why organizing the preamble is important for maintainability.

2. **Using Macros and Custom Commands**: Refactor a LaTeX document by creating custom macros for

frequently used formatting or commands. Replace repetitive code with your macros and explain how this improves the readability of the document.

3. **Minimizing Hardcoding**: Write a LaTeX document that minimizes hardcoding of layout or formatting elements (e.g., avoid direct `\vspace`, `\hspace`). Use packages like `geometry` and `setspace` to manage margins, spacing, and other layout properties.

6.4 Collaborating on LaTeX Documents (Git, Overleaf)

1. **Using Git for Version Control**: Set up a Git repository for a LaTeX project. Commit changes as you edit the document. Write a short explanation of how version control can help with collaborative LaTeX projects.

2. **Collaborating on Overleaf**: Create a project on Overleaf and share it with a collaborator. Both contributors should make edits to the document, and you should track the changes. Write a reflection on the experience of using Overleaf for collaboration.

3. **Managing Branches in Git**: Use Git to create separate branches for different sections of a LaTeX project (e.g., one branch for editing the introduction, another for the conclusion). Merge the branches back into the main branch once the edits are complete, and describe how Git manages the merge process.

Chapter 7

Advanced LaTeX Packages and Domain-Specific Applications

Contents

Md. Aquib, *Advanced LaTeX*, University Texts in the Mathematical Sciences, https://doi.org/10.1007/978-981-96-9322-1_7

Abstract: As users become more proficient in LaTeX, the focus naturally shifts from mastering foundational syntax to exploring the powerful ecosystem of packages that extend its capabilities across specialized domains. This chapter focuses on advanced LaTeX packages not only as tools for enhancing document quality but also as enablers of discipline-specific workflows in fields such as electrical engineering, computer science, chemistry, and more. It explores how tailored packages simplify the inclusion of complex diagrams, algorithms, circuit schematics, and domain-specific notations. Moreover, it guides readers through the process of creating and managing custom packages, offering insights into the internal mechanics of LaTeX development. By the end of this chapter, readers will have a practical understanding of how to leverage existing packages efficiently, adapt them to specialized needs, and even contribute their own to the broader TEX community.

Keywords: Advanced packages, Scientific typesetting, LaTeX for engineering, LaTeX in humanities, LaTeX for music, LaTeX for chess

7.1 Useful LaTeX Packages for Various Fields

LaTeX is widely used across different fields such as academia, science, engineering, and even business, owing to its flexibility and extensibility. To cater to the needs of specific fields, numerous LaTeX packages have been developed. These packages help users simplify complex tasks like typesetting advanced mathematical equations, creating professional tables, producing high-quality graphics, and more. In this section, we will explore some of the most useful LaTeX packages tailored to various fields.

7.1.1 Mathematics Packages

One of the most powerful and widely used extensions in the LaTeX ecosystem for mathematical typesetting is the `amsmath` package. Developed by the American Mathematical Society, this package extends LaTeX's default math capabilities with a suite of commands and environments designed to support the typesetting of complex mathematical expressions with professional-quality formatting.

At the core of its usefulness is the `align` environment, which makes it easy to write multiple equations that need to be aligned, for example, by their equal signs. This environment not only improves the visual structure of related equations but also helps preserve semantic clarity when reading through a document. Consider the following example, which demonstrates how two well-known physical laws can be aligned for comparison:

Example: Aligning Equations Using amsmath

LaTeX Code:

```
\usepackage{amsmath}

\begin{align}
    E &= mc^2 \\
    F &= ma
\end{align}
```

Output

$$E = mc^2 \tag{7.1}$$
$$F = ma \tag{7.2}$$

In this case, the ampersand symbol (&) in each line determines the alignment point, so both equations are visually aligned at the equal sign. This is particularly helpful in derivations, proofs, or when listing a system of equations.

Beyond alignment, the `amsmath` package also includes environments such as `gather` for centering multiple equations, `multline` for breaking long equations across several lines, and `cases` for representing piecewise-defined functions. Additionally, `amsmath` provides enhanced matrix environments, improves spacing in complex formulas, and introduces intuitive commands for common mathematical constructs like fractions, roots, integrals, summations, and more.

Because of its rich features and widespread support, `amsmath` is considered a foundational package for writing any mathematically intensive document in LaTeX, from undergraduate problem sets to research-level papers and dissertations.

7.1.2 Physics Packages

For writers in the physical sciences, particularly physics, typesetting complex equations with clarity and brevity is crucial. The `physics` package is designed specifically to simplify this task by offering a more natural and expressive syntax for many frequently used notations. Unlike the more general-purpose `amsmath` package, which lays the foundational structures for mathematical typesetting, the `physics` package provides user-friendly commands tailored for expressing derivatives, vector quantities, quantum states, and operators—core components of physics notation.

One of the most appreciated features of the package is the simplified command structure for derivatives. Instead of constructing a derivative using nested fraction and differential symbols manually, the command `\dv` allows for an elegant, one-line definition of both total and partial derivatives. For instance, the equation for velocity as the derivative of position with respect to time becomes exceptionally easy to write and visually appealing.

Vector notation is also handled gracefully with the command `\va`, which automatically bolds vector variables in a consistent typographic style. Moreover, quantum mechanics expressions such as bras, kets, and inner products can be typeset using familiar operator-like commands such as `\bra`, `\ket`, and `\braket`. This not only saves time but also makes the LaTeX source code more readable for those familiar with the subject.

To illustrate the utility of the package, consider the following example. It demonstrates how a basic Newtonian equation and a derivative can be written compactly using the `physics` package:

Example: Expressing Physical Laws with `physics`

LaTeX Code:

```
\usepackage{physics}

\begin{equation}
    \dv{x}{t} = v,\quad
    \va{F} = m \va{a}
\end{equation}
```

In this example, the command `\dv{x}{t}` produces a neatly formatted total derivative, while `\va{F}` and `\va{a}` render bold-faced vector quantities. The resulting equation is both typographically clean and conceptually aligned with standard physics notation.

What makes the `physics` package particularly useful is that it combines expressive power with visual consistency, minimizing the need to manually format frequently used constructs. Moreover, the package is designed to be compatible with `amsmath`, so it can be integrated into existing mathematical workflows without disruption. For anyone writing a document that includes substantial physics content, whether lecture notes, research papers, or textbooks, this package offers a modern and efficient approach to high-quality typesetting.

7.1.3 LaTeX for Chemical Diagrams and Equations

Precise and elegant presentation of chemical formulas, reaction mechanisms, and molecular structures is essential in chemistry, particularly in scientific documents. LaTeX offers dedicated packages such as `mhchem`, `chemfig`, and `chemmacros`, each designed for different aspects of chemical typesetting. This subsection introduces their usage, providing examples with both code and output side by side.

Chemical Formulas and Reactions Using mhchem

The `mhchem` package is widely used for typesetting chemical equations and formulas. It simplifies input through intuitive syntax while automatically handling subscripts, charges, and arrows. Add it to the preamble as follows:

```
\usepackage[version=4]{mhchem}
```

Here is how basic chemical formulas are written:

Chemical Formulas with mhchem

LaTeX Code:

```
\ce{H2O}, \ce{C6H12O6},
\ce{Na+}, \ce{SO4^2-}
```

Output:

$$H_2O, \quad C_6H_{12}O_6, \quad Na^+, \quad SO_4^{2-}$$

Chemical reactions, including reversible and precipitation reactions, are equally simple:

Typesetting Reactions with mhchem

LaTeX Code:

```
\ce{2H2 + O2 -> 2H2O}

\ce{CO2 + H2O <=> H2CO3}

\ce{Ag+ + Cl- -> AgCl v}
```

Output:

$$2\,H_2 + O_2 \longrightarrow 2\,H_2O$$
$$CO_2 + H_2O \rightleftharpoons H_2CO_3$$
$$Ag^+ + Cl^- \longrightarrow AgCl\downarrow$$

Drawing Molecules with `chemfig`

For molecular structures, `chemfig` is the package of choice. It allows users to draw structural formulas and control bond angles and branching.

To use it, include the package in the preamble:

```
\usepackage{chemfig}
```

Below is an example of methane:

Drawing Methane with chemfig

LaTeX Code:

```
\chemfig{C(-[2]H)(-[6]H)(-[0]H)(-[4]H)}
```

Output:

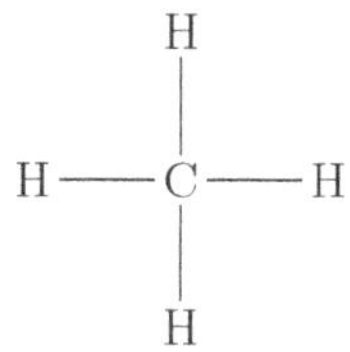

Aromatic compounds like benzene are also easy to illustrate:

Drawing Benzene with chemfig

LaTeX Code:

```
\chemfig{*6(=-=-=-)}
```

Output:

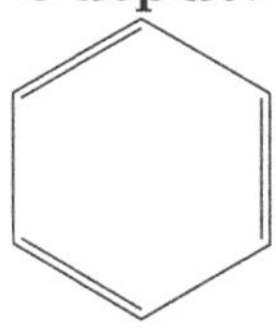

Other molecules and functional groups such as ethanol and the carboxyl group can be written as:

Functional Groups in chemfig

LaTeX Code:

```
\chemfig{CH_3-CH_2-OH}

\chemfig{C(=O)-OH}
```

Output:

CH_3 — CH_2 — OH

C ═ OH

Reaction Mechanisms with chemmacros

The `chemmacros` package is useful for more advanced reaction formatting, including mechanisms and annotated reaction arrows. It can be activated using:

```
\usepackage{chemmacros}
\chemsetup{modules=all}
```

Here is a mechanism-style example:

Reaction Arrows with chemmacros

LaTeX Code:

```
\schemestart
A \arrow{->} B \arrow{<->} C
\schemestop
```

Output:

A ⟶ B ⟷ C

You can also include reaction conditions:

Reaction Conditions

LaTeX Code:

```
\reaction{A + B ->[heat] C}
```

Output:

$$A + B \xrightarrow{\text{heat}} C \qquad \{1\}$$

Advanced Examples: Glucose and Polymers

Complex organic molecules like glucose or polymer chains can also be rendered with `chemfig`.

Drawing Glucose

LaTeX Code:

```
\chemfig{
CH_2OH-[:90]CH(-[:180]OH)-[:90]
CH(-[:180]OH)-[:90]CH(-[:180]H)-[:90]
CH(-[:180]OH)-[:90]C(=[:0]O)-[:180]H}
```

Output:

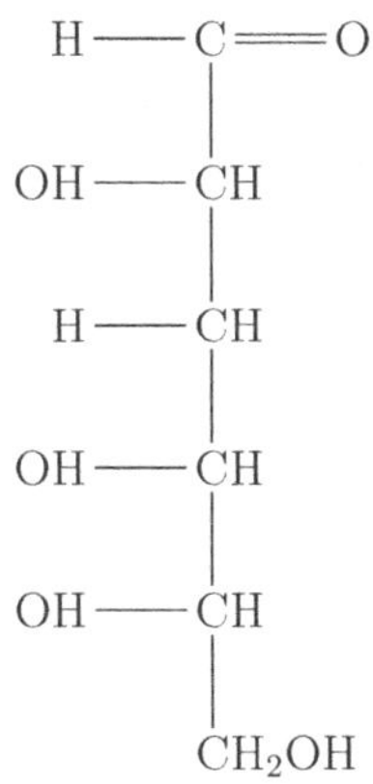

Polymers with repeated units and angled bonds:

Drawing a Polymer Chain

LaTeX Code:

```
\chemfig{-[:30](-[:90]
O-[:30])-[::+60](-[:90]
O-[:30])}
```

Output:

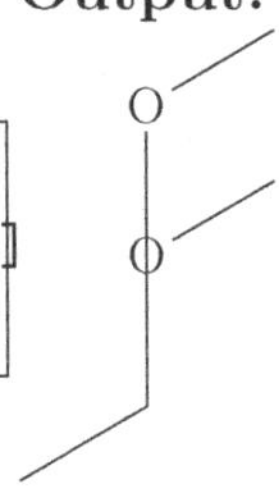

These tools provide chemists and educators the means to prepare professional, publication-ready documents with well-structured chemical content.

7.1.4 LaTeX for Music Notation

Typesetting music within LaTeX documents is an exciting feature that bridges the gap between music and mathematical precision. Whether one is writing a music theory textbook, a research article on composition, or simply wishes to embed musical excerpts in an academic document, LaTeX offers powerful tools for high-quality musical notation.

Three prominent approaches to music typesetting in LaTeX are through the use of LilyPond, MusixTeX, and ABC notation. Each has unique advantages depending on the level of complexity, output quality, and ease of use required. This subsection explores these tools in detail, showing how they integrate with LaTeX environments and how musical examples can be embedded seamlessly alongside text.

Engraving Music with LilyPond and `lilypond-book`

LilyPond is a professional music engraving system that can produce beautifully formatted scores with elegance comparable to published sheet music. Although it is a standalone tool, it integrates with LaTeX using the "lilypond-book" utility, which processes LilyPond code blocks embedded in LaTeX documents.

To use LilyPond with LaTeX, you must first install LilyPond from the official website (https://lilypond.org), or via a package manager such as `apt` for Linux users. After installation, documents are compiled using:

```
lilypond-book --pdf myfile.tex
pdflatex myfile.tex
```

Here is a complete LaTeX example demonstrating how to embed a simple melody using LilyPond:

Embedding a Melody with LilyPond

LaTeX Code:

```
\documentclass{article}
\usepackage{graphicx}
\begin{document}
Here is an example of a simple melody:
\begin{lilypond}
\relative c' {
  \key c \major
  \time 4/4
  c d e f | g a b c |
}
\end{lilypond}
\end{document}
```

LilyPond is ideal for users who need publication-quality musical scores and are comfortable working with an external toolchain. It supports virtually all classical notation features including dynamics, articulations, lyrics, transpositions, and even microtonal notation.

Composing Music Directly in LaTeX with MusixTeX

For those who wish to typeset music scores entirely within the LaTeX environment, without depending on external graphical tools, `MusixTeX` offers a powerful and mature solution. Unlike graphical notation software like MuseScore or LilyPond, which are primarily visual in their approach, MusixTeX adheres closely to LaTeX's typesetting principles, allowing users to build scores by writing code that describes the musical content in logical steps.

MusixTeX excels in providing granular control over every aspect of the musical layout: the spacing between notes, vertical alignment of staves, positioning of lyrics, and arrangement of polyphonic voices. This level of precision makes it highly suitable for scholarly or critical editions where exact representation matters. However, this control comes at the cost of complexity, the syntax is quite verbose, and the learning curve can be steep for newcomers to music typesetting or LaTeX itself.

To get started with MusixTeX, you first need to include the required packages in your preamble. These packages define the macros and fonts used for music symbols and layout:

Required Packages

```
\usepackage{musixtex}
\usepackage{musixcr}
%optional:enables additional symbol
support
```

Once the packages are loaded, the musical content is placed within a `music` environment, which acts similarly to environments like `equation` or `figure`. Each piece of the score, clefs, key signatures, time signatures, notes, and bar lines, is explicitly declared using specialized commands. For example, let us consider a simple 4/4 measure with a C major melody line:

Simple Melody in C Major

LaTeX Code:

```
\documentclass{article}
\usepackage{musixtex}
\begin{document}

\begin{music}
\parindent10mm
```

```
\generalmeter{\meterfrac{4}{4}}
% Time signature
\startextract
% Begin musical extract
\notes \qu c \qu d \qu e \qu f |
% Four quarter notes
\enotes
\zendextract
% End extract
\end{music}

\end{document}
```

Output:

In this example, the command `\generalmeter{\meterfrac{4}{4}}` sets the time signature, while `\notes ... \enotes` defines the actual musical content. Each note is represented by a command: `\qu` for quarter notes (crochets), followed by the pitch (e.g., c, d, e, f). A bar line is indicated with the `|` character. This concise example illustrates MusixTeX's building-block philosophy: the user constructs music semantically, one note or measure at a time.

For more sophisticated compositions, MusixTeX supports an extensive range of musical elements: multi-stave systems for piano or orchestral writing, and lyrics aligned below the staves, tuplets, beams, slurs, and ornaments. It also allows precise manual spacing, critical for aligning text and notes or for reproducing historically accurate layouts.

However, working with MusixTeX demands patience. Unlike visual tools, mistakes in spacing, alignment, or syntax may not become obvious until the document is compiled, which often requires multiple passes using the traditional LaTeX + dvips + ps2pdf workflow. Furthermore, users must often consult the documentation or examples for more complex notational constructs, especially when dealing with polyphony or counterpoint.

That said, for users who are comfortable in LaTeX and prefer a code-centric approach to composition, MusixTeX remains a powerful option. It integrates smoothly into existing LaTeX documents, enabling the typesetting of musical examples directly alongside academic text, a feature especially useful in music theory papers, historical musicology, and pedagogy.

As with many LaTeX packages, community support and templates play an important role. Beginners are encouraged to study working examples, modify them incrementally, and consult resources like the MusixTeX manual or the CTAN archive for guidance.

Below is a table that shows MusixTeX code snippets alongside their corresponding melody lines (interpreted musically).

MusixTeX code	**Corresponding melody line**
`\notes \qu c \qu d \qu e \qu f`	C – D – E – F (ascending quarter notes)
`\notes \qu g \qu f \qu e \qu d`	G – F – E – D (descending quarter notes)
`\notes \hl c \hl g`	C – G (half notes)
`\notes \qu c \enotes \barno=2 \notes \qu e \qu g`	C — E – G (bar number 2 appears)
`\notes \qu c \qu e \qu g \qu c'`	C – E – G – C' (C major arpeggio)
`\notes \qqqq cdef`	C – D – E – F (four sixteenth notes using

	shorthand)
`\notes \ibu0c2 \qb0c \qb0d \tbu0\qb0e`	Triplet: C – D – E (grouped triplet using beams)

Simple and Readable Input with ABC Notation

For users needing a fast and lightweight solution for entering melodies, particularly for folk music, tunes, or educational examples, the ABC notation system provides a highly readable format. The `abc` LaTeX package allows embedding this notation directly into documents.

After adding the following line to your preamble:

```
\usepackage{abc}
```

You can typeset a short melody as follows:

Using ABC Notation

LaTeX Code:

```
\documentclass{article}
\usepackage{abc}

\begin{document}

\begin{abc}
X:1
T:Simple Tune
M:4/4
L:1/4
K:C
C D E F | G A B c |
\end{abc}

\end{document}
```

ABC notation is widely used in folk music communities due to its plain text format. Though it lacks the typographic finesse of LilyPond or MusixTeX, it is perfect for basic melodies, chord charts, and classroom exercises.

Choosing the Right Tool

The ideal tool for music notation in LaTeX depends on your goals. LilyPond excels in typographic quality and supports full musical scores with lyrics and layout customizations. MusixTeX is excellent for users who prefer to remain fully within the LaTeX workflow and require precise control. ABC notation, on the other hand, is best suited for simpler pieces and is particularly attractive for its ease of use.

Method	Best for	Pros	Cons
LilyPond	Professional engraving	High-quality output	Requires external compilation
MusixTeX	Complex scores in pure LaTeX	Full control over layout	Verbose and complex syntax
ABC Notation	Simple melodies	Easy to write and learn	Limited formatting capabilities

Ultimately, the choice comes down to the complexity of the musical material and the workflow preferences of the author. LaTeX, through these tools, proves itself capable of integrating rich musical content into scholarly writing with clarity and precision.

7.1.5 Typesetting Chess in LaTeX

LaTeX provides powerful tools for chess typesetting, allowing users to render **chessboards** with positions, to write **chess moves** using algebraic notation, and to display **game sequences** in a structured format.

We will explore these features using the `\chessboard` and `\skak` packages.

Rendering Chessboards with Positions

The `\chessboard` package allows us to create **chessboards** and set up positions using **Forsyth-Edwards Notation (FEN)**.

Chessboard Example

LaTeX Code:

```
\documentclass{article}
\usepackage{chessboard}
\begin{document}

\chessboard[
  setfen=rn1qkb1r/ppp2ppp/
  3p1n2/4p3/2B1P3/2NP1Q2/
  PPP2PPP/R1B1K1NR w KQkq
  - 2 5,
  showmover=true
]
\end{document}
```

Output:

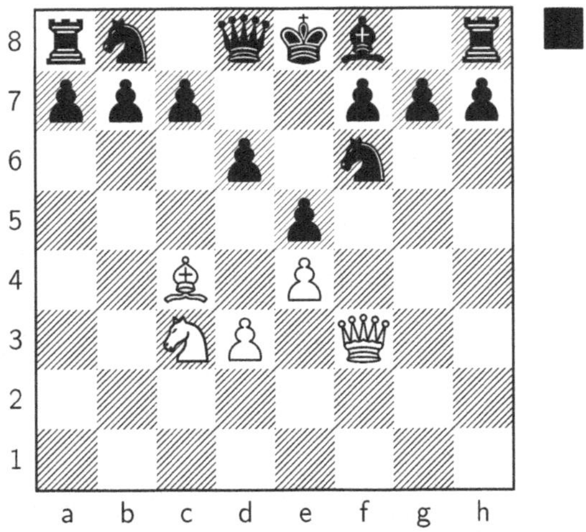

Writing Chess Moves Using Algebraic Notation

The \skak package enables us to write **chess moves** in **standard algebraic notation**.

Chess Notation Example

LaTeX Code:

```
\documentclass{article}
\usepackage{skak}
\begin{document}

\newgame
\mainline{1.e4 e5 2.Nf3 Nc6
 3.Bb5 a6}
\mainline{4.Ba4 Nf6 5.O-O
Be7 6.Re1 b5}

\end{document}
```

Output:
1 e4 e5 2 ♘f3 ♘c6 3 ♗b5 a6 4 ♗a4 ♘f6 5 O-O ♗e7 6 ♖e1 b5

Displaying Game Sequences in a Structured Format

We can present **chess game sequences** in a structured format, adding annotations, move numbers, and chess diagrams.

Chess Game Example

LaTeX Code:

```
\documentclass{article}
\usepackage{skak}
\usepackage{chessboard}
\begin{document}

\newgame
\mainline{1.e4 e5 2.Nf3 Nc6
3.Bb5 a6}
\chessboard[
  setfen=r1bqkbnr/pppp1ppp/
  2n5/8/4P3/5N2/
  PPPP1PPP/RNBQKB1R w KQkq
  - 2 3
]
\mainline{4.Ba4 Nf6
5.O-O Be7 6.Re1 b5}
\end{document}
```

Output:

1 e4 e5 2 ♘f3 ♘c6 3 ♗b5 a6

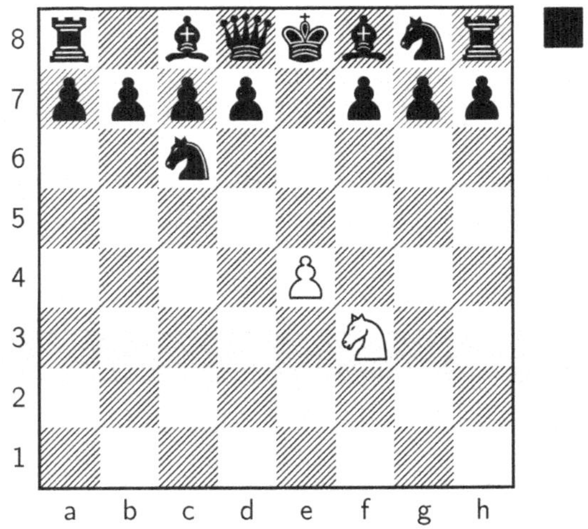

4 ♗a4 ♘f6 5 O-O ♗e7 6 ♖e1 b5

Advanced Chessboard Customization

The `\chessboard` package allows advanced customization, such as highlighting moves, changing pieces' colors, and marking specific squares.

Advanced Customization Example

LaTeX Code:

```
\documentclass{article}
\usepackage{skak}
\usepackage{chessboard}
\begin{document}

\chessboard[
  setfen=8/8/8/3p4/4P3/8/8/
  8 w - - 0 1,
```

```
  pgfstyle=straightmove,
  markmove={e4-d5},
  color=red
]
\end{document}
```

Output:

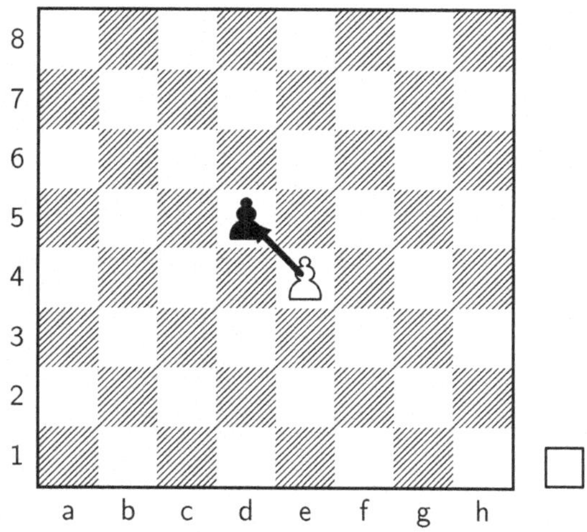

The visual output of each piece using the chessboard package.

Code	**Piece name**	Uses	**Output**
`P`	White Pawn	`\chess -board [setpieces ={Pa1}`	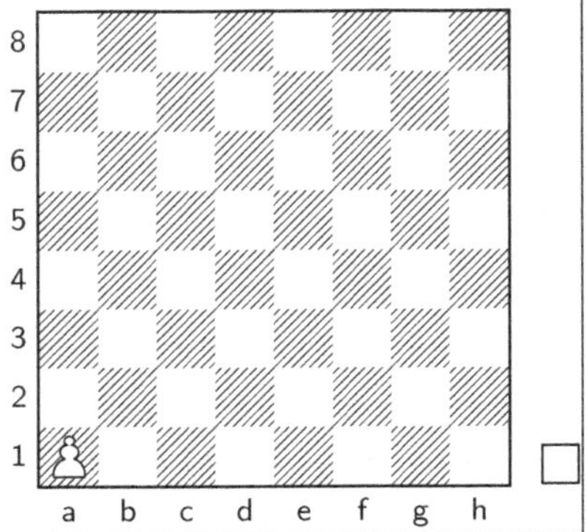
`N`	White Knight	`\chess -board [setpieces ={Na1}`	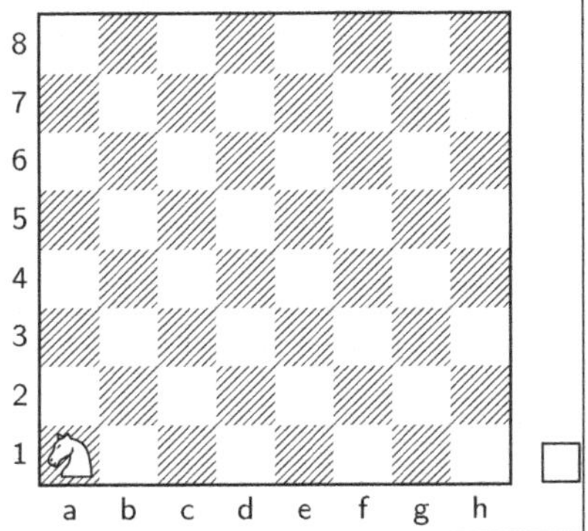
`B`	White Bishop	`\chess -board [setpieces ={Ba1}`	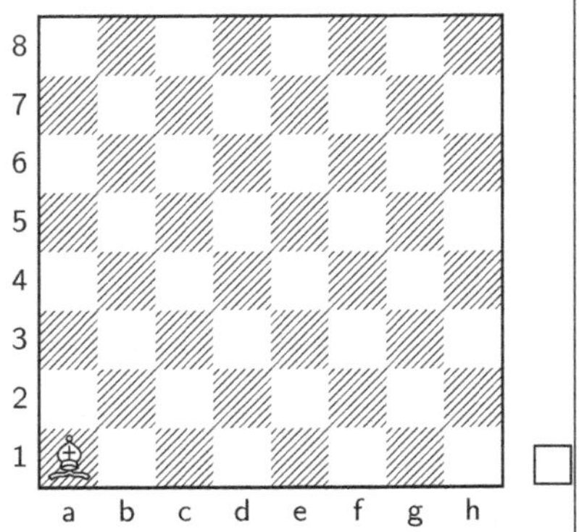

R	White Rook	\chess-board [setpieces ={Ra1}	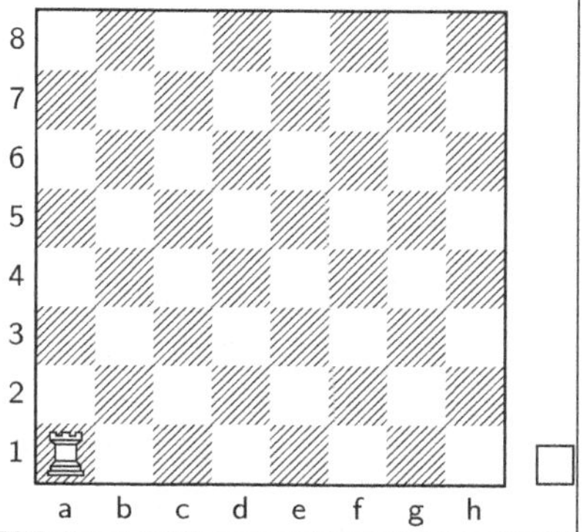
Q	White Queen	\chess-board [setpieces ={Qa1}	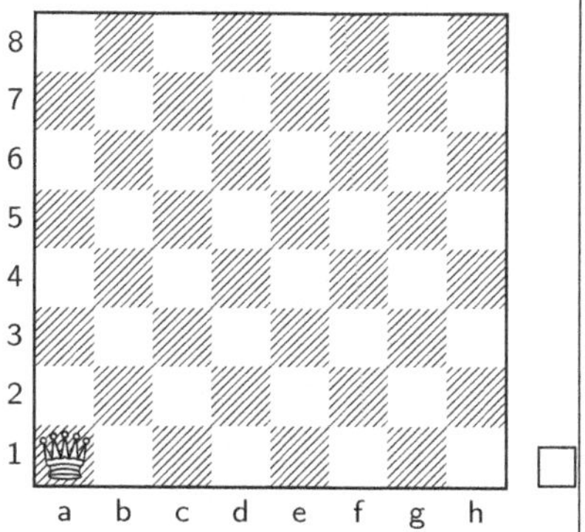
K	White King	\chess-board [setpieces ={Ka1}	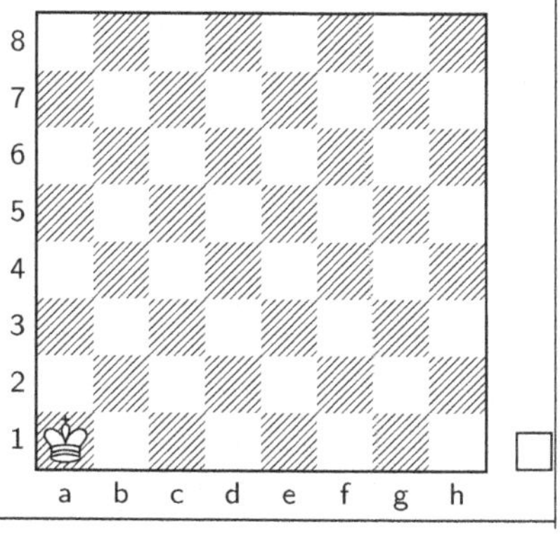

p	Black Pawn	\chess -board [setpieces ={pa1}	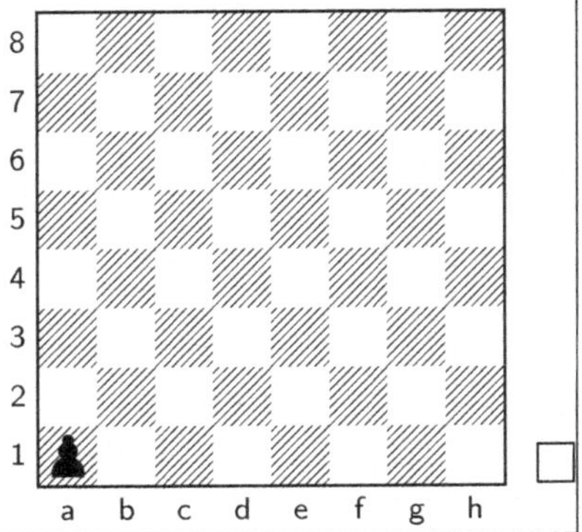
n	Black Knight	\chess -board [setpieces ={na1}	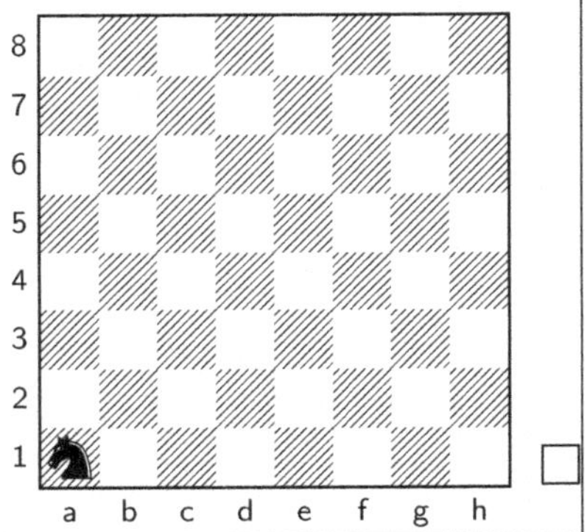
b	Black Bishop	\chess -board [setpieces ={ba1}	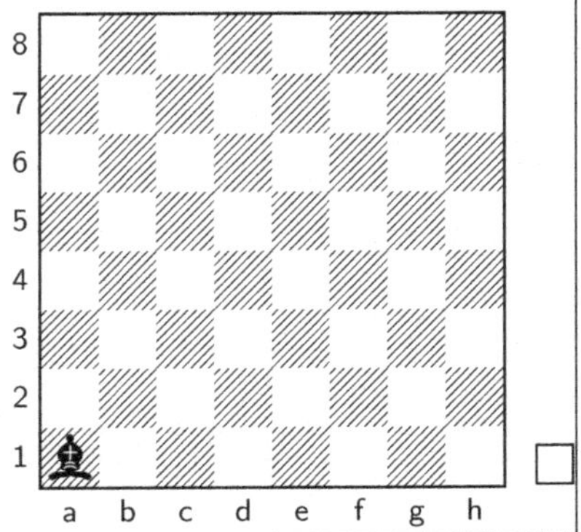

r	Black Rook	\chess -board [setpieces ={ra1}	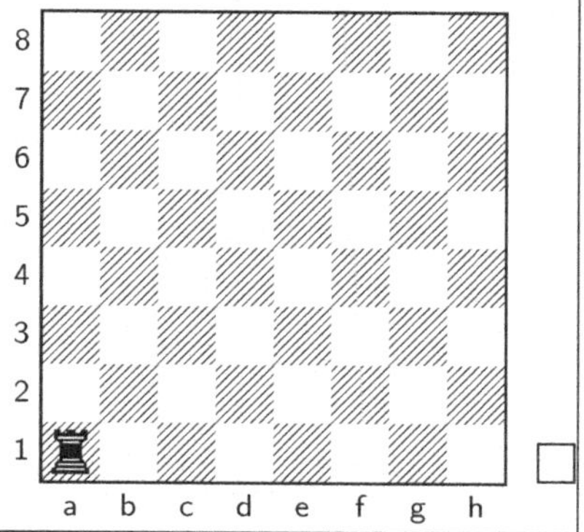
q	Black Queen	\chess -board [setpieces ={qa1}	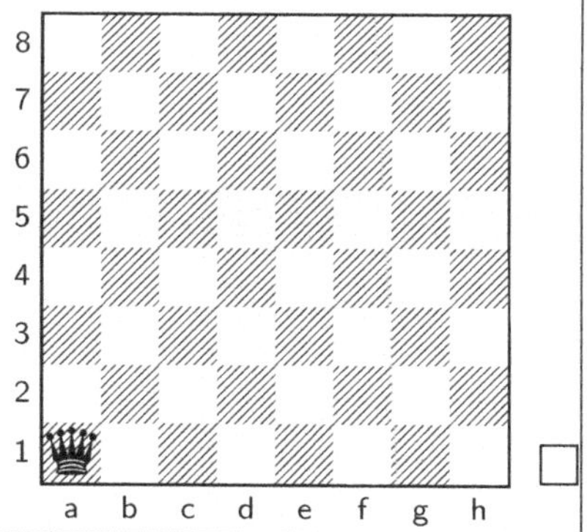
k	Black King	\chess -board [setpieces ={ka1}	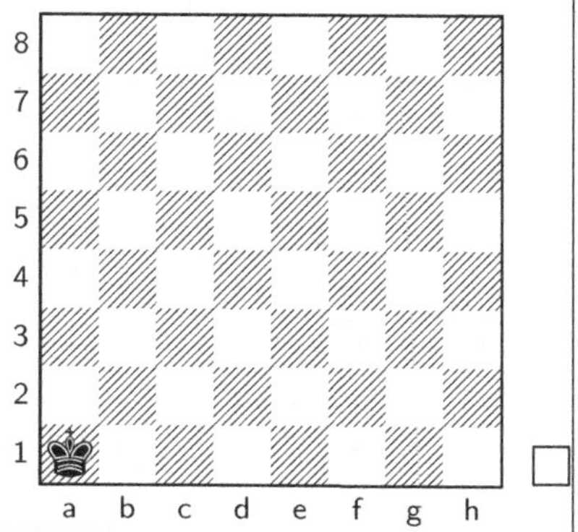

Here, each piece appears visually on the a1 square of a mini chessboard. You can adjust smallboard or change the square (like e4, etc.) if needed.

7.2 Electrical Engineering in LaTeX

LaTeX provides powerful tools for electrical engineering, enabling users to draw circuit diagrams using `\circuitikz`, to create signal processing plots using `\pgfplots`, and to design logic circuits using `\tikz`. We explore these tools with examples.

Drawing Circuit Diagrams with `circuitikz`

The `\circuitikz` package allows easy creation of electrical circuits with resistors, capacitors, transistors, and operational amplifiers.

Circuit Diagram Example

LaTeX Code:

```
\documentclass{article}
\usepackage{circuitikz}
\begin{document}

\begin{circuitikz}
 \draw (0,0) to[sinusoidal
voltage source, l=$V_s$] (0,3)
to[R, l=$R_1$] (3,3)
to[C, l=$C_1$] (3,0) -- (0,0);
\end{circuitikz}

\end{document}
```

Output:

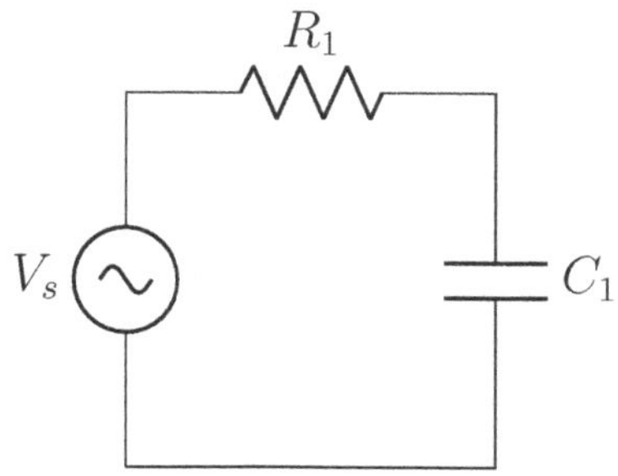

7.2.1 2. Plotting Signal Processing and Waveforms

Using \`pgfplots`, we can plot signals, sine waves, and filter responses.

Signal Processing Example

LaTeX Code:

```
\documentclass{article}
\usepackage{pgfplots}
\begin{document}

\begin{tikzpicture}
\begin{axis}[
    xlabel={$t$ (seconds)},
    ylabel={$V(t)$ (Volts)},
    grid=major,
]
 \addplot[domain=0:6.28,
   samples=100,smooth,blue]
        {sin(deg(x))};
\end{axis}
\end{tikzpicture}

\end{document}
```

Output:

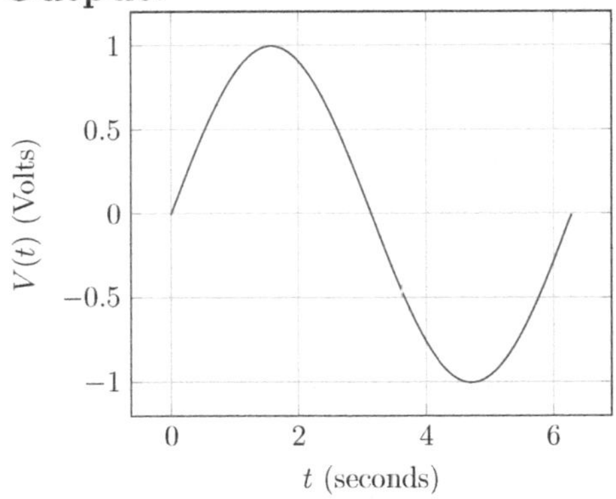

Designing Logic Circuits with tikz

Using `\tikz`, we can create logic gates, truth tables, and digital circuits.

Logic Circuit Example

LaTeX Code:

```
\documentclass{article}
\usepackage{tikz}
\usetikzlibrary{circuits.logic.US}
\begin{document}

\begin{tikzpicture}
 \node (A) at (0,1) {A};
 \node (B) at (0,-1) {B};
 \node (AND) at (2,0)
       [and gate] {};
 \node (OUT) at (4,0) {Output};

 \draw (A) -- (AND.input 1);
 \draw (B) -- (AND.input 2);
 \draw (AND.output) -- (OUT);
```

```
\end{tikzpicture}

\end{document}
```

Output:

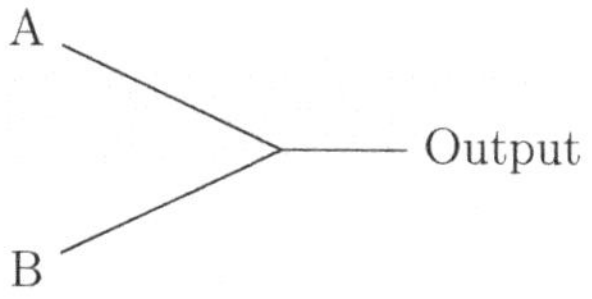

7.2.2 Engineering and Computer Science Packages

Engineering and computer science documents often require more than just text and mathematical formulas. Authors frequently need to include structured algorithms, source code with syntax highlighting, and well-crafted diagrams to communicate ideas effectively. LaTeX provides robust packages specifically designed to support these tasks in a visually appealing and technically accurate way.

In this subsection, we explore three essential packages: `algorithm2e` for writing algorithms in pseudocode, `listings` for displaying source code, and `tikz` for creating diagrams and technical illustrations. Each offers deep customizability and professional output, making them valuable tools in any technical writer's LaTeX toolkit.

Typesetting Algorithms with `algorithm2e`

The `algorithm2e` package is designed to help authors present algorithms in a structured and readable format. Unlike traditional environments that simply show code, this package emphasizes logical flow through built-in formatting for loops, conditions, and comments, closely mimicking how pseudocode appears in textbooks and research papers.

To begin using it, include the following in your document preamble:

```
\usepackage{algorithm2e}
```

Here is an example that demonstrates a basic algorithm structure:

Writing an Algorithm with `algorithm2e`

LaTeX Code:

```
\begin{algorithm}
    \SetAlgoLined
    \KwData{Input data}
    \KwResult{Processed data}
    Initialize variables\;
    \For{each element in list}{
        Process element\;
    }
    \caption{Basic Algorithm}
\end{algorithm}
```

Output:

A boxed environment showing a title, input/output description, loop structure, and clearly formatted pseudocode that resembles textbook-style algorithms

The environment supports many features such as line numbering, comments, indentation, and styling. These features make it ideal for presenting algorithms in a form suitable for academic publication or technical documentation.

Displaying Source Code with `listings`

Presenting source code in a LaTeX document requires more than just a monospaced font. Syntax highlighting, indentation, and line numbers improve readability and professionalism. The `listings` package offers extensive functionality for including code snippets from various programming languages directly within the LaTeX document.

To activate the package, add the following in your preamble:

```
\usepackage{listings}
```

Below is a simple example of a recursive Python function using the listings environment:

Simple Diagram with tikz

LaTeX Code:

```
\begin{lstlisting}[language
      =Python]
def factorial(n):
    if n == 0:
        return 1
else:
    return n * factorial(n-1)
```

Output:

A syntax-highlighted Python function with indentation and line numbers (optional), making the code clean and easy to follow

The `listings` package supports a wide variety of programming languages, including C++, Java, Python, MATLAB, and more. You can customize colors, fonts, and styles to match the aesthetic of your document or publication guidelines.

Creating Diagrams with `tikz`

The `tikz` package is one of LaTeX's most powerful tools, capable of generating everything from basic vector graphics to intricate circuit diagrams and data plots. It is particularly valuable in engineering and scientific disciplines where custom illustrations are often required.

To use TikZ, include the following in the preamble:

```
\usepackage{tikz}
```

The example below demonstrates a simple coordinate system with a line segment:

Simple Diagram with `tikz`

LaTeX Code:

```
\begin{tikzpicture}
\draw[thick, ->] (0, 0) --
(4, 0) node[anchor=north west]
{x};
\draw[thick, ->] (0, 0) --
(0, 4)
 node[anchor=south east] {y};
    \draw (0, 0) -- (3, 3);
\end{tikzpicture}
```

Output:

A coordinate system with labeled x and y axes, and a diagonal line from the origin to the point $(3, 3)$

TikZ offers extremely fine control over positions, labels, shapes, colors, and mathematical annotations. It is widely used for figures in theses, research articles, and presentations. More advanced features include 3D drawings, animation, and integration with plotting tools like PGFPlots.

7.2.3 Economics and Business Packages

LaTeX is increasingly popular in economics and business due to its precision, professional layout capabilities, and extensive package ecosystem. It is particularly valued for its ability to create data-driven documents such as reports, working papers, charts, and tables. Two especially useful packages in this context are `pgfplots`, for generating visualizations, and `datatool`, for working with structured data sets. This subsection explores both packages in depth, illustrating how they can be used to typeset data analysis and economic modeling directly in LaTeX.

Data Visualization with `pgfplots`

The `pgfplots` package is one of the most powerful tools available in LaTeX for plotting data. It is built on top of TikZ and allows users to generate high-quality 2D and 3D plots directly from LaTeX code. For economists and business analysts, this is especially useful when preparing visualizations of market trends, comparative data, and time series within the same environment as your written analysis.

To use `pgfplots`, the package must be included in the preamble:

```
\usepackage{pgfplots}
\pgfplotsset{compat=1.18}
```

Suppose we want to illustrate sales revenue over 3 months. The following example shows how to construct a simple line plot:

Line Chart with pgfplots

LaTeX Code:

```
\begin{tikzpicture}
\begin{axis}[
    title={Sales Data},
    xlabel={Months},
    ylabel={Revenue (in USD)},
    xtick={1,2,3},
    xticklabels={Jan, Feb, Mar},
    ymin=0, ymax=6000
```

```
]
\addplot coordinates {(1,2000)
(2,3000) (3,5000)};
\end{axis}
\end{tikzpicture}
```

Output:
A line chart titled "Sales Data" with three points for January, February, and March showing upward revenue growth from \$2,000 to \$5,000

This package supports extensive customization, including color schemes, multiple plot overlays, shaded areas for confidence intervals, and interactive legends. It also integrates smoothly with external data sources for larger data sets, making it suitable for formal academic or business reporting.

Managing and Displaying Data with `datatool`

While `pgfplots` focuses on visual representation, the `datatool` package offers powerful capabilities for importing and processing tabular data. This is particularly relevant in economics and business contexts where data often resides in spreadsheets or CSV files. `datatool` allows LaTeX to read such data, manipulate it, and display it dynamically within the document, which is ideal for generating periodic reports or statistical summaries.

To use `datatool`, include the package in the preamble:

```
\usepackage{datatool}
```

One way to create and use a small internal data set (without reading from a file) is demonstrated in the following example. It creates a database named `sales`, adds rows to it, and displays it in tabular form.

Creating and Displaying a Data Set with datatool

LaTeX Code:

```
\DTLnewdb{sales}
\DTLaddrow{sales}{January,2000}
\DTLaddrow{sales}{February,3000}
\DTLaddrow{sales}{March,5000}
\DTLdisplaydb{sales}
```

Output:

January	2000
February	3000
March	5000

This simple usage already reveals the potential of the package. For more advanced tasks, `datatool` supports conditional logic, data sorting, filtering, and even generating summary statistics such as averages, maxima, and minima. One could also import a `.csv` file using:

```
\DTLloaddb{salesdata}{sales.csv}
```

This feature is particularly useful for automating report generation where the numerical values in the tables and plots are kept up-to-date without manual edits to the LaTeX source.

Integrating Data and Narrative

What makes these packages so valuable in business and economics is their ability to integrate data analysis directly with explanatory text. For example, one can define commands that calculate statistics from a data set and then insert those values into a paragraph automatically. This ensures consistency throughout a document especially in documents where the data might change frequently (such as monthly reports or annual economic reviews).

Instead of relying on copy-pasting from spreadsheets, users can structure their entire document pipeline in LaTeX: input data, generate visuals, display tables, and refer to numerical results all in one place. This approach not only increases reproducibility but also minimizes human error and maintains a clean, consistent style throughout the document.

7.2.4 Humanities and Social Sciences Packages

In humanities and social sciences, clarity, credibility, and scholarly rigor depend heavily on proper referencing, quotation handling, and precise language formatting. LaTeX supports these needs through powerful packages that go beyond basic typesetting, offering rich control over citation styles, multilingual quotation formatting, and bibliographic data integration. This subsection explores two key packages: `biblatex` for citation and bibliography management, and `csquotes` for handling quotations in a language-sensitive and typographically accurate way.

Citation and Bibliography Management with `biblatex`

Academic writing in the humanities and social sciences often follows specific citation styles such as MLA, APA, or Chicago. The `biblatex` package, along with its companion backend processor `biber`, offers a flexible and modern framework for citations and bibliographies. Unlike older systems such as `BibTeX`, `biblatex` allows for full customization of citation formats, multilingual support, and fine-tuned control over how entries are displayed and sorted.

To get started with `biblatex`, include the following in your document preamble:

```
\usepackage[backend=biber,
style=authoryear]{biblatex}
\addbibresource{references.bib}
```

This command specifies the use of the `authoryear` citation style (common in social sciences) and declares the source `.bib` file containing the bibliographic data. Citations in the text are then created using high-level commands that separate the formatting logic from the citation logic.

Here is a simple example of a textual citation using `\textcite`, which formats the author's name in the sentence and the year in parentheses:

Textual Citation with biblatex

LaTeX Code:

```
\textcite{smith2023} discusses
the importance of accurate data
in ethnographic studies.

\printbibliography
```

Output:

Smith (2023) discusses the importance of accurate data in ethnographic studies.
References: Smith, John. 2023. *Data and Fieldwork in Cultural Anthropology.* Cambridge University Press.

This modularity allows different parts of the citation, such as author, year, title, and publisher, to be styled independently, making `biblatex` highly adaptable to discipline-specific requirements. It also supports annotations, sorting by criteria such as type or year, and sub-bibliographies for different sections of a document (e.g., primary sources vs. secondary sources).

Quotation Formatting with `csquotes`

Quotations are central to scholarship in fields such as literature, history, and philosophy. The `csquotes` package provides a robust framework for managing quotation marks, especially in multilingual documents or texts requiring nested quotations. One of its main benefits is that it automatically adjusts quotation marks based on the document's language and the nesting level, eliminating the need to manually enter typographically correct quotes.

To begin using `csquotes`, load it with:

```
\usepackage{csquotes}
```

Once active, the package offers commands like `\enquote` for inline quotations and `\blockquote` for longer excerpts. Here is an example of the former:

Inline Quotation with `csquotes`

LaTeX Code:

```
\enquote{To be or
not to be, that is
the question.}
```

Output:

"To be or not to be, that is the question."

If the document uses a non-English language (e.g., German or French), quotation marks will automatically adjust to the typographic norms of that language. This is particularly useful in comparative literature, translation studies, or when citing works in the original language.

For longer passages, `csquotes` also provides block quotation environments such as `\blockquote`, which apply indentation and spacing appropriate for prose analysis:

Block Quotation with csquotes

LaTeX Code:

```
\blockquote{The history of all
hitherto existing society is
the history of class struggles.}
```

Output:

A visually separated block with: "The history of all hitherto existing society is the history of class struggles."

These features ensure that quotations are handled consistently and professionally throughout a document while reducing the cognitive load on the author.

7.2.5 General-Purpose Packages

While many LaTeX packages are domain-specific, there are a number of general-purpose packages that are invaluable across all academic and professional disciplines. These packages enhance the structure, readability, and functionality of documents and are especially useful for customizing layout, incorporating color, and enabling interactive elements like hyperlinks. This subsection explores three of the most widely used general-purpose packages: `geometry`, `xcolor`, and `hyperref`.

Customizing Page Layout with `geometry`

Controlling the layout of a document is an essential aspect of high-quality typesetting. The `geometry` package provides a flexible and intuitive way to define the page size, margins, and orientation of your document. Rather than manually adjusting settings with multiple commands, `geometry` allows for a centralized declaration in the preamble.

A common use case is setting uniform one-inch margins around the page. This can be achieved as follows:

Setting Margins with `geometry`

LaTeX Code:

```
\usepackage[margin=1in]{geometry}
```

Effect:

Applies 1-inch margins on all sides of every page, conforming to common manuscript guidelines and submission standards

Beyond basic margins, `geometry` supports page orientation (portrait or landscape), custom paper sizes (A4, letter, legal, etc.), and asymmetric settings for binding and double-sided printing. This makes it an essential package for thesis writing, journal submissions, and formatted reports.

Color Control and Highlighting with `xcolor`

Visual structure is crucial for highlighting key content, and the `xcolor` package offers a powerful interface for color customization. This package goes beyond the basic `color` package, enabling authors to define custom colors, use predefined palettes, and apply colors to text, tables, page elements, and mathematical content.

To enable its features, load the package in the preamble:

```
\usepackage{xcolor}
```

Here is a basic example of applying color to inline text:

Using Text Color with xcolor

LaTeX Code:

```
\textcolor{blue}{This
text will be blue.}
```

Output:

This text will be blue.

Colors can also be defined using RGB, CMYK, or HTML-style hex codes, allowing complete control over document branding or styling. For example, authors preparing teaching materials may use different colors for emphasis, code annotations, or alert messages.

Interactive Documents with `hyperref`

Modern documents often contain internal navigation elements, such as clickable references, and external hyperlinks to websites or digital archives. The `hyperref` package automatically turns section titles, figure references, citations, and even URLs into clickable links in the output PDF.

To activate it, include in the preamble:

```
\usepackage{hyperref}
```

One of the most common use cases is linking to an external website, as shown below:

External Hyperlink with hyperref

LaTeX Code:

```
\href{https://www.example.com}
{Click here to visit Example.com}
```

Output:

Click here to visit Example.com

The package also supports back-referencing from bibliographies to citations, colored link styles, and the creation of document outlines in PDF readers. This makes it a vital package for navigation-heavy documents such as books, theses, and technical manuals.

Conclusion and Further Exploration

Each of these general-purpose packages, `geometry`, `xcolor`, and `hyperref`, adds critical value to any LaTeX document, improving visual design, accessibility, and compliance with formatting standards. They are not limited to technical disciplines; humanities, sciences, and business documents all benefit from fine-grained control over layout and interactivity.

7.2.6 Full LaTeX Example

Simple Melody with MusixTeX

```
\documentclass{article}
\usepackage{amsmath}
% For mathematical formulas
\usepackage{physics}
% For physics notation
\usepackage{algorithm2e}
% For algorithms
\usepackage{pgfplots}
% For plotting
\usepackage{biblatex}
% For bibliographies and citations
\addbibresource{references.bib}

\title{Useful LaTeX Packages for Various
Fields}
\author{Dr. LaTeX}
\date{\today}
```

```
\begin{document}

\maketitle

\section{Mathematics and Physics}
Using the \texttt{amsmath} package,
we can write complex mathematical
expressions:
\begin{align}
    E &= mc^2 \\
    F &= ma
\end{align}

With the \texttt{physics} package,
we can simplify physics notation:
\begin{equation}
    \dv{x}{t} = v, \quad
    \va{F} = m \va{a}
\end{equation}

\section{Engineering and Computer
Science}
With the \texttt{algorithm2e} package,
we can write algorithms in a structured
way:
\begin{algorithm}
    \SetAlgoLined
    \KwData{Input data}
    \KwResult{Processed data}
    Initialize variables\;
    \For{each element in list}{
        Process element\;
    }
```

```
    \caption{Basic Algorithm}
\end{algorithm}

Using the \texttt{listings} package,
we can easily include formatted source
code with syntax highlighting. Here is
an example of a Python function:
\begin{lstlisting}[language=Python]
def factorial(n):
    if n == 0:
        return 1
    else:
        return n * factorial(n-1)
\section{Economics and Business}
The \texttt{pgfplots} package is ideal
for creating charts and plots. Below is
an example of a line chart:
\begin{tikzpicture}
    \begin{axis}[
        title={Sales Data},
        xlabel={Months},
        ylabel={Revenue (in USD)}
    ]
    \addplot coordinates {(1,2000)
    (2,3000) (3,5000)};
    \end{axis}
\end{tikzpicture}

\section{Humanities and Social Sciences}
The \texttt{biblatex} package makes it
easy to manage citations and references
in research documents:
\begin{verbatim}
\usepackage[backend=biber,
```

```
style=authoryear]{biblatex}
\addbibresource{references.bib}
\end{verbatim}

With the \texttt{csquotes} package,
you can handlequotations efficiently:
\begin{verbatim}
\enquote{To be or not to be, that is the
question.}
\end{verbatim}
\begin{verbatim}

\printbibliography
\end{document}
\end{verbatim}
```

7.3 Developing Your Own LaTeX Packages

While LaTeX offers thousands of ready-made packages for almost every imaginable task, there are scenarios, especially in specialized academic or technical contexts, where existing packages may not fully meet your needs. In such cases, developing your own LaTeX package becomes both a powerful and a practical solution. This section provides a foundational guide to creating custom packages, starting with basic structuring and command definitions, and progressing to more advanced topics such as managing package options, interacting with counters, and ensuring compatibility with other packages. Whether you are streamlining repetitive formatting tasks or building tools for a broader user base, writing your own LaTeX package opens new possibilities for customization and efficiency in document preparation.

7.3.1 Developing a Custom LaTeX Package

LaTeX allows users to create their own **packages** to extend functionality. A LaTeX package typically defines **new commands** and **environments**, customizes **document styles and formatting**, and provides **additional macros** for document automation. A package is written in **plain TeX/LaTeX** and saved with a `.sty` extension.

A LaTeX package starts with `\ProvidesPackage{name}`, which identifies the package, and `\RequirePackage{name}`, which loads the necessary dependencies. Below we give a basic package structure.

Basic Package Structure

```
% mypackage.sty
\ProvidesPackage{mypackage}
[2025/02/16 Custom LaTeX Package]
\RequirePackage{xcolor}
% Load required package

\newcommand{\highlight}[1]{%
  \colorbox{yellow}{#1}%
}

\newenvironment{important}{%
  \par\noindent\textbf{Important: }
  \itshape%
}{%
  \par
}
```

This defines a **new command** `\highlight{}` that highlights text in yellow and a **new environment** `important` that bolds text.

To use a package, we need to follow the following steps:

1. **Save the file** as `mypackage.sty`.
2. **Place it in the document folder** or the local `texmf` directory.
3. **Load the package** in your document:

   ```
   \usepackage{mypackage}
   ```

Using the Package

```
\documentclass{article}
\usepackage{mypackage}

\begin{document}

This is a \highlight{highlighted} text.

\begin{important}
This section is marked as important!
\end{important}

\end{document}
```

%sectionAdding Package Options

We can define **custom options** using `\DeclareOption` and `\ProcessOptions`.

Adding Package Options

```
% mypackage.sty
\ProvidesPackage{mypackage}
[2025/02/16 Custom LaTeX Package]
```

```
\DeclareOption{red}{\def\mycolor{red}}
\DeclareOption{blue}{\def\mycolor{blue}}
\ProcessOptions\relax

\newcommand{\highlight}[1]{%
  \colorbox{\mycolor}{#1}%
}
```

Now, the user can choose an **option when loading the package**:

```
\usepackage[red]{mypackage}
% Highlights in red
\usepackage[blue]{mypackage} % Highlights
                             % in blue
```

A package should include a **documentation file** in `.dtx` format.

To generate **package documentation**, use `docstrip`:

Package Documentation

```
\documentclass{article}
\usepackage{mypackage}

\begin{document}

\title{mypackage: A Custom LaTeX Package}
\author{Your Name}
\date{\today}

\maketitle

\section{Introduction}
The \texttt{mypackage} package provides:
- Text highlighting.
- An \texttt{important} environment.
```

```
- Customization via package options.

\end{document}
```

LaTeX packages **enhance productivity** and make documents **modular and reusable.**

7.3.2 Advanced LaTeX Package Development

This document covers how to create an advanced LaTeX package called `advpackage.sty`. This package provides custom counters to numbering systems for elements like definitions and theorems, custom environments to automatically formatted content such as warnings and examples, auto-numbered lists to dynamic lists with automatic numbering, and automated styling to predefined styles for sections, tables, and figures.

7.3.3 Creating a Custom Counter

A counter in LaTeX is used for numbering objects like theorems, exercises, or examples.

Define a Counter

```
% advpackage.sty
\ProvidesPackage{advpackage}
[2025/02/16 Advanced LaTeX Package]

\newcounter{example}
\renewcommand{\theexample}
{Example \arabic{example}}

\newcommand{\example}[1]{
```

```
    \refstepcounter{example}
    \textbf{\theexample:} #1
}
```

To use the counter above, first include the command \usepackage{advpackage} and write

```
\example{This is a custom example.}
\example{Another numbered example.}
```

Output:

Example 1: This is a custom example.
Example 2: Another numbered example.

7.3.4 Creating Custom Environments

A custom environment allows structured content with predefined formatting. This is how we define the custom environment.

Define a Custom Environment

```
% Define an "alertbox" environment
\newenvironment{alertbox}[1]{%
\par
\noindent
\begin{tcolorbox}[colframe=red!75!black,
colback=red!10, boxrule=1pt, title=#1]
}{%
\end{tcolorbox}
}
```

We can use the environment as:

```
\begin{alertbox}{Warning}
Be careful with unbalanced curly braces in LaTeX.
\end{alertbox}
```

and the output will be

> **Warning**
>
> Be careful with unbalanced curly braces in LaTeX.

7.3.5 Auto-Numbered Lists

Here, we demonstrate dynamic auto-numbered lists where the numbers adjust automatically.

Auto-Numbered List

```
% Define a numbered list
\newcounter{numlist}
\newcommand{\itemnum}[1]{
    \refstepcounter{numlist}
    \textbf{(\thenumlist)} #1
}
```

We can use the auto-numbered lists as:

```
\itemnum{First auto-numbered item.}
\itemnum{Second auto-numbered item.}
```

and the output will be:

> (1) First auto-numbered item
> (2) Second auto-numbered item

7.3.6 Automated Styling for Sections

We can automate section styling using the `titlesec` package.

Automated Section Formatting

```
% Load titlesec and customize
section format
\RequirePackage{titlesec}
\titleformat{\section}
{\Large\bfseries\color{blue}}
{\thesection.}{0.5em}{}
```

We can use the section as:

```
\section{Styled Section}
This section title is automatically blue and
bold.
```

7.3.7 Automated Table Styling

We can automate table formatting to ensure professional styling.

Automated Table Styling

```
% Define a command for professional
tables
\newcommand{\proftable}[2]{%
    \begin{table}[h]
        \centering
        \renewcommand{\arraystretch}{1.5}
        \begin{tabular}{|c|c|}
        \hline
        #1 \\
```

```
            \hline
            #2 \\
            \hline
            \end{tabular}
        \end{table}
}
```

We can use the Automated Table Formatting as:

`\proftable{Column 1 & Column 2}{Data 1 & Data 2}`

and the output will be

Column 1	Column 2
Data 1	Data 2

Full LaTeX Document Using the Package

Full Document

```
% Define a command for professional
tables
\begin{verbatim}
\documentclass{article}
\usepackage{advpackage}

\begin{document}

\title{Advanced LaTeX Package Demo}
\author{Your Name}
\date{\today}
\maketitle

\section{Introduction}
This document demonstrates the features
of \texttt{advpackage.sty}.
```

```
\section{Examples of Features}

\example{This is a custom example using
numbered counters.}

\begin{alertbox}{Caution}
This is an alert box with a warning
message.
\end{alertbox}

\itemnum{First auto-numbered item.}
\itemnum{Second auto-numbered item.}

\section{Styled Section}
This section is formatted with automated
styling.

\proftable{Header 1 & Header 2}
{Value 1 & Value 2}

\end{document}
\end{verbatim}
```

7.4 Commonly Used Packages

Now, we will list 100 commonly used packages and their functionalities for many applications.

1. amsmath and amssymb

Usage: The `amsmath` and `amssymb` packages are widely used in mathematical typesetting to extend LaTeX's core capabilities. Provided by the American Mathematical Society (AMS), these packages are designed to meet the demands of authors working in mathematics, engineering, and sciences, where complex notation and precise formatting are essential.

The `amsmath` package enhances the input and display of mathematical expressions. It refines the appearance and logic of equation structures, offering additional environments and macros that produce clearer, more consistent results. It is typically loaded in the preamble of a LaTeX document and is considered a standard requirement for any document involving structured mathematics.

The `amssymb` package complements `amsmath` by providing access to an extended range of mathematical symbols. These symbols are especially useful in disciplines such as algebra, logic, and number theory, where standard LaTeX might not provide sufficient options.

Features: The `amsmath` package introduces a collection of mathematical environments that improve the layout and readability of equations. These include tools for aligning multiline equations, displaying systems of equations, managing piecewise functions, and formatting equations that span multiple lines. The package also refines spacing rules in math mode, ensuring that expressions look natural and professionally typeset.

Additionally, `amsmath` provides structured environments for numbered and unnumbered equations, and it allows users to control equation numbering and referencing more flexibly than standard LaTeX. It also introduces commands for inserting text within equations and for adjusting the size of brackets and delimiters according to content.

On the other hand, the `amssymb` package extends the symbol library available to the author. It includes a variety of symbols for logic (e.g., implication, equivalence), set theory (e.g., subset, superset, set membership), and number systems (e.g., blackboard bold fonts for sets like

$\mathbb{R}$, $\mathbb{N}$, and $\mathbb{Z}$). These symbols are not available in standard LaTeX and require `amssymb` to be loaded explicitly.

Together, `amsmath` and `amssymb` form the foundation of mathematical typesetting in LaTeX, offering both structural tools and symbolic richness necessary for producing high-quality mathematical documents.

2. graphicx

Usage: The `graphicx` package is the standard tool in LaTeX for importing and manipulating external image files. It allows authors to seamlessly embed graphics—such as plots, illustrations, and photographs—into their documents. This package is especially useful in academic and technical writing, where visual elements are often essential for explaining concepts or presenting data.

To use `graphicx`, the package must be loaded in the preamble of the LaTeX document. Once included, it enables support for various image formats (such as PDF, PNG, and JPG, depending on the compilation engine used) and introduces a set of flexible commands to incorporate those images at precise locations within the text.

Features: The primary feature provided by `graphicx` is the `\includegraphics` command, which inserts image files into the document. However, the package offers more than just basic inclusion. It supports a range of powerful customization options to control the appearance and placement of images.

Users can resize images by specifying exact width or height values or by scaling them proportionally. Additionally, the package allows for image rotation by arbitrary angles and provides options to clip or trim image content. These adjustments make it easier to achieve precise formatting and visual alignment in figures.

Another key feature of `graphicx` is its compatibility with the floating figure environment. This means that inserted images can be captioned, labeled, and referenced elsewhere in the document using standard LaTeX cross-referencing mechanisms. The package is also fully compatible with other figure-related packages and workflows, making it an essential component in the preparation of professional documents that involve any form of graphical content.

3. geometry

Usage: The `geometry` package is a widely used LaTeX tool that provides fine control over page layout. Its primary function is to redefine the dimensions of the document's printable area, such as the margins, paper size, and overall positioning of text on the page. Unlike the default settings provided by most document classes, which are often rigid or overly conservative, the `geometry` package empowers users to tailor the layout according to specific formatting needs or institutional requirements.

It is particularly helpful when preparing documents like research articles, technical reports, or theses that require precise alignment and spacing specifications. By loading this package with appropriate options, users can ensure consistency and conformity with style guidelines, especially for submissions to journals, publishers, or academic institutions.

Features: The `geometry` package introduces a highly flexible interface for modifying document layout. It supports standard paper sizes, including A4, letter, legal, and custom dimensions. Users can easily adjust the margins on all four sides of the page either uniformly or individually. For instance, it is possible to set wider outer margins for binding or to increase the top margin to accommodate headers and titles.

Beyond margins, the package allows for the customization of additional parameters such as text height and width, column separation, header and footer spacing, and binding offsets. It also supports landscape orientation and can dynamically recalculate layout dimensions in response to changes in other formatting settings.

A noteworthy feature is the package's compatibility with different document classes and its ability to work seamlessly with other layout-related packages. It interprets a wide variety of option formats, numerical, named, or relative, and provides informative feedback when conflicts or ambiguities arise. This makes it especially useful for users seeking both simplicity in typical use cases and robustness for more advanced typesetting demands.

The `geometry` package plays an essential role in producing clean, professional documents with customized layouts, offering both accessibility for beginners and depth for experienced users seeking precise typographical control.

4. hyperref

Usage: The `hyperref` package is a fundamental tool in LaTeX for producing documents with interactive and navigable features. Its main purpose is to enable hyperlinks within the PDF output, making references, citations, URLs, and document structure elements like sections and chapters clickable. This dramatically improves the usability of digital documents, especially lengthy or technical texts where readers frequently navigate between different parts.

To use the package, it is typically loaded in the preamble of the document. Although it can be loaded with default settings, it also accepts a wide range of options that control the behavior and appearance of links. These include the link colors, border styles, destination styles, and metadata information such as the document title and author in the PDF file.

Features: The most visible and important feature of `hyperref` is its automatic conversion of internal references, such as those created with `\ref`, `\cite`, or `\pageref`, into clickable links. When the document is compiled to PDF (via `pdflatex`, `xelatex`, or `lualatex`), these links allow readers to jump directly to the associated section, figure, table, or citation.

In addition to internal referencing, the package handles external hyperlinks seamlessly. When users include a URL or email address using commands like `\url{}` or `\href{}`, the text is rendered as a live link that opens in a Web browser or email client when clicked in the PDF.

The package also enriches the document with navigational aids by adding bookmarks to the PDF's sidebar. These bookmarks mirror the document's structural hierarchy (sections, subsections, chapters, etc.), making it easier for readers to browse the document interactively.

Furthermore, `hyperref` supports customization of link aesthetics. By default, links can be boxed or colored, but users can opt to suppress visual cues or modify the color schemes to match the document's design. The package is also capable of encoding PDF metadata such as the title, author, keywords, and subject, which enhances the accessibility and searchability of the final PDF document.

5. `babel`

Usage: The `babel` package is the standard tool in LaTeX for multilingual typesetting. It enables users to set the primary language of the document and, optionally, switch between multiple languages within the same file.

When a language is specified, `babel` automatically applies language-specific typographical rules, adjusts hyphenation patterns, and modifies certain terms (like "Chapter" or "Contents") to match the selected language.

A basic usage example involves loading the package with a language option in the preamble:

```
\usepackage[english]{babel}
```

This line sets the entire document's language to English. Other common options include `french`, `german`, `spanish`, `russian`, and many more, depending on what language support is installed in your LaTeX distribution.

Features: The core feature of `babel` is its ability to manage language-specific conventions seamlessly. When you choose a language, it ensures correct hyphenation according to the language's rules, which is especially important for texts in languages with complex syllabic structures. It also adjusts punctuation spacing where required (for example, in French, certain punctuation marks are preceded by a non-breaking space).

Another key feature is the automatic localization of document elements. Section titles, figure and table captions, and the table of contents headings are all translated into the appropriate language. For example, in German, "Chapter" becomes "Kapitel"; in Spanish, it becomes "Capítulo."

For multilingual documents, `babel` provides commands such as `\selectlanguage` and `\foreignlanguage`, which allow you to switch language settings mid-document, or even for specific phrases. This is especially useful in academic and literary contexts where quotations or citations appear in various languages.

6. fancyhdr

Usage: The `fancyhdr` package is used to redefine and customize the headers and footers in LaTeX documents. While the default LaTeX layout provides basic page numbering, `fancyhdr` allows much greater flexibility. It enables users to insert specific content into the left, center, and right parts of both headers and footers on odd and even pages, making it especially valuable in academic reports, books, theses, and professional documents where uniformity and visual clarity are important.

To use the package, it is loaded in the preamble with:

```
\usepackage{fancyhdr}
```

This provides the necessary tools to modify the layout of headers and footers. Once loaded, the user can switch to the `fancy` page style using:

```
\pagestyle{fancy}
```

Features: The primary feature of `fancyhdr` is its fine-grained control over each section of the header and footer. You can independently define the content of the left (`\lhead`, `\lfoot`), center (`\chead`, `\cfoot`), and right (`\rhead`, `\rfoot`) parts of the header and footer. For example, you might want to display the chapter title on the left of the header and the page number on the right, or place the author's name at the bottom center of every page.

Another useful feature is support for different layouts on odd and even pages, critical in double-sided (book) printing. This allows for mirrored headers and footers suitable for binding. You can even insert custom rules (lines) above or below headers and footers, adjust their spacing, or remove them entirely.

The package is also compatible with other packages like `geometry` and `titlesec`, making it a powerful tool in any document design workflow. Whether you're designing a professional thesis, formatting an article for publication, or assembling a custom report, `fancyhdr` provides the tools to give your document a polished and consistent appearance.

7. xcolor

Usage: The `xcolor` package is used to introduce and manage color within LaTeX documents. It significantly extends the functionality provided by the older `color` package, offering both backward compatibility and a wide range of advanced features. With `xcolor`, authors can apply color to text, backgrounds, tables, rules, and graphical elements, making it an essential tool for enhancing visual appeal and clarity in both printed and digital documents.

To begin using the package, include the following line in your preamble:

```
\usepackage{xcolor}
```

Features: One of the most important features of `xcolor` is its support for both predefined color names (like `red`, `blue`, `green`, `cyan`, `gray`, etc.) and custom color definitions. Users can define their own colors using RGB, CMYK, grayscale, or HTML-style hexadecimal notation. This flexibility allows precise control over document aesthetics.

Text can be easily colored using the `\textcolor` command, and entire paragraphs or page elements can be shaded using environments like `colorbox` or `fcolorbox`. In tables, rows and columns can be shaded for readability using commands like `\rowcolor` or `\cellcolor`, especially in conjunction with the `colortbl` or `tcolorbox` packages.

`xcolor` also allows for the creation of color themes and palettes, making it useful in presentations, teaching materials, and documents that follow branding guidelines. It is highly customizable and integrates well with other layout and formatting packages, providing both simplicity for beginners and depth for advanced users.

Whether the goal is to highlight code snippets, differentiate table rows, mark corrections in collaborative documents, or simply improve readability, `xcolor` is the standard package for applying and managing color in LaTeX.

8. fontenc

Usage: The `fontenc` package is used to specify the output font encoding in LaTeX documents. Font encoding determines how characters are represented internally, and this choice directly affects the quality of the output, particularly for documents containing accented or special characters. While the default encoding used by LaTeX is OT1 (which supports only a limited range of characters), switching to T1 encoding via `fontenc` greatly enhances typographic results, especially for documents written in languages that use Latin-based alphabets.

To activate T1 encoding, which is widely recommended for multilingual support and better hyphenation of words with diacritics, one simply includes the package as follows:

```
\usepackage[T1]{fontenc}
```

Features: By enabling T1 encoding, `fontenc` allows LaTeX to access a broader character set that includes accented characters and special glyphs directly from the font, rather than constructing them from individual accent marks. This results in cleaner, more consistent text output and significantly improves automatic hyphenation in languages such as French, German, Spanish, or Polish.

In addition to improving linguistic support, the use of proper font encodings contributes to the overall quality of the typeset document. This is particularly important when preparing professional publications, theses, or multilingual texts. While `fontenc` does not alter the appearance of the font directly, it works in conjunction with font packages (such as `lmodern`, `newtx`, or `times`) to ensure that the appropriate glyphs are rendered accurately.

9. inputenc

Usage: The `inputenc` package allows authors to write their LaTeX documents using a specific input encoding directly in the source file. This means that characters such as accents, umlauts, or other diacritical marks can be typed as is, rather than being entered through LaTeX escape sequences. This greatly improves the writing experience and readability of the source code, especially for users writing in languages other than English.

The most commonly used encoding today is `utf8`, as it supports the full range of Unicode characters. To enable this, you can load the package in your preamble as follows:

```
\usepackage[utf8]{inputenc}
```

This setting instructs LaTeX to interpret the document's source as UTF-8 encoded, which is the default encoding for most modern text editors and systems.

Features: The main advantage of using `inputenc` is its ability to directly support the use of non-ASCII characters in the LaTeX source code. Instead of using commands like `\'e` for é or `\ss` for ß, the user can simply type these characters directly. This leads to a more natural and readable workflow, especially when collaborating on multilingual documents.

Besides `utf8`, the package also supports older encodings such as `latin1`, `applemac`, and `ansinew`, which may be useful when working with legacy documents or systems.

Although newer LaTeX engines like `XeLaTeX` and `LuaLaTeX` handle Unicode natively and no longer require `inputenc`, the package remains essential when working with the traditional `pdfLaTeX` engine. Its inclusion ensures consistent character handling, minimizes encoding-related errors, and enhances compatibility across platforms and document sources.

10. array

Usage: The `array` package is used to extend the capabilities of LaTeX's default tabular and array environments, offering improved control over the formatting and alignment of columns. This is particularly useful when typesetting mathematical arrays or creating complex tables that require precise alignment or styling beyond the default capabilities provided by LaTeX.

To use the package, include it in your document preamble with the following command:

```
\usepackage{array}
```

Once loaded, the `array` package enhances the standard `tabular` and `array` environments without changing their basic syntax.

Features: The key contribution of the `array` package lies in its ability to define custom column types and to allow for more flexible formatting within tables and arrays. One of its most useful features is the `>...` and `<...` syntax, which enables the insertion of arbitrary LaTeX code before or after the contents of a column. This is especially helpful for aligning columns with mathematical symbols or custom styling.

Additionally, the package introduces the `m`, `b`, and `p` column specifiers, which allow vertical alignment to the middle, bottom, or fixed-height paragraphs, features that are not available in standard LaTeX.

In mathematical contexts, the `array` environment behaves similarly to `tabular`, but it is used within math mode to typeset matrices and other structures. With the enhancements from the `array` package, users gain finer control over spacing and alignment, enabling more aesthetically pleasing and readable mathematical layouts.

11. mathptmx

Usage: The `mathptmx` package is used to switch the default font of the entire document to a Times-like typeface, not only for body text but also for mathematical expressions. This package is particularly valuable when a consistent, professional font such as Times New Roman is required throughout a document, including in equations and math symbols, such as in academic theses, dissertations, or journal submissions.

To activate the Times font, simply include the package in the preamble of your LaTeX document:

```
\usepackage{mathptmx}
```

Once loaded, this package overrides the default Computer Modern font family and applies a font similar to Times Roman to both the text and math content.

Features: The primary feature of `mathptmx` is that it provides Times Roman fonts not only for body text but also attempts to adapt mathematical fonts to visually match the serif style of Times. This eliminates the inconsistency that often arises when text and math use different font families.

It adjusts the appearance of operators, symbols, variables, and Greek letters so they harmonize with the surrounding Times-style text. Although some math symbols remain from the default LaTeX fonts, `mathptmx` makes intelligent substitutions to preserve a coherent visual style.

While modern alternatives such as `newtxtext` and `newtxmath` offer more flexibility and broader Unicode support, `mathptmx` remains a lightweight, easy-to-use solution for quickly applying Times Roman to an entire document with minimal configuration.

This package is especially useful when publishers or institutions require strict font guidelines that mandate the use of Times New Roman throughout the document, including within all mathematical content.

12. `tikz` and `pgfplots`

Usage: The `tikz` and `pgfplots` packages are essential tools for authors who wish to incorporate high-quality illustrations, technical diagrams, and plots into their LaTeX documents. The `tikz` package serves as a comprehensive framework for creating vector-based graphics directly within the LaTeX source code, offering precision and flexibility that rivals external graphic software. On the other hand, `pgfplots`, which builds upon the `pgf/tikz` infrastructure, is designed specifically for generating two- and three-dimensional plots of functions and data sets.

To use both packages, include the following in the preamble of your document:

```
\usepackage{tikz, pgfplots}
```

This enables a wide range of drawing and plotting commands to be used seamlessly in your LaTeX environment.

Features: The `tikz` package provides an extensive graphical syntax for drawing geometric shapes and creating flowcharts, electrical circuits, trees, mind maps, automata, and more, all using plain LaTeX commands. Its high degree of programmability makes it possible to write reusable code for complex drawings and to dynamically generate visuals that reflect underlying mathematical logic or computations.

One of its key strengths is the integration with LaTeX text and math environments: all labels and annotations in a `tikzpicture` use the same font and layout settings as the rest of the document, ensuring perfect consistency.

The `pgfplots` package complements `tikz` by offering tools for creating publication-quality scientific and mathematical plots. It can render plots of functions, data tables, histograms, bar charts, contour maps, and 3D surfaces, all with LaTeX precision. It supports logarithmic scales, automatic axis labeling, legends, grid lines, color maps, and a wide variety of customizable plot markers and line styles.

An additional advantage of using `pgfplots` is its compatibility with external data files, making it suitable for use cases in scientific publications, thesis work, or reports that require accurate and reproducible visual representations of experimental results or theoretical functions.

Together, `tikz` and `pgfplots` offer a unified system for integrating high-quality graphics into LaTeX documents without relying on external drawing tools. They are widely adopted in fields such as mathematics, computer science, engineering, and the physical sciences for their precision and visual coherence.

13. booktabs

Usage: The `booktabs` package is specifically designed to improve the typographic quality of tables in LaTeX documents. It is most commonly used in academic writing, technical documentation, and publishing where clarity and professionalism in data presentation are essential. Unlike the default horizontal rules generated with `\hline`, which often appear visually heavy or cluttered, `booktabs` provides commands that yield cleaner, more elegant table layouts.

To include it in your document, add the following line to your preamble:

```
\usepackage{booktabs}
```

Features: The `booktabs` package offers several refined tools for creating high-quality tables. Its most notable feature is the introduction of three specialized commands: `\toprule`, `\midrule`, and `\bottomrule`. These commands replace the traditional `\hline` used in standard tables, and they are carefully designed to align with established rules of good table design, such as those advocated by the typesetting community and in typographic references like *The Elements of Typographic Style* by Robert Bringhurst.

The `\toprule` command draws a bold horizontal line at the top of the table, clearly distinguishing the table from the surrounding text. The `\midrule` is used to separate the header row from the body of the table and provides a subtler line with less visual weight. The `\bottomrule`, used at the bottom of the table, complements the `\toprule` with the same line weight, visually closing the table with balance and clarity.

Importantly, `booktabs` discourages the overuse of vertical rules and multiple horizontal lines. The philosophy behind the package promotes simplicity and alignment of information through spacing and positioning rather than graphical clutter. This results in tables that are easier to read and aesthetically pleasing.

In addition, the package provides spacing commands such as `\addlinespace`, which allows extra vertical space between rows without adding lines. This can be particularly helpful when trying to increase legibility in dense tables.

14. biblatex

Usage: The `biblatex` package is a modern and highly versatile solution for managing bibliographies and citations in LaTeX documents. Unlike older bibliography systems such as `natbib` or the traditional BibTeX workflow, `biblatex` is designed to work seamlessly with the `biber` backend and provides full control over both citation styles and bibliography formatting.

To use the package, you typically load it in the document preamble with:

```
\usepackage{biblatex}
```

You must also specify the accompanying `.bib` file that contains your bibliography entries, for example:

```
\addbibresource{references.bib}
```

This method ensures that your reference data is stored separately from the document itself, improving organization and reusability.

Features: One of the strongest features of `biblatex` is its extensive customizability. It supports a wide range of citation styles (numeric, author-year, alphabetic, etc.) and allows users to define or tweak formatting rules for in-text citations and reference lists through a consistent and readable interface.

The package distinguishes between citations and bibliography styles, meaning that users can independently customize how citations appear in the text (e.g., parenthetical or footnoted) and how references are formatted in the bibliography (e.g., sorting order, name format, title style). This modularity is especially helpful for adapting documents to different publisher or academic style requirements.

In addition to basic citation commands like `\cite`, `\parencite`, and `\footcite`, `biblatex` includes advanced commands for citing specific pages, chapters, or even custom fields. It also supports localization, enabling multilingual bibliography output without manual changes.

Another advantage of `biblatex` is its integration with the `biber` backend, which allows for richer data processing, such as automatic sorting, filtering, and cross-referencing. This backend handles complex tasks like name disambiguation and provides more reliable Unicode support.

15. tcolorbox

Usage: The `tcolorbox` package is a highly versatile tool for creating boxed content in LaTeX documents. It provides a wide range of customization options, allowing users to design colored boxes with titles, borders, background shading, and more. It is especially useful in educational or technical documents where certain content needs to be visually emphasized, such as theorems, definitions, remarks, examples, or even full custom environments.

To begin using it, the package is loaded with:

```
\usepackage{tcolorbox}
```

Once included, users can define and use simple boxes immediately or configure elaborate designs with custom styles.

Features: One of the main strengths of `tcolorbox` lies in its flexibility. It supports both inline and display boxes and offers extensive control over colors, fonts, borders, padding, alignment, shadows, and breakable content. It integrates seamlessly with packages like `amsmath` and `listings`, making it possible to wrap equations, code snippets, or verbatim text inside a visually styled box.

For example, a box can have a title bar with a specific font and color scheme, a shaded background, and a surrounding border. The style can be reused and even defined globally for consistency throughout a document. Boxes can also be breakable across pages, which is essential for long content like lists or code blocks.

Furthermore, `tcolorbox` allows the creation of custom environments that behave just like native LaTeX environments. This is particularly valuable for structuring documents where different types of content (e.g., notes, warnings, summaries) need distinct visual treatments. These custom environments can be defined once and reused multiple times, enhancing both the appearance and maintainability of the document.

Advanced users can define dynamic and conditional content using built-in keys and programmable settings, and the package even supports external skin themes, TikZ integration, and layering.

16. enumitem

Usage: The `enumitem` package is designed to provide fine control over the formatting and layout of lists in LaTeX. While the default environments, `itemize`, `enumerate`, and `description`, are sufficient for many documents, they offer limited flexibility when it comes to customizing spacing, indentation, label formatting, or nesting behavior. The `enumitem` package addresses this limitation by allowing authors to tailor list environments to fit specific stylistic or structural needs.

To begin using it, the package must be loaded in the preamble:

```
\usepackage{enumitem}
```

Once included, users can modify both the appearance and structure of lists directly within the document or by defining new environments.

Features: With `enumitem`, one can adjust the spacing above and below list environments, the indentation of items and labels, the label format (such as using roman numerals, alphabetical characters, or custom symbols), and the alignment of text. This is done via key-value options that can be passed either globally or locally to each list.

For example, if the default list indentation is too wide or too tight for the surrounding content, it can be adjusted easily using the `leftmargin` key. Additionally, vertical space between items or between lists and surrounding text can be controlled with the `topsep`, `itemsep`, and `parsep` keys.

The package also enables the creation of custom list environments that behave like standard lists but carry predefined styles and spacings. This is particularly helpful when a document uses specific list formatting conventions repeatedly, such as in academic papers, instructional materials, or legal documents.

A particularly useful feature is the ability to resume a numbered list after an interruption. For instance, an `enumerate` list can be split across multiple sections while preserving the correct numbering sequence.

Finally, the `enumitem` package ensures compatibility with most LaTeX document classes and works well alongside other formatting tools. It is widely regarded as essential for authors who wish to exert precise typographic control over list presentation in their documents.

17. csquotes

Usage: The `csquotes` package is a versatile tool for managing quotations in LaTeX documents. Unlike basic quotation formatting using the standard LaTeX commands such as `\quote` or manually entering quote marks, `csquotes` ensures that all quotations are rendered in typographically correct forms. It is particularly useful in documents that require multilingual support, quotation nesting, or consistent stylistic formatting across various types of quotations.

To begin using it, simply include the package in your preamble:

```
\usepackage{csquotes}
```

Features: One of the primary advantages of the `csquotes` package is its ability to automatically adapt quotation marks to the language of the document. For instance, English quotations might use "double quotes," whereas German uses „Guillemets" or other locale-specific styles. This language-aware behavior is seamlessly integrated with the `babel` or `polyglossia` packages, making `csquotes` a perfect choice for multilingual typesetting.

The package provides several key commands, such as `\enquote{}` for inline quotes, which handles the formatting of both primary and nested quotations automatically. For example, a nested use of `\enquote{\enquote{...}}` would correctly alternate between outer and inner quotation styles as expected in the chosen language.

In addition to inline quotations, `csquotes` also supports block quotations using environments like `displayquote` or `foreigndisplayquote`. These allow longer quotations to be set off from the main text with proper indentation and formatting, which is ideal for academic or literary works that include extended cited passages.

Customization is another core strength of `csquotes`. Users can define their own quotation styles if the defaults do not meet specific formatting guidelines. This is particularly valuable for publishers, academic institutions, or journals that enforce strict typographic standards.

18. beamer

Usage: The `beamer` class is specifically designed for creating professional-quality presentations directly within LaTeX. Unlike other packages, which are loaded into an existing document class via `\usepackage`, `beamer` is itself a full-fledged document class. To use it, you replace the typical document class declaration with:

```
\documentclass{beamer}
```

This transforms your LaTeX source into a dynamic, slide-based presentation format suitable for academic talks, lectures, and conference presentations.

Features: The `beamer` class provides an extensive array of features tailored to presentation design. At its core, it uses a frame-based system where each `frame` represents a single slide. These frames can include standard LaTeX elements like text, lists, equations, images, tables, and figures while also supporting overlays and stepwise disclosure through incremental uncovering of content.

One of the standout capabilities of `beamer` is its built-in support for themes and color schemes. Users can choose from a wide selection of predefined themes—such as `Madrid`, `Berkeley`, or `CambridgeUS`, to control the visual appearance of slides. These themes manage not only color and font choices but also layout details like header bars, footers, and navigation symbols.

Moreover, `beamer` integrates smoothly with other packages like `graphicx`, `tikz`, `pgfplots`, and `hyperref`, allowing users to insert graphics, create complex diagrams, plot data, and add clickable hyperlinks or navigation links within the presentation.

It also supports advanced structuring of the presentation via sections and subsections, which can be reflected in navigation bars or table-of-contents slides for better audience orientation.

Another powerful feature is its overlay specification mechanism, which makes it easy to create effects like progressive itemization or dynamic emphasis. For example, one can reveal bullet points or equations piece by piece across several slides, helping to maintain focus and clarity during a talk.

`beamer` presentations compile to PDF and are highly portable, making them an excellent alternative to traditional tools like PowerPoint or Keynote, particularly for those already familiar with LaTeX syntax and academic formatting.

19. setspace

Usage: The `setspace` package is widely used to control the line spacing throughout a LaTeX document. It is particularly useful in academic, legal, and professional documents where specific spacing (such as double spacing for thesis submissions or manuscript formatting) is required. By loading this package in the preamble, the user gains access to commands that conveniently switch between single, one-and-a-half, and double line spacing, either globally or within specific environments.

To activate the package, simply include it in the preamble:

```
\usepackage{setspace}
```

Features: Once the package is loaded, the most common line spacing options are accessed through the commands `\singlespacing`, `\onehalfspacing`, and `\doublespacing`. These commands can be placed in the preamble to apply the chosen spacing throughout the document, or used locally within environments or groups to apply spacing selectively.

For example, using `\doublespacing` after `\begin{document}` ensures that the entire document is double spaced. Alternatively, if only a specific section, such as the body of a letter or an appendix, needs to use a different spacing, one can enclose the desired text within a spacing environment:

```
\begin{onehalfspace}
 This section uses one-and-a-half line
 spacing.
 \end{onehalfspace}
```

The `setspace` package ensures consistent spacing adjustments without disrupting other formatting elements in the document. It works well in conjunction with common classes like `article`, `report`, and `book` and is frequently required by publishers, journal submission guidelines, and academic institutions.

In addition, the package is compatible with footnotes and bibliography sections, which often have their own spacing requirements. For example, it is possible to keep the main body of the text double spaced while maintaining single spacing in footnotes for compactness and clarity.

20. `titlesec`

Usage: The `titlesec` package is designed to provide fine-grained control over sectioning commands in LaTeX documents. This includes not only major structural elements like `\section` and `\chapter` but also smaller divisions such as `\subsection` and `\paragraph`. It is particularly useful in cases where the default appearance of headings does not match the desired style of the document, for instance, when a publication requires headings in all caps, boldface, centered, or a different font size and color.

To begin using the package, it must be loaded in the document preamble:

```
\usepackage{titlesec}
```

Features: The core feature of `titlesec` lies in its ability to redefine how headings appear. The command `\titleformat` allows users to specify the style of a given sectioning level. With this command, one can modify the font family, font size, alignment, indentation, spacing before or after the heading, and more.

For example, the appearance of `\section` headings can be modified to use a larger font size and be centered on the page, while `\subsection` headings can be made bold and left-aligned with custom spacing.

Another powerful command is `\titlespacing`, which controls the vertical space before and after headings, as well as indentation from the left margin. This is particularly useful when the default spacing creates too much or too little white space, or when trying to comply with strict formatting requirements (such as journal templates or thesis guidelines).

The package also supports conditional formatting of headings depending on whether the document is in the main body or appendix, enabling distinct styles to be applied for different parts of a document.

In addition, `titlesec` integrates well with color and font-related packages, allowing one to style section headings with colored text, custom fonts, or underlines for visual emphasis. This makes it ideal for designing highly customized documents such as resumes, reports, course notes, and institutional templates.

21. `fontspec` (only in XeLaTeX and LuaLaTeX)

Usage: The `fontspec` package is used for selecting and customizing fonts in LaTeX documents compiled with either XeLaTeX or LuaLaTeX. Unlike pdfLaTeX, which relies on a limited set of Type 1 fonts and requires additional packages like `mathptmx` or `helvet` to change font families, XeLaTeX and LuaLaTeX allow direct access to system-installed OpenType and TrueType fonts. The `fontspec` package acts as the interface for this functionality, making font selection and modification more intuitive and flexible.

To use `fontspec`, it must be loaded in the document preamble:

```
\usepackage{fontspec}
```

Note that this package is incompatible with pdfLaTeX and will only compile correctly with engines that support Unicode natively—namely XeLaTeX and LuaLaTeX.

Features: One of the core features of `fontspec` is its ability to select fonts by name using system font identifiers, which means you can use the same fonts in your LaTeX document that you use in word processors. For example, setting the main font to Times New Roman or Calibri can be done with a single line:

```
\setmainfont{Times New Roman}
```

Beyond selecting fonts, `fontspec` allows extensive customization of font features, such as small caps, ligatures, numeral styles (old-style, lining), and alternate characters.

This is achieved using the optional arguments of the font selection commands:

```
\setmainfont[
  Ligatures=TeX,
  Numbers=OldStyle,
  BoldFont={Times New Roman Bold},
  ItalicFont={Times New Roman Italic}
]{Times New Roman}
```

The package supports different font roles in a document: `\setmainfont` for the primary (serif) font, `\setsansfont` for the sans-serif font, and `\setmonofont` for monospace (typewriter) text. You can switch between them using the standard commands `\textrm`, `\textsf`, and `\texttt` or by invoking the font commands directly.

`fontspec` also plays a critical role in multilingual documents, as it enables proper rendering of complex scripts and right-to-left languages when used alongside packages like `polyglossia` or `babel` (with LuaLaTeX).

22. subcaption

Usage: The `subcaption` package is used when a single figure or table contains multiple components that each of which requires its own individual caption. This situation commonly arises in scientific or technical documents where comparisons between several plots, diagrams, or data sets are presented side by side. Rather than creating separate figures, `subcaption` allows all the components to be grouped into a single figure or table environment while still giving each component its own label and caption.

To use this package, it must be loaded in the document preamble using:

```
\usepackage{subcaption}
```

It is important to note that `subcaption` is a modern and preferred alternative to the older `subfigure` package, which is now considered obsolete. The `subcaption` package is fully compatible with the standard `caption` package and integrates well with most figure and table environments.

Features: The main feature of `subcaption` is its support for the `subfigure` and `subtable` environments. These allow authors to create composite figures or tables, where each sub-element can be labeled and referenced independently. For instance, two related graphs can be shown side by side in one figure, each with its own subcaption (e.g., "(a) Comparison at time t_1" and "(b) Comparison at time t_2"), while also being referred to in-text as Figure 1(a) and Figure 1(b).

It also provides fine control over the formatting of subcaptions, including the style of labeling (alphabetic, numeric, Roman, etc.), positioning (above or below the subfigure), spacing between elements, and alignment within the figure or table.

The `subcaption` package improves the clarity of multipart visual presentations and simplifies the referencing of complex layouts. This makes it particularly useful in academic theses, scientific publications, and technical documentation where structured and interpretable visual representation is essential.

23. `mhchem`

Usage: The `mhchem` package is specifically designed to simplify the typesetting of chemical equations, molecular formulas, and reaction mechanisms in LaTeX documents. Chemists, educators, and students often need to represent chemical compounds such as H_2O or reactions like $2\,H_2 + O_2 \longrightarrow 2\,H_2O$ in a clean, readable, and semantically correct way. Without a dedicated package, such expressions can be difficult to write and interpret in LaTeX. The `mhchem` package addresses this problem by introducing an intuitive and readable syntax for rendering chemical notation.

To use the package, simply include the following line in the document preamble:

```
\usepackage{mhchem}
```

Once loaded, the `\ce` command provided by `mhchem` allows authors to enter chemical expressions using conventional chemical syntax that closely resembles handwritten notation.

Features: The `mhchem` package offers a range of features that make it an indispensable tool for typesetting chemistry-related documents. First and foremost, it provides the `\ce` macro, which intelligently parses chemical expressions and formats them according to chemical typesetting conventions. It automatically handles subscripts and superscripts (e.g., oxidation states or isotopes), corrects spacing around symbols and reaction arrows, and supports charges, equilibrium signs, and other common chemical notations.

For example, to render a chemical reaction such as hydrogen gas reacting with oxygen to form water, one can simply write:

```
\ce{2H2 + O2 -> 2H2O}
```

This will result in a properly spaced and aligned chemical reaction. The package supports a wide range of arrow types (e.g., reversible, equilibrium, resonance), conditions above or below arrows (e.g., catalysts, temperature), and physical state symbols such as (s), (l), (g), and (aq).

In addition, `mhchem` works seamlessly in both text and math mode and can be combined with other mathematical symbols when needed. This versatility makes it especially useful in documents that mix chemistry and mathematics, such as physical chemistry reports, quantum chemistry derivations, or lab manuals.

The `mhchem` package significantly improves the readability, consistency, and professional appearance of chemical notation in LaTeX and is highly recommended for any document involving chemical content.

24. cleveref

Usage: The `cleveref` package is used in LaTeX documents to enhance the process of cross-referencing. In standard LaTeX, referencing numbered elements such as figures, tables, sections, or equations typically requires explicitly stating the type of object (e.g., "Figure \ref{fig:label}"). This can be repetitive and error-prone, especially in large documents with many references. The `cleveref` package streamlines this process by automatically detecting the type of object being referenced and formatting the reference appropriately.

To enable this functionality, the package must be loaded in the document preamble using the following command:

```
\usepackage{cleveref}
```

Once loaded, authors can replace `\ref` with `\cref` for singular references and `\Cref` for capitalized references, and LaTeX will take care of including the correct label such as "Figure," "Table,", "Section," or "Equation" along with the appropriate number.

Features: The key feature of `cleveref` is its ability to automatically determine the type of reference and prepend the correct label. For instance, when referencing a figure labeled as `fig:example`, using `\cref{fig:example}` would yield "Figure 1" without needing to write the word "Figure" manually. Similarly, `\cref{eq:main}` would result in "Equation (1)," assuming the label corresponds to an equation environment.

Another powerful feature is its support for multiple references. When passing multiple labels to `\cref`, it automatically combines and formats them into a concise, human-readable list, such as "Figures 1–3" or "Sections 2 and 3.'

Additionally, the package allows full customization of reference names, capitalization styles, and punctuation. This makes it highly valuable for documents that must adhere to specific formatting or editorial guidelines.

The `cleveref` package works well with many other common LaTeX packages, including those for math, figures, and tables. It is particularly beneficial in technical or academic writing, where numerous cross-references appear throughout a document and where consistency and automation are essential for maintaining quality and clarity.

25. `algorithm` and `algorithmic`

Usage: The `algorithm` and `algorithmic` packages are widely used in LaTeX documents to present algorithms and pseudocode in a clean and structured format. They are especially useful in computer science, engineering, mathematics, and other fields where documenting computational procedures is essential. The `algorithm` package provides a floating environment similar to figures and tables, allowing algorithms to be positioned and captioned within a document, while `algorithmic` provides the actual syntax and structure for the algorithmic steps themselves.

To begin using these packages, they must be included in the document's preamble:

```
\usepackage{algorithm}
\usepackage{algorithmic}
```

Once loaded, users can wrap their pseudocode inside an `algorithm` environment to treat it like a float and then insert the actual code using the `algorithmic` environment. The result is a numbered, captioned algorithm that is easy to cross-reference and aesthetically integrate with the rest of the document.

Features: The primary feature of these packages is the ability to typeset pseudocode using familiar programming constructs such as `IF–THEN–ELSE`, `FOR` loops, `WHILE` loops, and procedure calls. The environment supports indentation, line numbering, and labeling of steps or blocks for reference within the text.

Additionally, users can provide custom captions using `\caption{}` and refer to algorithms using standard LaTeX referencing commands such as `\ref` or `\cref` (when used with the `cleveref` package).

Although functional and widely used, the `algorithmic` package has limited customization capabilities. For more flexibility in formatting, including customization of keywords and layout, alternatives such as `algorithm2e` may be preferable. Nonetheless, `algorithm` and `algorithmic` remain a reliable and widely supported choice for typesetting pseudocode in professional and academic documents.

26. physics

Usage: The `physics` package is designed to simplify the typesetting of common mathematical and physical expressions, particularly those frequently used in physics, such as derivatives, integrals, vector notation, and quantum mechanical symbols. It significantly reduces the need to manually define repetitive macros and ensures consistent notation throughout the document. The package is especially helpful for students, educators, and researchers in physics and applied mathematics.

To use it, you simply include the package in your preamble:

```
\usepackage{physics}
```

Features: One of the primary advantages of the `physics` package is its clean and concise syntax for a wide range of physics-related operations. For example, it provides shorthand commands for ordinary and partial derivatives through `\dv` and `\pdv`, allowing the user to write derivatives without worrying about formatting or placement of the differential operators.

In addition, the package offers intuitive commands for Dirac bra-ket notation, such as `\bra`, `\ket`, and `\braket`, which are heavily used in quantum mechanics. It also supports vector notation, inner products, expectation values, and many more mathematical structures relevant to physics.

The `physics` package automatically handles proper spacing in expressions and is compatible with most standard math environments, making it a practical and efficient tool for producing clear and professionally formatted physics documents. While it is highly convenient, users should also be mindful that it loads many macros, so care should be taken when integrating it with other specialized math packages.

27. multirow

Usage: The `multirow` package is used to create table cells that span multiple rows within the `tabular` environment. This is especially useful when presenting hierarchical or grouped data in a compact and structured format. When used in conjunction with the `array` package, it offers even more flexibility for customizing alignment and spacing within complex tables.

To activate this functionality in your document, the package should be loaded in the preamble:

```
\usepackage{array, multirow}
```

Features: The `multirow` package introduces the `\multirow` command, which allows a single table entry to span multiple rows, vertically centering the content by default. This is especially beneficial in tables where data categories repeat, such as in multilevel labels, grouped rows, or when describing shared characteristics across several rows.

The basic syntax of the command `\multirow{n}{width}{content}` specifies the number of rows the content should span, the width of the cell (which may be set to `*` for natural width), and the actual content. This not only reduces redundancy in table content but also improves readability and presentation.

Together with column alignment enhancements from the `array` package, `multirow` can be used to construct sophisticated tables suitable for academic papers, reports, and theses that require fine-grained control over tabular structure.

28. pgf and pgfplots

Usage: The `pgf` and `pgfplots` packages are widely used in LaTeX for creating high-quality vector-based graphics and plots. These packages are particularly valuable in academic, scientific, and technical documents where clear, precise, and scalable figures are essential. While `pgf` provides a lower-level interface for drawing shapes and paths programmatically, `pgfplots` builds on top of it to offer a user-friendly environment for generating publication-ready plots.

To use these packages, they should be included in the document preamble as follows:

```
\usepackage{pgf, pgfplots}
```

Features: The `pgf` package is part of the larger PGF/TikZ framework and supports the construction of lines, curves, geometric shapes, and even custom diagrams using Cartesian or polar coordinates. It is a versatile tool that allows authors to control every aspect of the graphic directly from the LaTeX source code.

The `pgfplots` package, which depends on `pgf`, provides an intuitive interface for plotting data and mathematical functions. It supports a variety of plot types such as line plots, scatter plots, bar charts, contour plots, and surface plots. Users can customize axes, legends, ticks, labels, color maps, and grid lines with great precision.

One of the most powerful aspects of `pgfplots` is its ability to generate 2D and 3D plots directly from raw data or analytic expressions. It integrates well with LaTeX's math typesetting system, making it easy to include mathematical annotations and labels within figures.

These packages eliminate the need for external image files, ensuring that the entire figure creation and customization process is encapsulated within the LaTeX document itself, maintaining consistency in font, style, and layout throughout.

29. siunitx

Usage: The `siunitx` package is designed to provide a comprehensive and consistent way of typesetting physical units and numbers according to the International System of Units (SI). In scientific and technical writing, clarity and uniformity in presenting numerical values and units are critical. The `siunitx` package allows authors to maintain this consistency automatically, both in inline math and in tables or displayed equations. It can also handle uncertainty notation, number alignment, and scientific notation formatting.

To use the package, include the following line in the preamble of your document:

```
\usepackage{siunitx}
```

Features: The `siunitx` package offers a robust set of tools that simplify the task of writing units and measurements. It automatically applies correct spacing between numbers and units and formats them according to international typographic standards. For example, using the command $9.81\,\mathrm{m\,s^{-2}}$ will produce the acceleration due to gravity in a uniform and readable format.

In addition to formatting single values, the package can display numbers with uncertainties (e.g., $5.43(21)\,\mathrm{g}$), format numbers in scientific notation, and align columns of numbers within tables. The syntax is flexible yet consistent, ensuring that units such as joules, amperes, and kelvin are presented correctly and clearly.

With powerful configuration options, users can customize output style, digit grouping, decimal marker (e.g., switching between dot and comma), rounding behavior, and the treatment of exponents. The `siunitx` package is thus indispensable for documents that involve significant numerical data, providing both semantic clarity and typographic precision.

30. mathrsfs

Usage: The `mathrsfs` package is used in mathematical documents to provide access to an elegant and distinctive script font. This font is especially useful when the default calligraphic font provided by LaTeX (via the `\mathcal` command) does not suffice for stylistic or clarity purposes. The script letters provided by `mathrsfs` are often preferred in advanced mathematical writing to denote particular types of structures, such as sheaves, families of sets, or script-style function spaces, especially when a visual distinction is necessary.

To use the package, include it in your preamble as follows:

```
\usepackage{mathrsfs}
```

Features: Once loaded, the package introduces the `\mathscr` command, which produces uppercase Latin letters in a flowing script style that is more ornate than the default `\mathcal` font. For example, while both `\mathcal{F}` and `\mathscr{F}` denote the letter "F" in a calligraphic style, the output from `\mathscr` is more decorative and typically better suited for formal contexts such as algebraic geometry or category theory.

The `mathrsfs` package does not require additional configuration and works seamlessly in both math mode and display math environments. It is compatible with most other mathematics-related packages, making it a lightweight and reliable enhancement to mathematical typesetting in LaTeX.

31. mathtools

Usage: The `mathtools` package is an essential extension of the widely used `amsmath` package. It inherits all of `amsmath`'s capabilities and adds many refinements and enhancements, particularly for mathematical typesetting. Its primary role is to provide more flexible tools for constructing and aligning equations, as well as offering a variety of new commands and environments that simplify common mathematical expressions. For those writing technical or mathematical documents, `mathtools` is often loaded in place of `amsmath` since it automatically includes it.

To enable it, simply add the package in the document preamble:

```
\usepackage{mathtools}
```

Features: One of the key features of `mathtools` is its inclusion of additional symbols and operators that are not available in the base `amsmath` package. For instance, it defines the command `\coloneqq` to denote definitions (i.e., :=) in a typographically consistent way. It also introduces tools for fixing the alignment and spacing of math expressions, such as improved versions of `\xrightarrow` and `\xleftarrow` that can accommodate annotations above or below arrows.

Beyond symbols, `mathtools` enhances the equation alignment environments. It includes utilities like `\mathclap` and `\mathrlap`, which help reduce excess space in math formulas caused by wide symbols or superscripts. This is especially helpful in dense formulas where precision and compactness are essential.

Additionally, `mathtools` provides better handling of paired delimiters (such as parentheses, brackets, or absolute value signs). With commands like `\DeclarePairedDelimiter`, users can define custom macros that automatically resize delimiters or keep them fixed, allowing for more elegant and consistent formatting of expressions involving norms, inner products, or floor/-ceiling functions.

32. footmisc

Usage: The `footmisc` package is used to enhance and customize the appearance and behavior of footnotes in

LaTeX documents. While LaTeX handles footnotes well by default, there are cases, especially in scholarly and formal writing, where more refined control is desired. This package allows users to modify how footnotes are formatted, spaced, numbered, and placed.

To use the package, include it in the preamble:

```
\usepackage{footmisc}
```

Features: The `footmisc` package provides a wide range of options for tailoring footnotes to fit the stylistic or typographic needs of a document. One of its most important capabilities is adjusting the layout and spacing of footnotes. For instance, users can reduce the space between footnotes, control the indentation, or choose to display footnotes in a single block of text rather than as a list.

It also supports different footnote number styles, including symbols (†, §, etc.), roman numerals, or alphabets. With the `symbol` or `alph` options, authors can format footnote markers in ways that correspond to editorial standards or journal requirements.

Another powerful feature is the ability to change the placement of footnotes. The `bottom` option, for example, forces footnotes to appear at the bottom of the text block (rather than at the bottom of the page), aligning them more closely with the surrounding paragraph layout. This is particularly useful in multicolumn layouts or narrow page formats.

The package also enables users to create footnotes in a paragraph-like style (using the `para` option), where all footnotes run together as continuous text rather than being displayed as a vertical list. This can save space and is commonly used in compact documents or publications with strict layout constraints.

In combination with other packages like `fancyhdr` or `geometry`, `footmisc` can help produce finely tuned and visually consistent documents where footnotes enhance rather than interrupt the reading flow.

33. `caption`

Usage: The `caption` package is used to enhance and customize the appearance of captions for figures and tables in LaTeX documents. By default, LaTeX generates basic captions that appear below figures and above tables, with little control over layout or formatting. This package allows authors to modify various aspects of captions, including font size, alignment, label format, spacing, and position.

To begin using it, include the package in the preamble as follows:

```
\usepackage{caption}
```

Features: The most notable feature of the `caption` package is the ability to customize how captions are styled and displayed. It enables fine control over the label (e.g., "Figure", "Table"), the numbering style, and the text that follows the label. For instance, authors can choose whether the label and caption text appear on the same line or on separate lines, or whether to use bold or italic formatting.

With this package, the spacing between the figure/table and the caption can be adjusted to improve layout aesthetics. This is particularly useful in documents that require precise visual consistency, such as theses or journal submissions.

In multilingual documents, the `caption` package also integrates well with packages like `babel` or `polyglossia`, automatically adapting the caption labels to the selected language.

Another useful feature is the ability to configure global or local styles for captions. You can apply a specific format to all captions in a document or override it for individual figures or tables using the optional arguments provided by the package. The package even allows numbering to be suppressed or modified, and custom separators (such as colons, dashes, or line breaks) can be used between the label and the caption text.

For advanced layouts, `caption` can be used in conjunction with the `subcaption` package to manage complex caption hierarchies, such as when a figure contains multiple subfigures, each requiring its own descriptive text.

Ultimately, the `caption` package helps authors produce professional-quality documents where figure and table captions are consistent, clear, and aligned with publication or institutional guidelines.

34. musixtex

Usage: The `musixtex` package is used for typesetting complex musical scores directly within LaTeX documents. It is well-suited for classical music notation, including multi-staff arrangements and polyphonic music.

To use it, include in the preamble:

```
\usepackage{musixtex}
```

Features: `musixtex` supports detailed musical notation such as notes, rests, clefs, time signatures, slurs, ties, beams, lyrics, and multiple staves. It allows fine control over spacing and layout and can handle orchestral scores or solo parts. The package requires a three-pass compilation using `musixtex`, `musixflx`, and `latex` to position elements accurately.

This package is ideal for users needing high-quality, professional-looking sheet music within academic or performance-related LaTeX documents. It is often combined with helper packages like `musixlyr` for lyrics and `musixgch` for guitar chords.

35. rotating

Usage: The `rotating` package is designed to give authors more flexibility in rotating content such as figures, tables, or even entire blocks of text. This is particularly useful in cases where horizontal space is limited, such as when presenting wide tables or large diagrams that would not fit comfortably in the normal portrait orientation of a document page. Rather than manually adjusting every line, the `rotating` package provides structured environments and commands to rotate elements with minimal effort.

To use the package, include the following line in the preamble:

```
\usepackage{rotating}
```

Features: The primary feature of the `rotating` package is the ability to rotate content at any angle, though 90° and 180° are most commonly used. It provides both inline rotation through commands and page-level rotation via special floating environments.

For inline rotation, the `\rotatebox` command allows users to rotate any content, text, or graphics, by a specified angle:

```
\rotatebox{90}{Rotated Text}
```

More advanced and document-friendly features come in the form of floating environments: `sidewaysfigure` and `sidewaystable`. These are analogous to the standard `figure` and `table` environments but render the content rotated by 90° (typically counter-clockwise) and centered on a landscape-oriented page. This is particularly helpful for including wide tables in printed documents without reducing font size.

The package also cooperates with standard LaTeX floats and honors page breaks, captions, and labels for cross-referencing. Moreover, it respects document margins and can be used in combination with the `caption`, `graphicx`, and `float` packages to refine layout and positioning.

By offering both precision control (via angle specifications) and high-level automated tools (via rotated floats), `rotating` is ideal for users who require well-aligned, rotated content without compromising the structure and flow of the document.

36. microtype

Usage: The `microtype` package is one of the most subtle yet powerful tools in LaTeX for enhancing the typographic quality of a document. Its primary role is to refine the appearance of text by applying fine-grained adjustments to character spacing, kerning, and margin alignment. These improvements are carried out automatically, requiring little to no manual intervention, making the package an excellent choice for those aiming to produce professionally typeset documents. To enable its features, one typically loads the package in the preamble with:

```
\usepackage{microtype}
```

Features: The `microtype` package provides two principal mechanisms for typographic enhancement: protrusion and font expansion.

Protrusion allows certain characters, such as punctuation marks (periods, commas, quotation marks), to slightly extend beyond the text block's margins. This optical adjustment results in cleaner-looking paragraph edges, particularly in justified text, where lines might otherwise appear uneven due to short characters near the margin.

Font expansion enables LaTeX to make very small adjustments to the width of individual glyphs, typically within a fraction of a percent, so that text can better fill a line. This helps reduce awkward spacing between words and minimizes typographic issues like rivers or visually distracting gaps in justified paragraphs. Although these width changes are minute and imperceptible to the eye, they can significantly improve the overall flow of the document.

Additionally, `microtype` enhances kerning, the spacing between specific pairs of letters, further improving text legibility and rhythm. It is compatible with most font encodings and works particularly well with modern font families. The package can also be customized extensively using optional arguments to enable or disable specific features or adjust their intensity.

While its effects may not be immediately visible, the `microtype` package makes a substantial difference in the visual polish of a document. It is especially useful in books, academic reports, journal articles, and other formal documents where typographic excellence is expected.

37. `wrapfig`

Usage: The `wrapfig` package is used to wrap text around figures or tables, enabling a layout that is often seen in magazines and newspapers. Instead of having figures occupy an entire line or page, this package allows you to place them to the left or right of the text, so the surrounding content can flow around the figure, creating a more compact and visually integrated layout. This is especially useful in documents where space optimization is important or when integrating small illustrative images inline with the explanation.

To use the package, add the following to the preamble:

```
\usepackage{wrapfig}
```

Features: The `wrapfig` package introduces the `wrapfigure` environment, which lets you specify the horizontal alignment (left or right), width of the figure, and the number of lines of text that should wrap around it. This environment automatically calculates the appropriate vertical space and adjusts the text flow accordingly. Figures inserted using `wrapfig` can be placed mid-paragraph or at paragraph boundaries, depending on how seamless you want the integration to be.

In addition to figures, `wrapfig` can be used for tables as well, enabling compact layouts even when dealing with tabular data. The package also supports fine adjustments such as controlling the horizontal offset, vertical spacing, and whether the figure should start on the current or next line.

While the package enhances the visual layout significantly, care must be taken when using it in complex documents or with narrow margins, as the wrapping behavior can occasionally interfere with paragraph spacing or justification. When used appropriately, however, `wrapfig` adds a polished, professional look to content-rich documents.

38. `longtable`

Usage: The `longtable` package is specifically designed to create tables that can span across multiple pages. Unlike the standard `tabular` environment, which renders tables as fixed blocks that cannot break across page boundaries, `longtable` provides a way to construct large tables with automatic continuation and consistent formatting over several pages. This is particularly useful in reports, technical documentation, or data sets where large amounts of tabular information must be presented without interruption.

To use the package, include the following in the preamble:

```
\usepackage{longtable}
```

Features: The core feature of the `longtable` environment is its ability to break tables across page boundaries while retaining full control over formatting. It supports repeated header and footer rows on every page, which helps maintain readability in long data sets. This is done by specifying separate sections of the table for the first page header, continued page headers, and footers.

The package is fully compatible with most of the standard table customization tools and works well with column alignment options such as `l`, `c`, `r`, and `p{}`. Additionally, `longtable` can be combined with other packages such as `booktabs` for high-quality typesetting or `xcolor` for row shading.

Because it is a float-less environment, `longtable` does not need to be enclosed in a `table` environment and begins rendering content exactly where it is placed in the source file. This direct placement ensures that tables appear in the intended position within the text, even if they extend over multiple pages.

39. multicol

Usage: The `multicol` package enables authors to divide sections of text into multiple columns, making it especially useful for creating newspaper-style layouts, dense academic notes, or formatted sections in posters and presentations. It is often employed in documents where space efficiency or visual parallelism is required.

To begin using the package, include it in the preamble:

```
\usepackage{multicol}
```

Once included, the document can include multi-column sections using the `multicols` environment. The number of desired columns is passed as an argument:

```
\begin{multicols}{2}
 This text will be typeset in two columns.
\end{multicols}
```

Features: The `multicol` package provides flexible control over column formatting. It allows you to set the number of columns dynamically, manage column balancing (so that the columns are of approximately equal height), and customize spacing between columns using parameters like `\columnsep` and `\columnseprule`.

It supports column breaks using the `\columnbreak` command and integrates well with sectioning commands and environments like `itemize`, `enumerate`, and math environments.

Unlike standard page-wide formatting, the `multicols` environment ensures that content is compact and visually organized in narrow spaces, making it an excellent tool for publications or documents with spatial constraints.

40. sectsty

Usage: The `sectsty` package is used to modify the appearance of sectional headings in a LaTeX document. It provides a simple and convenient interface for customizing fonts, styles, and colors of section-level commands such as `\section`, `\subsection`, and so on. This is especially useful in documents that require personalized or visually distinctive section titles, such as presentations, reports, or design-oriented projects.

To start using it, add the following line to your preamble:

```
\usepackage{sectsty}
```

Features: The package allows you to apply a uniform style to all section headings or target individual sectioning commands. You can change the font family (such as `sf` for sans-serif or `tt` for monospace), apply font shapes (bold, italic), or use custom colors when combined with the `xcolor` package.

For example, if you want all section titles to appear in blue and in sans-serif font, you can write:

```
\allsectionsfont{\sffamily\color{blue}}
```

This will affect `\section`, `\subsection`, `\subsubsection`, and other levels uniformly. Alternatively, if you only want to modify a specific level, such as just the top-level sections, you can use:

```
\sectionfont{\color{blue}\bfseries}
```

The `sectsty` package provides an intuitive way to improve the aesthetic quality of your document's structure without complex redefinitions or low-level formatting commands.

41. chngcntr

Usage: The `chngcntr` package is used to modify the behavior of LaTeX counters, especially when working with nested or hierarchical numbering schemes. It is particularly useful in documents where figures, tables, or equations should be numbered within sections or chapters, or conversely, when that behavior needs to be removed.

To use the package, include it in the preamble of your document:

```
\usepackage{chngcntr}
```

Features: One of the main features of `chngcntr` is its ability to decouple or couple counters from each other. For example, in a document where figures are automatically numbered as "Figure 1.1," "Figure 1.2," etc., within Section 1, you can use this package to change that behavior so that figures are numbered continuously across the entire document (e.g., "Figure 1," "Figure 2,", etc.).

This is accomplished using the `\counterwithout` and `\counterwithin` commands:

- `\counterwithin{figure}{section}` will number figures within sections.
- `\counterwithout{figure}{section}` will remove section-based numbering from figures.

This flexibility is helpful when adhering to publication or institutional formatting guidelines that require specific numbering schemes.

The package also works well in conjunction with other layout or formatting tools, making it a lightweight but powerful addition for users needing granular control over numbering in complex documents.

42. adjustbox

Usage: The `adjustbox` package is used to modify the appearance and layout of boxes containing text or graphics. It acts as a general-purpose tool for adjusting the size, orientation, trimming, and framing of content—especially useful when integrating external figures or when fine-tuning the placement of elements in complex layouts.

To load the package, include the following in your preamble:

```
\usepackage{adjustbox}
```

Features: The `adjustbox` package extends the functionality of `graphicx` and similar packages by offering a unified interface for manipulating boxes. With this package, users can resize content proportionally, scale it to a specific width or height, rotate it by an arbitrary angle, clip its edges, or even add borders and backgrounds to framed elements. The commands can be used inline or in combination with environments like `minipage` or `figure`.

It is particularly valuable when creating slides, posters, or technical documentation where precise control over layout and presentation is essential. The ability to combine multiple transformations in one command makes `adjustbox` a versatile tool for producing polished and visually consistent documents.

43. marginnote

Usage: The `marginnote` package is designed to allow users to place notes in the document margins. Unlike the standard command, which can have placement conflicts in some environments (like inside footnotes or within floats), `marginnote` offers greater flexibility and consistency when adding annotations alongside the main text.

To use the package, include the following line in your preamble:

```
\usepackage{marginnote}
```

Features: The package provides a single command, `\marginnote`, which inserts a note into the margin without disrupting the layout of the surrounding text. You can choose whether the note appears in the left or right margin, and you can also control vertical placement for more precise alignment with the body content.

This is especially useful for academic and editorial work, such as adding brief commentary, referencing glossary terms, highlighting important observations, or inserting short side notes without cluttering the main body of the document. The package also plays well with multicolumn or asymmetric page layouts where traditional margin note behavior may not function as expected.

44. pdfpages

Usage: The `pdfpages` package is used to insert entire pages or selected pages from an external PDF file into a LaTeX document. This is particularly helpful when you want to append a finished document (such as a certificate, scanned form, or published article) into your compiled output without altering its formatting or recreating its layout.

To use the package, add the following line to your preamble:

```
\usepackage{pdfpages}
```

Features: The `pdfpages` package offers fine-grained control over PDF inclusion. It allows you to:

1. Insert all pages or a specific range of pages from a PDF file.
2. Scale the imported pages to match the current page dimensions or a desired size.
3. Rotate, center, or crop pages before including them.
4. Insert multiple PDF pages per LaTeX page (useful for compact layouts).
5. Choose between single-page and double-page (spread) layout options.

This package is essential for creating composite documents, such as reports with appendices, publications with supplemental material, or portfolios that merge LaTeX-generated content with preexisting PDF documents.

45. epigraph

Usage: The `epigraph` package is used for elegantly typesetting epigraphs, short quotations, or sayings, commonly placed at the beginning of a chapter, section, or even a standalone page. These epigraphs can serve as a thematic prelude to the content that follows, providing historical, literary, or philosophical context in a visually distinguished format.

To use this package, include the following line in your document preamble:

```
\usepackage{epigraph}
```

Features: This package offers the `\epigraph` command, which allows the user to specify a quotation and its source, typically the author. By default, the epigraph is right-aligned and separated from the main text, often using a smaller font size to distinguish it from the body content. The package provides customization options for the positioning, alignment, and font of the epigraphs.

Additionally, the `\setlength` and `\renewcommand` commands can be used in conjunction with `epigraph` to change the indentation, width, or spacing of epigraphs throughout the document. This makes it particularly well-suited for books, dissertations, or essays that benefit from atmospheric or thematic quotations at the start of chapters.

46. appendix

Usage: The `appendix` package is designed to assist in formatting and managing appendices in a structured document. In academic writing, appendices are commonly used to provide supplementary material, such as raw data, additional figures, tables, or code, that supports the main content but is too detailed for inclusion in the main body of the text.

To enable this functionality, load the package in the preamble of your document using:

```
\usepackage{appendix}
```

Features: Once included, the `appendix` package introduces enhanced control over the way appendices are labeled, titled, and displayed. It allows you to use the `\appendix` command to switch from the regular sectioning structure to a specific appendix format. By default, sections following the `\appendix` declaration are labeled alphabetically (e.g., Appendix A, Appendix B), and the numbering style can be easily customized.

Moreover, the package allows for fine-tuned formatting of appendix titles, table of contents entries, and numbering schemes, which is particularly useful for theses, reports, and technical documentation. The clarity and professionalism of well-formatted appendices contribute to the overall readability of formal documents, and the `appendix` package makes it much easier to achieve that goal.

47. float

Usage: The `float` package enhances LaTeX's ability to manage the positioning of floating elements such as figures and tables. In standard LaTeX, float environments like `figure` and `table` are governed by placement rules that try to optimize page layout. While this automatic behavior is useful, it can sometimes cause floats to appear far from their intended position in the source code.

To gain precise control over float placement, you can load the package using:

```
\usepackage{float}
```

Features: The primary feature of the `float` package is the introduction of the `H` placement specifier. Unlike the default placement options, such as `h` (here), `t` (top), `b` (bottom), and `p` (page of floats), the `H` option instructs LaTeX to place the float exactly at the point where it appears in the code, without attempting to move it elsewhere. This can be particularly helpful in tightly formatted documents, exams, or when alignment with nearby text is crucial.

In addition to the `H` option, the package supports the creation of custom float environments, giving users even more flexibility in designing their document structure. Overall, `float` is a lightweight yet powerful tool for authors who need precise placement of graphical and tabular content.

48. glossaries

Usage: The `glossaries` package is used for creating glossaries, lists of terms, and abbreviations within a LaTeX document. It is particularly useful in academic, technical, and scientific writing, where precise terminology and consistent definitions enhance the clarity and professionalism of the content.

To activate the package, add the following line in your preamble:

```
\usepackage{glossaries}
```

This package requires an additional command to initialize glossary management:

```
\makeglossaries
```

Features: The `glossaries` package supports the automatic creation and formatting of multiple glossaries, acronym lists, and abbreviation sets. Each entry can include a name, a description, and optionally a symbol or notation. Once defined, glossary terms can be referenced throughout the document using specific commands that ensure the term is printed consistently, and that it is added to the glossary index.

An especially powerful feature is the handling of acronyms. When first referenced, acronyms can appear in full form with the abbreviation in parentheses, and in abbreviated form thereafter. This improves readability while maintaining formality.

The final glossary or list of abbreviations is generated at the end of the document (or in a desired location) using:

```
\printglossaries
```

It is worth noting that compiling documents with glossaries typically requires running additional steps, such as using the `makeglossaries` tool or invoking glossary support through an integrated LaTeX editor.

49. `textcomp`

Usage: The `textcomp` package is used to expand LaTeX's ability to typeset a wide range of textual symbols that are not available in the default font encoding. This includes symbols that are often needed in technical and academic writing, such as degree signs, currency markers, and certain punctuation characters that enhance the typographic quality of the document.

To use the package, load it in the preamble of your document as follows:

```
\usepackage{textcomp}
```

This line grants access to a set of additional symbols specifically intended for use in text mode.

Features: The primary feature of the `textcomp` package is its support for an extended set of textual symbols, many of which are not available in standard LaTeX without this package. These symbols include:

- The degree symbol (`\textdegree`), commonly used in scientific contexts such as temperature or angles
- Currency symbols such as the Euro (`\texteuro`), cent (`\textcent`), and others that might not be part of the standard font set
- Typographically correct quotation marks, old-style numerals, and text arrows

Another benefit is that the package automatically adapts to the font encoding in use (e.g., T1, OT1), ensuring proper rendering of the supported symbols without any manual configuration.

It is often used in combination with the `fontenc` package, especially when using T1 encoding, to make sure all glyphs are rendered accurately across different font families.

50. pstricks

Usage: The `pstricks` package is used to create sophisticated, high-quality graphics and illustrations directly within LaTeX. Unlike basic image inclusion or simple vector diagrams, `pstricks` allows for detailed control over graphic elements, including line styles, shapes, arrows, plots, shading, and even function graphs. It is particularly favored in scientific and technical documents where precise, customizable visual representations are required.

To use the package, add the following line in the preamble of your document:

```
\usepackage{pstricks}
```

Note: `pstricks` relies on PostScript for rendering. As such, it does not work natively with pdfLaTeX. To compile documents using `pstricks`, one must use workflows like `latex -> dvips -> ps2pdf` or alternatively compile with `XeLaTeX`, which supports PostScript natively.

Features: The `pstricks` package offers an extensive toolkit for producing complex illustrations and diagrams. Key capabilities include:

- Drawing geometric shapes (lines, circles, ellipses, polygons, Bézier curves)
- Customizing colors, line widths, dash styles, fill patterns, and arrowheads
- Placing and rotating text within figures, including mathematical expressions
- Generating coordinate axes, grid systems, and function plots
- Composing complex diagrams with layers and clipping paths
- Combining multiple graphic elements to produce composite illustrations

`pstricks` is often extended with auxiliary packages such as `pst-plot`, `pst-node`, and `pst-tree`, each designed for more specific tasks like function plotting, node-link diagrams, or tree structures.

Because of its PostScript dependency, users working on PDF workflows should consider using `tikz` as a modern, PDF-compatible alternative unless the specific power of `pstricks` is essential.

51. subfig

Usage: The `subfig` package is used for placing multiple related figures within a single floating figure environment, known as subfigures. This is particularly useful in scientific and technical documents where comparisons or variations of a single concept are best displayed side by side or in a structured layout. The package enables authors to present several graphics or diagrams under one main caption, while each subfigure retains its own individual caption.

To enable this functionality, the package must first be loaded in the preamble using:

```
\usepackage{subfig}
```

Once loaded, the `subfloat` command can be used within the `figure` environment to insert individual subfigures.

Features: The `subfig` package provides a powerful mechanism to group and label multiple images in a single figure environment. Each subfigure is automatically labeled with a lowercase letter (a), (b), (c), etc., making it easier to reference each component independently using LaTeX's cross-referencing system.

A key advantage of this package is the ability to create neat and aligned visual structures where all subfigures share a common baseline or are arranged in rows or columns. Authors can customize spacing between subfigures, control alignment, and decide how captions are formatted beneath each subfigure or beneath the entire figure block.

Furthermore, subfigures remain compatible with floating behavior in LaTeX, allowing the entire figure to move to an optimal position in the document without breaking layout consistency. This flexibility, along with its integration with packages like `graphicx`, makes `subfig` a practical and visually appealing choice for organizing related visual content.

52. datetime2

Usage: The `datetime2` package is used to display dates and times in a flexible, customizable format within a LaTeX document. It replaces the older `datetime` package and provides extensive localization and formatting capabilities. This package is particularly valuable in formal documents, multilingual publications, or any context where standardized or human-readable date and time output is required.

To begin using the package, include it in your preamble with:

```
\usepackage{datetime2}
```

Once loaded, it provides commands like `\today` and `\DTMnow` to display the current date and time, respectively, in customizable formats.

Features: The `datetime2` package offers a wide array of options for presenting dates and times, including the choice of numeric, textual, or abbreviated formats. It supports the customization of separators (e.g., slashes, hyphens, dots), ordering (e.g., day-month-year or year-month-day), and padding (e.g., with or without leading zeros).

One of its key strengths lies in multilingual support. By default, it supports several predefined language modules such as English, German, French, Spanish, and many others. The formatting conventions for dates and times automatically adapt based on the chosen language, ensuring proper cultural and regional display formats.

The package also allows fine control over the appearance of the time component, including options to show or hide seconds, choose between 12-hour or 24-hour clock formats, and specify the level of precision. Advanced users can define their own custom styles or override the existing formats using a combination of package options and configuration commands.

53. `parskip`

Usage: The `parskip` package is used to modify the way LaTeX handles the spacing between paragraphs. By default, LaTeX indicates the start of a new paragraph through indentation. However, in some typesetting styles, particularly in technical reports, articles, or modern layouts, it is preferable to use vertical spacing instead of indentation. The `parskip` package enables this alternative formatting behavior by inserting vertical space between paragraphs and removing the paragraph indentation.

To activate the package, simply include it in your preamble:

```
\usepackage{parskip}
```

Features: The primary function of `parskip` is to ensure that paragraphs are visually separated using space rather than indentation. It automatically adjusts both the vertical space following a paragraph and the removal of any paragraph indent (`\parindent`). This results in a cleaner, more contemporary layout that is especially suitable for documents like business reports, instructional manuals, and design-heavy documents.

In addition to spacing changes, the package also corrects spacing around environments such as itemized lists and block quotations to maintain visual consistency. It makes sure that these elements do not create excessive gaps or interfere with the overall document layout.

The `parskip` package is easy to use and integrates well with most standard document classes. However, users should be aware that certain class or package combinations may redefine paragraph behaviors, so compatibility should be tested when using highly customized layouts.

54. makeidx

Usage: The `makeidx` package is used to generate indexes in LaTeX documents. An index provides a list of keywords or phrases with references to the pages where they appear, which is extremely valuable in textbooks, technical manuals, and comprehensive reference works. The process of indexing helps readers quickly locate specific terms or topics in a long document. To begin using it, the package must be loaded in the preamble with:

```
\usepackage{makeidx}
\makeindex
```

The first command loads the indexing functionality, while the second, `\makeindex`, initializes index creation for the document.

Features: The `makeidx` package provides a straightforward mechanism for marking terms to appear in the index. Within the body of the document, indexing is done by using the `\index{...}` command next to the word or phrase that should be included. For instance, writing:

```
\index{differential geometry}
```

next to a discussion of differential geometry ensures that this term will appear in the final index, along with the page number where it occurs.

To place the actual index at the end of the document, the following command is used:

```
\printindex
```

This command generates and displays the compiled index in its proper location, typically near the end of the document or after the bibliography.

The indexing process involves one additional compilation step. After running LaTeX, a separate index generation tool (such as `makeindex`) must be run to process the entries and prepare the index for inclusion. Most modern LaTeX editors handle this automatically or provide a command-line option for manual use.

The `makeidx` package also supports subentries and hierarchical indexing, such as:

```
\index{curvature!Gaussian}
```

which would create an index entry for "curvature" and list "Gaussian" as a subentry beneath it.

55. pdfcomment

Usage: The `pdfcomment` package enables authors to embed PDF annotations such as comments, highlights, and notes directly into their LaTeX documents. These annotations are not visible in printed copies but appear interactively in a PDF viewer that supports commenting, such as Adobe Acrobat Reader. This functionality is especially useful in collaborative writing, peer review, or instructional materials where the author may want to provide supplementary commentary or suggestions without cluttering the document itself.

To use the package, add the following line to the document preamble:

```
\usepackage{pdfcomment}
```

Once loaded, you can begin inserting comments at any location in the document using commands like `\pdfcomment`, which attach the comment to a word, phrase, or object in the text.

Features: The primary feature of the `pdfcomment` package is its ability to place interactive annotations in a compiled PDF file. These annotations are rendered as small icons or highlights, and the comment content is revealed when a user hovers over or clicks on the annotated area in a compatible PDF viewer. This makes it easy to provide feedback or clarifications without altering the visible content or layout of the document.

The package supports several types of annotations, including standard pop-up comments, in-text notes, highlights, and stamps. It also allows customization of the comment icon, color, author name, and even the open/close state of comments when the PDF is opened. For example, a simple usage would look like:

```
This sentence includes a
\pdfcomment{Clarify this point.}comment.
```

In addition to basic commenting, `pdfcomment` can also be configured to add tooltips or invisible metadata-like notes. It is important to note that the visual representation of comments depends on the PDF viewer; while most desktop applications handle them well, browser-based PDF viewers may offer limited support.

In summary, `pdfcomment` enhances collaboration and document review in LaTeX by embedding professional-grade annotations directly into the final PDF output, making it a valuable tool for academics, editors, and coauthors.

56. `amsfonts`

Usage: The `amsfonts` package is part of the suite of tools developed by the American Mathematical Society (AMS) and is used to provide access to additional mathematical fonts. It complements packages such as `amsmath` and `amssymb`, and its main role is to enhance the typographical range of mathematical expressions, particularly by offering access to specialized font sets such as blackboard bold, fraktur, and other calligraphic styles often used in mathematical writing.

To use the package, include the following line in the preamble of your LaTeX document:

```
\usepackage{amsfonts}
```

This line makes the extended font features available for use throughout the document.

Features: The key feature of the `amsfonts` package is its ability to provide additional math-specific fonts that are not available in the standard LaTeX setup. These include blackboard bold characters, which are typically used to represent number sets such as $\mathbb{R}$ (real numbers), $\mathbb{Z}$ (integers), and $\mathbb{N}$ (natural numbers). It also gives access to fraktur fonts, which are often used to denote ideals in algebra or elements of certain mathematical structures.

While packages like `amssymb` also load the `amsfonts` internally, it can be useful to load `amsfonts` directly if only the font features are needed without the additional symbols.

The use of these fonts contributes significantly to the clarity and expressiveness of mathematical documents, allowing authors to conform to traditional notations used in textbooks and academic literature. As such, `amsfonts` is widely used in formal mathematical and scientific documents where typographical precision is essential.

57. minted

Usage: The minted package is designed for typesetting source code with syntax highlighting in LaTeX documents. It leverages the powerful Python-based Pygments library to support a wide range of programming languages, making it ideal for technical and academic documents that need to include code with proper formatting and color differentiation.

To use minted, you must include it in the document preamble with the following command:

```
\usepackage{minted}
```

Since minted relies on external processing by Pygments, the document must be compiled using the -shell-escape option, which allows LaTeX to execute external programs. This means the document must be compiled from the command line or using an editor that supports this compilation flag.

Features: The most significant feature of the minted package is its ability to provide high-quality syntax highlighting across dozens of programming languages, including but not limited to Python, Java, C++, HTML, and LaTeX itself. It uses semantic parsing to apply color to keywords, strings, comments, and other language constructs, greatly improving readability and visual structure.

minted also allows for extensive customization, including line numbering, frame styling, background coloring, font size adjustments, and code highlighting. Users can define their own color schemes or use any of the predefined Pygments styles.

Another powerful aspect of minted is the listing environment it provides, which is similar to the one from the listings package but with more advanced and visually appealing output. For authors who frequently write technical documentation involving source code, minted is a highly flexible and aesthetically pleasing option that produces professional-quality results.

58. blindtext

Usage: The `blindtext` package is used to insert placeholder text into a LaTeX document. It is especially useful when testing or designing a layout before the actual content is available. The package allows authors to focus on document structure, typography, and spacing without being concerned about what content will eventually fill each section.

To begin using it, include the package in your preamble with:

```
\usepackage{blindtext}
```

After this, you can generate dummy text on demand using commands such as `\blindtext` or `\Blinddocument`.

Features: The primary feature of the `blindtext` package is the generation of "Lorem ipsum" style filler text that resembles the flow and structure of natural language. This helps writers and designers evaluate how the final output might look once the real content is inserted.

In addition to paragraphs, the package can also simulate full documents using the `\Blinddocument` command, which produces multiple sections and subsections filled with dummy content. You can also control how many paragraphs or sections are generated by passing optional arguments, making it flexible for quick layout testing.

Another useful feature is its multilingual support; `blindtext` can generate placeholder text in several languages when used in conjunction with language packages such as `babel`. This ensures that the layout can be tested under different language settings, especially for documents intended for international use.

59. comment

Usage: The `comment` package is used to selectively exclude portions of content from being typeset in the final output. This is especially useful during the drafting or editing stages of document preparation, where certain sections need to be temporarily disabled without removing them entirely from the source file. Instead of manually commenting every line using the percent symbol (%), this package allows users to define environments to ignore entire blocks of text.

To begin using it, include the package in your document preamble:

```
\usepackage{comment}
```

After that, you can define a custom comment environment using:

```
\begin{comment}
This entire block will not appear in the
final document.
\end{comment}
```

Features: The `comment` package offers a flexible and efficient mechanism for excluding sections of content. It accepts any length of content, including nested environments, and does not require each line to be individually marked. This can be particularly helpful when working on large projects or collaboratively editing a document, as it keeps the source file organized and readable while controlling what is rendered in the output.

In addition to the default `comment` environment, the package allows the creation of named comment environments, which can be conditionally activated or deactivated. This makes it ideal for selectively including or suppressing content depending on the target audience, versioning, or internal reviews.

60. `tabularx`

Usage: The `tabularx` package is used for creating tables that automatically adjust their column widths to fit the available line width. It is especially helpful when typesetting wide tables where fixed-width columns may either overflow the page or leave too much whitespace. This package builds on the traditional `tabular` environment by introducing a new column type that stretches to occupy remaining horizontal space.

To use this package, add the following to your preamble:

```
\usepackage{tabularx}
```

Then, within your document, you can define a `tabularx` environment similar to a regular `tabular` table, but specifying the desired total width (typically `\textwidth`) as its first argument.

Features: The main feature of `tabularx` is the introduction of the `X` column specifier. Unlike fixed-width columns such as `l`, `c`, or `r`, the `X` column will expand or contract its width as needed to fill the available space. This makes it ideal for formatting tables with columns that contain long text entries, such as descriptions, while maintaining control over the table's total width.

You can mix `X` columns with regular column types and even customize the alignment of `X` using advanced declarations. The package is highly useful in professional typesetting scenarios such as reports, articles, and data-driven documents, where table formatting must remain both flexible and aesthetically consistent.

By automatically balancing column widths, `tabularx` helps ensure your tables remain well-proportioned without manual trial-and-error adjustments.

61. ulem

Usage: The `ulem` package is used for advanced underlining and text decoration in LaTeX documents. While the standard LaTeX command `\underline` allows basic underlining, the `ulem` package expands on this by offering a variety of underline styles and strikeout capabilities. It is especially useful in editing drafts, preparing annotated documents, or emphasizing text in creative layouts.

To enable its functionality, include the package in your document preamble:

```
\usepackage{ulem}
```

Features: The `ulem` package provides a suite of commands that go beyond simple underlining. It includes:

1. `\uline` for normal underlining that breaks at line ends
2. `\uuline` for double underlining
3. `\uwave` for wavy underlining
4. `\sout` for striking through text with a horizontal line
5. `\xout` for crossing out text with a diagonal line

These enhancements offer significantly more control over how emphasis is applied, particularly when compared to the limitations of standard LaTeX.

However, one important note is that `ulem` redefines the `\emph` command to use underlining instead of italics. This behavior can be restored to default italics using the `[normalem]` option when loading the package:

```
\usepackage[normalem]{ulem}
```

The `ulem` package is a powerful tool when visual distinction of text is important, whether for stylistic or editorial purposes. It is widely used in both academic and publishing environments when clarity and text emphasis are key.

62. showkeys

Usage: The `showkeys` package is used during the document drafting process to display label names in the margins. It is particularly useful for authors and editors working with cross-references, equations, and citations, as it makes all `\label`, `\ref`, and `\cite` tags visible in the compiled document without affecting the final layout.

To activate this functionality, include the package in your preamble:

```
\usepackage{showkeys}
```

Features: Once loaded, the `showkeys` package automatically prints the names of all defined labels adjacent to their respective references in the output PDF. This includes labels for sections, equations, figures, tables, and any other environments that support referencing. These label tags appear in the document margins or inline, depending on the context.

This capability is invaluable when checking for consistency, identifying missing labels, or resolving ambiguous references in complex documents. It helps streamline the editing process by giving immediate visual feedback on how references are defined and used.

The output produced by `showkeys` is purely for draft and editorial purposes. For final versions, the package should be removed or commented out to restore the clean formatting of the document. Additionally, this package is compatible with most document classes and requires no special configuration, making it an easy yet powerful debugging aid in any LaTeX workflow.

63. mathptmx

Usage: The `mathptmx` package is used to set Times as the default font for both text and mathematical content in a LaTeX document. This package is particularly helpful in academic and professional writing, where the Times font family is often preferred for its readability and formal appearance. By enabling Times across both regular text and mathematical expressions, the document achieves a unified and consistent typographic style.

To use the package, include the following line in your preamble:

```
\usepackage{mathptmx}
```

Features: The primary feature of `mathptmx` is its ability to switch the document's font family to Times Roman, including math fonts. This helps create documents that look more polished and are visually aligned with the standards of many journals and institutions that request the use of Times New Roman.

Specifically, the package replaces the default Computer Modern fonts with Times Roman for the main text and applies compatible math fonts that resemble Times-style numerals, symbols, and operators. Although it does not support all Unicode characters or advanced math symbols as modern font packages like `newtxtext` or `unicode-math` might, it remains a lightweight and effective solution for traditional LaTeX workflows.

The `mathptmx` package is widely supported and integrates well with other packages. However, for more comprehensive font customization, users may consider using newer alternatives such as `newtx` or `txfonts`, which offer broader support for Times-compatible fonts and enhanced math typography.

64. dcolumn

Usage: The `dcolumn` package is used to align numbers in tabular columns on the decimal point. This is particularly useful when presenting numerical data, such as scientific measurements or financial figures, where proper alignment significantly enhances readability and comparison across rows.

To activate the package, include the following in your preamble:

```
\usepackage{dcolumn}
```

Features: The key feature of `dcolumn` is the introduction of a new column specifier, typically denoted by `D`, which allows the user to specify how numbers should be aligned, particularly on a specific symbol such as the decimal point. This ensures that digits before and after the decimal are vertically aligned, regardless of their length.

The column specification for `dcolumn` takes three arguments: the input decimal marker (usually `.`), the output decimal marker, and the number of decimal digits to align. This gives precise control over the visual structure of numerical data in tables.

This package is ideal for tables in academic, scientific, and technical documents where consistent numerical presentation is essential. It integrates seamlessly with standard LaTeX tabular environments and can be used alongside other formatting tools for professional-quality tables.

By using `dcolumn`, authors can produce visually appealing, well-aligned tables that emphasize the clarity and accuracy of numeric data.

65. afterpage

Usage: The `afterpage` package is used to defer the execution of certain commands, such as inserting large figures, tables, or page-breaking content, until the beginning of the next page. This capability is particularly useful in situations where you want to ensure that certain elements appear cleanly at the top of the following page without disrupting the flow of the current one.

To enable this functionality, add the package to your preamble with:

```
\usepackage{afterpage}
```

Features: The primary feature of `afterpage` is the command `\afterpage{<commands>}`. This command queues the enclosed instructions and delays their execution until the start of the next page. It is especially helpful in long documents, where careful control over content placement can improve visual balance and readability.

The package is compatible with most document classes and works well with floating environments like `figure` and `table`. However, authors should use it cautiously, especially in documents with frequent manual page breaks or complex float interactions, to avoid conflicts or unexpected behavior.

66. multind

Usage: The `multind` package is designed for documents that require more than one index. It enables authors to create multiple indexes based on different categories or types of content, such as subject indexes, name indexes, or specialized term lists. This makes it highly suitable for reference books, technical manuals, or comprehensive academic texts where organizing information across multiple dimensions improves navigation and usability.

To activate the package, include it in the preamble of your LaTeX document:

```
\usepackage{multind}
```

Features: The core functionality of `multind` is its ability to define and manage separate index streams within the same document. Once initialized, each index can be populated with entries independently using distinct indexing commands. The package provides mechanisms to define custom index types, write entries to the corresponding auxiliary files, and print each index in its own dedicated section.

When using `multind`, authors must run the indexing process separately for each index file (e.g., with the `makeindex` tool) and then include them in the final document. This flexibility is particularly useful when different audiences might benefit from distinct ways of locating content.

While modern packages like `imakeidx` or `splitidx` offer alternative approaches with extended capabilities, `multind` remains a lightweight and straightforward option for documents that require simple multi-indexing support.

67. pdflscape

Usage: The `pdflscape` package is used to rotate specific pages in a LaTeX document so that their contents appear in landscape orientation. It is especially useful when working with wide tables, large figures, or detailed diagrams that do not fit well in the standard portrait layout. What sets `pdflscape` apart is its integration with PDF viewers: when a page is rotated using this package, it appears automatically in landscape mode when the PDF is opened, ensuring an optimal viewing experience.

To activate the package, simply include the following in the document preamble:

```
\usepackage{pdflscape}
```

Features: The main feature of `pdflscape` is the provision of the `landscape` environment. Any content placed inside this environment is rotated by 90°, and the resulting page is flagged in the PDF metadata as a landscape page. This means that most PDF readers will automatically rotate the screen display to match the page orientation.

This is particularly helpful for multipage documents that include charts or data-intensive tables, which benefit from a wider format. Unlike manual rotation using graphic transformations, the `pdflscape` package works at the document structure level, ensuring compatibility with indexing, linking, and navigation features in the final PDF.

It is worth noting that while `pdflscape` is the preferred choice for PDF output, the similar `lscape` package may be used in contexts where PDF-specific functionality is not required. However, `pdflscape` is recommended for modern workflows due to its viewer-aware landscape handling.

68. pdfsync

Usage: The `pdfsync` package is designed to enable synchronization between a LaTeX source file and its compiled PDF output. This is especially helpful during the editing process, as it allows users to jump between the source code and the corresponding location in the output PDF and vice versa. It significantly improves the workflow in integrated development environments (IDEs) or PDF viewers that support this feature.

To use the package, include the following line in the preamble of your LaTeX document:

```
\usepackage{pdfsync}
```

Features: The core functionality of `pdfsync` is to embed special information in the generated PDF file, which can then be used by compatible editors and PDF viewers to establish a two-way link between the source code and the final output. This linking is done without altering the visible content of the document.

When enabled, clicking a location in the PDF file can highlight the corresponding line in the source code, and navigating to a section of the source code can show the relevant position in the output. This feature is particularly valuable for long or complex documents where manual tracking of edits would be cumbersome.

While `pdfsync` was more commonly used in earlier workflows, many modern editors (like TeXShop, TeXworks, Overleaf, and TeXstudio) now offer more advanced syncing through alternative technologies such as SyncTeX. Nonetheless, `pdfsync` remains useful in legacy systems or for those who prefer its lightweight integration.

69. numprint

Usage: The `numprint` package is used to format numbers in LaTeX documents, particularly large numbers that benefit from digit group separators such as commas or thin spaces. It is commonly used in scientific, financial, and technical writing where consistent numerical formatting improves readability and presentation quality.

To include the package in your document, add the following line in the preamble:

```
\usepackage{numprint}
```

Features: One of the key features of `numprint` is its ability to automatically insert thousands separators in large numbers, which helps reduce visual clutter and aids in numerical interpretation. For example, the number

1234567 can be typeset as 1 234 567 or 1,234,567, depending on the configuration.

The package is flexible and allows customization of the separator symbol, the number of decimal digits to display, and the formatting of numbers with units. Additionally, it provides specialized commands for printing tables with aligned numbers and for formatting numbers according to localized conventions (e.g., European or American styles).

The command `\numprint{1234567}` will format the number according to the defined rules, and users can configure settings globally using package options or the `\npthousandsep` and `\npdecimalsign` commands.

The `numprint` package is especially valuable in documents that contain large quantities of numerical data, offering clarity, consistency, and better typographical control over numeric formatting.

70. esint

Usage: The `esint` package is used to enhance the mathematical typesetting capabilities of LaTeX by providing a wider variety of integral symbols beyond the standard \\`int`. It is particularly valuable in advanced mathematical documents, such as those involving vector calculus, complex analysis, or differential geometry, where specialized integral notations are frequently required.

To activate the package, include the following line in your document preamble:

```
\usepackage{esint}
```

Features: The primary feature of `esint` is its extended set of integral symbols, which go beyond the conventional single, double, and triple integrals. It includes integral signs for contour integrals, clockwise and counterclockwise integrals, surface and volume integrals, and other specialized mathematical notations. These are particularly useful in fields such as physics and engineering where such operators have distinct meanings.

Once loaded, the package redefines or supplements the basic integral commands to support these more specialized forms. For instance, it provides commands like `\ointclockwise` and `\varoiint`, which represent path integrals and double integrals with customized styling.

By offering a more comprehensive range of integral symbols, the `esint` package helps ensure mathematical notation in LaTeX matches the precision and specificity expected in formal mathematical and scientific writing.

71. ifthen

Usage: The `ifthen` package introduces basic conditional logic into LaTeX documents, enabling authors to create dynamic content that responds to specific criteria or conditions. This can be particularly useful in large documents, templates, or documents that require different outputs based on user-defined flags or counters.

To use the package, load it in your preamble with:

```
\usepackage{ifthen}
```

Features: The `ifthen` package provides commands such as `\ifthenelse` and `\whiledo` that allow LaTeX to evaluate boolean expressions and make decisions accordingly. It supports comparisons between numbers, evaluation of boolean values, checking whether a command is defined, and much more.

For example, an author can create a condition that typesets different text depending on the value of a counter, or omit sections from the document entirely based on defined logical rules. This makes it possible to write reusable and modular LaTeX code, especially when designing templates or creating teaching materials where conditions like draft mode, solution inclusion, or language selection matter.

While not as powerful as the more modern `etoolbox` or `expl3` logic tools, `ifthen` remains widely used for its simplicity and ease of integration with traditional LaTeX workflows.

72. xr

Usage: The `xr` package, short for "external references," is used when a LaTeX document needs to reference labels from another separate LaTeX file. This is particularly useful when working on large projects that are split across multiple documents, such as a multivolume book, a set of supplementary files, or a thesis with separate appendices or articles.

To use this package, add the following line to your preamble:

```
\usepackage{xr}
```

Then, you must specify which external document to reference using the `\externaldocument` command, which takes the name of the external document (without the `.aux` extension). For example:

```
\externaldocument{supplement}
```

This command tells LaTeX to read label information from the file `supplement.aux`, allowing you to reference equations, theorems, sections, or figures from the external document using the standard `\ref` or `\eqref` commands.

Features: The main feature of the `xr` package is its ability to resolve cross-references across independent LaTeX source files without the need to merge them into a single compilation. This allows for modularity and clean organization in large writing projects. It supports:

- Standard label referencing across documents
- Prefixing labels (using an optional argument to `\externaldocument`) to avoid label name collisions between the main and external documents
- Compatibility with most standard referencing commands such as `\ref`, `\eqref`, and `\pageref`

For example, to prevent label conflicts, you can use:

```
\externaldocument[supp-]{supplement}
```

Then, referencing a label `{eq:energy}` from the supplement will require `\ref{supp-eq:energy}` in the main document.

The `xr` package works best when both documents are compiled in the same directory or the path to the auxiliary file is correctly specified. Note that the external document must be compiled at least once to generate the `.aux` file required for cross-referencing.

73. varioref

Usage: The `varioref` package extends LaTeX's referencing capabilities by automatically providing additional context about the location of a referenced item, such as whether it appears on the current page, the next page, the previous page, or a distant page. This is particularly helpful in long documents where the precise location of the referenced item contributes to better navigation and reader understanding.

To begin using `varioref`, include the package in your preamble with:

```
\usepackage{varioref}
```

After loading the package, you can use the command `\vref` in place of `\ref` to generate a reference that includes not only the label number but also a page cue if the referenced object is on a different page.

Features: The key feature of the `varioref` package is its ability to produce context-aware cross-references. For example, if you use `\vref{fig:example}`, the output might be:

"Figure 2.1 on the next page" or *"Figure 2.1 on page 23,"* depending on where the figure appears in relation to the referencing text.

Internally, the package enhances the user experience by reducing the reader's need to flip through pages or scan for figures, sections, or tables referenced without context. It works seamlessly with standard LaTeX environments such as `figure`, `table`, `equation`, and sectioning commands.

The package also supports configuration and localization of the page-cue phrases, such as replacing "on the next page" with other custom wording or adjusting them for different languages. For multilingual documents, it integrates with packages like `babel` to adapt these phrases accordingly.

Finally, while `varioref` works well on its own, it can also be used alongside other referencing packages such as `hyperref` and `cleveref`, although care must be taken to load them in the correct order to avoid conflicts.

74. fancyvrb

Usage: The `fancyvrb` package is used to enhance the way verbatim (literal) text is handled in a LaTeX document. It serves as a powerful extension to the standard `verbatim` environment and is especially useful when precise formatting is required, such as for source code, configuration snippets, or command-line output. To use it, the package must be loaded in the preamble using:

```
\usepackage{fancyvrb}
```

Once included, the package offers both an enhanced environment called `Verbatim` and an inline version `\verb`.
Features: The `fancyvrb` package provides a rich set of features for customizing verbatim text. It allows users to control nearly every aspect of formatting, including line numbering, font size, font family, and line spacing. One can frame verbatim blocks to visually separate them from the main text, which improves clarity in documents that contain code or instructional content. Another useful capability is reading verbatim content directly from external files, which keeps the source document cleaner and makes it easier to manage large code examples.

In addition, the package supports line highlighting for drawing attention to specific parts of a code block, particularly beneficial in teaching materials. You can also define custom styles to maintain consistent formatting across all verbatim environments in a document. Moreover, `fancyvrb` integrates well with other formatting tools, allowing users to combine it with color and box-styling packages like `xcolor` and `tcolorbox`. These advanced capabilities make it a preferred choice for authors who need fine-tuned control over textual representations in technical and academic writing.

75. natbib

Usage: The `natbib` package is widely used in academic and scientific writing for flexible and robust citation management. It is particularly favored in disciplines where author-year citation formats are common, such as the social sciences and natural sciences. To use it, simply include the package in your document preamble as follows:

```
\usepackage{natbib}
```

Once loaded, `natbib` allows authors to cite references in a variety of styles and formats, both inline and parenthetical, with consistent formatting controlled through citation style options.

Features: The `natbib` package supports both author-year and numeric citation modes, offering commands like `\citet` for textual citations (e.g., "Smith (2020)") and `\citep` for parenthetical citations (e.g., "(Smith, 2020)"). This dual-format capability gives authors significant flexibility in how citations are integrated into narrative text. In addition, it allows customization of punctuation and formatting between citations, provides support for multiple bibliographies, and works seamlessly with BibTeX for automatic bibliography generation.

The package includes advanced features such as sorting and compressing multiple citations into a single reference group, adding notes to citations, and using citation aliases for repeated references. Users can also define custom citation styles and bibliographic styles, making it easy to conform to specific journal or publisher requirements. `natbib` is compatible with a wide range of bibliography style files (.bst) and can be used alongside packages like `hyperref` to produce clickable citations in PDFs.

76. unicode-math

Usage: The `unicode-math` package is used for enabling direct use of Unicode characters in mathematical expressions. It is designed to work specifically with modern LaTeX engines such as XeLaTeX and LuaLaTeX, which support full Unicode input. This package is particularly beneficial for authors who prefer writing mathematical symbols directly in source files (e.g., using $\sum$ instead of `\sum`) or for multilingual documents requiring seamless integration of various scripts and math symbols.

To use the package, include the following line in your preamble:

```
\usepackage{unicode-math}
```

This package must be used with either the XeLaTeX or the LuaLaTeX engine, as it is not compatible with pdfLaTeX.

Features: The `unicode-math` package allows LaTeX users to write math using standard Unicode characters and simplifies the input of mathematical content by eliminating the need for traditional TeX commands for most symbols. It also introduces the possibility of changing the math font independently of the main text font using the `\setmathfont` command. With this feature, authors can select from a wide range of OpenType math fonts, such as `Latin Modern Math`, `STIX Two Math`, or `XITS Math`, providing both typographic variety and improved rendering across devices.

In addition to enabling Unicode character input, the package also redefines many standard LaTeX math commands to take full advantage of OpenType math capabilities. This includes improved kerning, glyph positioning, and access to alternative glyphs not available through legacy math font encodings. It supports both left-to-right and right-to-left math typesetting, making it ideal for use in international and multilingual publications.

77. scrlayer-scrpage

Usage: The `scrlayer-scrpage` package is a modern and powerful tool for customizing headers and footers in LaTeX documents. It is part of the KOMA-Script bundle and serves as an advanced alternative to the older `fancyhdr` package. This package is especially useful in documents that require refined typographic control, such as books, theses, or formal reports. It integrates seamlessly with KOMA-Script classes (`scrartcl`, `scrreprt`, `scrbook`) but is also compatible with standard classes like `article` and `report`.

To activate the package, simply include it in the preamble:

```
\usepackage{scrlayer-scrpage}
```

Features: The `scrlayer-scrpage` package provides a layered page style mechanism, allowing the user to define complex header and footer configurations in a modular and reusable way. Unlike `fancyhdr`, which requires manual management of head and foot elements, `scrlayer-scrpage` uses a declarative syntax that enables users to define page styles by specifying layers and content for each part of the header or footer.

It supports automatic updates to headers and footers based on chapter or section titles, page numbers, or custom text. These elements can be aligned independently (left, center, right) for even and odd pages, which is particularly important for double-sided documents.

Another key feature is its support for predefined page styles such as `plain.scrheadings` and `scrheadings`, which can be adapted and extended easily. The package also respects typographic guidelines of KOMA-Script, ensuring consistent appearance and layout.

78. endnotes

Usage: The `endnotes` package is designed to manage notes that appear at the end of a document rather than at the bottom of each page. This is particularly useful in academic or literary writing where endnotes are preferred over footnotes for stylistic or publishing reasons. Instead of using the standard LaTeX `\footnote` command, this package provides a dedicated command to create endnotes throughout the document and then display them all collectively at the end.

To begin using the package, it should be included in the preamble with:

```
\usepackage{endnotes}
```

Then, within the body of the document, use the `\endnote` command in place of `\footnote` to create individual notes:

```
This is some text.\endnote{This is the
corresponding endnote.}
```

At the location where all endnotes should be printed, typically at the end of the document before `\end{document}`, add the following command:

```
\theendnotes
```

Features: The `endnotes` package redirects footnotes into a separate list of endnotes that can be compiled and formatted like any other section. It provides compatibility with most document classes and supports customization of the appearance of endnotes. Users can reset counters, group notes by chapters in multipart documents, and control the numbering format. This makes it an effective tool for authors who require clean and structured referencing without cluttering the page layout with footnotes.

79. placeins

Usage: The `placeins` package is a valuable tool for managing the placement of floating elements in a LaTeXdocument, specifically figures and tables. By default, LaTeX tries to optimize the layout by floating figures and tables to positions it considers visually appropriate, which can sometimes result in floats appearing far from their reference point in the text. This can confuse the reader or break the logical flow of the document. The `placeins` package offers an elegant solution by allowing you to enforce stricter boundaries on where floats may appear.

To use the package, include the following in your preamble:

```
\usepackage{placeins}
```

Once loaded, the most important command it provides is:

```
\FloatBarrier
```

This command forces all figures and tables defined before it to be placed before the next section or point in the text. When inserted at logical breaks—such as at the end of a section, it ensures that floats do not move into the next section or appear unexpectedly late.

Features: The key feature of the `placeins` package is the `\FloatBarrier` command, which acts as a boundary preventing floats from crossing it. This is particularly useful in documents where each section must retain its own figures and tables without bleed-over from surrounding content. Additionally, if the `[section]` option is provided when loading the package, LaTeX automatically inserts a `\FloatBarrier` at every section boundary:

```
\usepackage[section]{placeins}
```

With this option, all floats are constrained to the section in which they are declared, eliminating the need to insert `\FloatBarrier` manually. This feature ensures consistent visual and logical structure, which is especially beneficial in academic writing, theses, or technical documentation that requires tight alignment between content and visuals.

80. background

Usage: The `background` package is used to place background elements, such as images, text, or decorative watermarks on every page of a document. It is especially helpful for documents that require branding, security markings (like "Confidential" or "Draft"), or visually appealing backdrops for slides, reports, or handouts.

To use this package, you must load it in the preamble of your document:

```
\usepackage{background}
```

Once included, the package allows the author to configure background elements globally or page by page using various options.

Features: The `background` package provides fine control over the appearance and position of background content. You can place either images or text behind the main document body and customize its location, scale, opacity, and rotation. Configuration is done using key-value pairs, which are set with the `\backgroundsetup` command.

For example, you can set a watermark that says "Confidential" by specifying the text, scaling it, and adjusting its opacity and rotation. Similarly, for full-page background images (e.g., letterheads or templates), the image file path can be specified along with options to control alignment and size.

The package supports advanced placement logic, including background content for all pages or just a specific page range. It also works well in conjunction with color and graphics packages such as `xcolor` and `graphicx`, allowing for consistent visual design.

This package is widely used in both academic and professional publishing when aesthetic and informative background elements are needed to enhance the layout without interfering with the main content.

81. diagbox

Usage: The `diagbox` package is designed for creating diagonally split table cells, which is particularly useful for labeling both the row and column of a table header in a single compact cell. This formatting is commonly seen in statistical tables, contingency tables, and data comparison grids, where both row and column headings need to be represented in the same cell.

To use the package, include the following line in the document preamble:

```
\usepackage{diagbox}
```

Once loaded, the package introduces the `\diagbox` command, which can be used inside a `tabular` environment to generate a cell that contains two labels separated by a diagonal line.

Features: The `diagbox` package provides elegant support for diagonal splitting within table cells. It allows you to specify the text that should appear in the top-left and bottom-right of the diagonally split box. The diagonal line automatically adjusts its angle based on the content, making the appearance neat and visually consistent.

It supports further customization such as setting the width and height of the diagonal box, adjusting the text alignment within each section, and adding additional styling to enhance the visual design of the table. It also integrates well with other table-related packages such as `booktabs`, `array`, and `colortbl`, offering flexibility for both simple and complex table layouts.

82. pifont

Usage: The `pifont` package provides access to the Dingbats font, which contains a wide variety of typographic symbols, including checkmarks, crosses, arrows, pointing hands, stars, and geometric shapes. These symbols are often used for marking tasks as complete, highlighting key points, or enhancing visual elements in documents such as forms, questionnaires, or instructional materials.

To use the package, include it in the preamble of your document as follows:

```
\usepackage{pifont}
```

Once loaded, the package allows you to invoke symbols by referencing their font slot number or by using predefined shortcuts.

Features: One of the key features of the `pifont` package is the ability to insert a variety of symbols that are not included in the standard LaTeX symbol set. For example, a common use case is the inclusion of checkmarks and crosses, often used in to-do lists or result tables. The package defines user-friendly commands like `\ding{51}` for a checkmark (✓) and `\ding{55}` for a cross ($\times$), making them easy to use and consistent across the document.

The symbols can also be customized in size and color using packages such as `xcolor` and `scalefnt`, allowing for flexible design. Moreover, since these symbols come from a dedicated font, they render cleanly and scale well with text, ensuring professional typographic quality.

The pifont package is especially useful in presentations, instructional guides, and academic documents where visual cues enhance reader understanding or interface-style interaction is required. Its integration with standard LaTeX tables and lists makes it a versatile tool for adding visual symbols without resorting to external graphics or images.

83. minted

Usage: The minted package is used for typesetting source code with syntax highlighting in LaTeX documents. It relies on the external Python-based tool Pygments to apply language-specific formatting rules, making it especially suitable for academic papers, programming books, technical reports, or any document that requires readable and well-styled code examples.

To use the package, it must be loaded in the preamble using:

```
\usepackage{minted}
```

Note that because minted depends on Pygments, documents using it must be compiled with the -shell-escape flag enabled in the LaTeX compiler. This allows LaTeX to execute the external Pygments script during compilation.

Features: The minted package supports a large number of programming languages and markup formats including Python, Java, C++, HTML, JSON, LaTeX itself, and many others. It provides fine-grained control over the appearance of code listings through numerous customization options such as line numbering, background shading, font size, frames, and syntax color schemes. Each code block is enclosed in the minted environment, which takes the language name as a parameter and then typesets the enclosed content accordingly.

For example, the environment

```
\begin{minted}{python}
def hello():
    print("Hello, world!")
\end{minted}
```

would produce syntax-highlighted Python code using colors and formatting that follow standard Python conventions. Beyond inline usage, the package also supports code listings from external files, enabling better separation of content and formatting, especially in longer documents or software manuals.

`minted` is highly customizable via options passed to the package or individual environments. Users can change the font size, highlight specific lines, and define custom Pygments styles. The appearance can be fine-tuned to match the visual style of the overall document, contributing to both clarity and aesthetic quality.

Because of its accuracy, extensibility, and visual appeal, `minted` is often preferred over older alternatives like `listings` when shell escape is available.

84. tabu

Usage: The `tabu` package is designed to enhance LaTeX's tabular capabilities by providing an extended and more flexible version of the standard `tabular` environment. It serves as a high-level interface for creating complex tables, especially those that require advanced column alignment, dynamic width adjustments, or mixed alignment styles. With `tabu`, authors can produce sophisticated table layouts while simplifying the underlying code structure.

To use the package, it should be loaded in the document preamble as follows:

```
\usepackage{tabu}
```

Once loaded, the tabu environment can replace the traditional tabular environment, with additional features and intuitive syntax.

Features: The tabu package introduces a highly adaptable table environment that allows users to define column widths in terms of percentages or stretchable lengths using the X column type. This makes it especially useful for tables that need to span the full width of the page or adjust automatically to the available space. It supports multiline cells and automatic text wrapping and can handle mixed column alignments such as left, center, and right justification all within a single table.

A notable benefit of tabu is that it integrates well with other packages like booktabs, allowing authors to include professional-quality horizontal rules while still leveraging dynamic spacing and alignment. It also supports rotating cells and applying alternating row colors when combined with the colortbl or xcolor packages.

Despite its flexibility and convenience, it is important to mention that the tabu package has not been actively maintained in recent years and may be incompatible with the latest versions of LaTeX. As such, users are advised to test it thoroughly or consider alternatives like longtable for multipage tables or tabularx and array for better compatibility in complex layouts.

Nonetheless, for projects where it works reliably, tabu offers a rich set of tools that can greatly simplify the creation of advanced tables with precise formatting requirements.

85. asymptote

Usage: The asymptote package provides support for embedding Asymptote vector graphics directly within a LaTeX document. Asymptote is a powerful descriptive graphics language similar to MetaPost but with advanced features suitable for producing publication-quality technical illustrations, particularly in mathematics, engineering, and computer science. By loading this package, users can include high-quality 2D and 3D diagrams defined using Asymptote's scripting syntax. This integration allows Asymptote code to be processed as part of the LaTeX compilation workflow.

To activate support for Asymptote graphics, the following line should be included in the preamble:

```
\usepackage{asymptote}
```

Once included, Asymptote environments can be placed in the document, typically using either external `.asy` files or inline Asymptote code blocks.

Features: The `asymptote` package enables precise control over vector graphics with support for scalable diagrams that remain sharp at any resolution. It allows the drawing of points, lines, curves, and surfaces in both two and three dimensions and supports labeling with LaTeX syntax using mathematical notation. Its programming interface includes variables, loops, conditionals, and functions, allowing for reusable and dynamically generated figures.

One of the key strengths of Asymptote is its native support for 3D perspective rendering, surface shading, and projections, which makes it particularly well suited for geometric and scientific visualization. Moreover, Asymptote graphics can interact seamlessly with LaTeX text and math, ensuring consistent font and typesetting quality across the entire document.

Compiling documents with Asymptote graphics requires additional compilation steps beyond standard `pdflatex`, such as using `latex + asymptote + pdflatex` or enabling shell escape for automated workflows in editors like Overleaf or TeXShop.

The combination of scripting flexibility and professional-quality rendering makes `asymptote` an excellent tool for users who require high-end technical illustrations directly embedded within their LaTeX documents.

86. filecontents

Usage: The `filecontents` package allows users to create and write to external files directly from within a LaTeX document. This functionality is particularly useful for generating auxiliary files, such as bibliography databases (`.bib`) or data sets (`.csv`), without requiring users to maintain them separately. It is often used in self-contained LaTeX documents, especially for sharing minimal examples or producing documents that can be compiled independently without external file dependencies.

To activate the functionality, add the following line to the document preamble:

```
\usepackage{filecontents}
```

After including the package, you can use the `filecontents` environment anywhere before `\begin {document}` to create a file.

Features: The `filecontents` package creates external files from within the LaTeX source by writing content to them during compilation. This is particularly advantageous when you want to embed bibliographic data or tabular data sets directly within the main document, eliminating the need for distributed file bundles.

Each file created using this package is saved in the working directory (or the output directory in some TeX systems). The environment ensures that the file is only created if it does not already exist, helping avoid unintentional overwriting. In addition, an enhanced version of the package, `filecontents*`, omits LaTeX comment headers, which is useful for generating raw data files like CSV or plain BibTeX entries.

The ability to embed and generate files during compilation is ideal for reproducible documents, especially in academic settings where submission guidelines require a single, standalone file. The `filecontents` package simplifies document portability while maintaining full functionality.

87. standalone

Usage: The `standalone` package is designed to allow specific parts of a LaTeX document, such as TikZ diagrams, plots, or tables, to be compiled as independent documents while also being seamlessly included within a larger main file. This is particularly useful in collaborative projects or when managing documents with multiple reusable figures and diagrams. By enabling modular document design, the `standalone` package promotes clean structure and faster compilation.

To use the package, include the following line in the preamble of your main document:

```
\usepackage{standalone}
```

Each sub-document (e.g., a TikZ diagram saved as its own `.tex` file) should use the `standalone` document class to compile on its own, like this:

```
\documentclass{standalone}
\usepackage{tikz}
\begin{document}
\begin{tikzpicture}
  \draw (0,0) -- (2,2);
\end{tikzpicture}
\end{document}
```

Then, in the main document, you can include the diagram using:

```
\input{diagram.tex}
```

Features: The `standalone` package supports independent compilation of sub-documents while maintaining compatibility with `\input` and `\include` in the main document. It automatically trims unnecessary white space around included files (such as diagrams), ensuring they are tightly cropped and neatly integrated into the layout.

Additionally, it supports the use of conditional compilation, where a subfile can detect whether it is being compiled independently or as part of a parent document. This is ideal when the same code needs to behave differently depending on the compilation context, for example, applying a specific font size or document class only in standalone mode.

In large projects or graphics-heavy documents, using `standalone` improves modularity, simplifies collaboration, and significantly reduces compilation time during iterative development. It is widely adopted in documents that involve numerous TikZ illustrations, PGFPlots charts, or segmented content meant to be reused across multiple files.

88. animate

Usage: The `animate` package is used to embed frame-based animations within PDF documents generated by LaTeX. These animations are constructed from a sequence of images or drawings, which are played back in supported PDF viewers (such as Adobe Acrobat). This functionality is particularly useful for displaying time-dependent simulations, step-by-step visualizations, and educational illustrations.

To use the package, include it in the preamble of your document with:

```
\usepackage{animate}
```

Animations can be created either by using a series of external image files (e.g., PNG, PDF) or by dynamically generating frames within LaTeX using graphics packages such as TikZ or PSTricks.

Features: The `animate` package provides a flexible interface for defining animations in PDF output. It supports various playback options including start and stop controls, frame rate adjustment, looping, and reversible playback. Users can specify how animations begin, whether on click, automatically upon opening the document, or manually using control buttons.

When using external files, the package allows batch inclusion of sequentially numbered images. For instance, a series of files named `frame1.pdf`, `frame2.pdf`, ... can be loaded into an animation environment to create a smooth visual presentation.

Internally generated frames, such as those drawn with TikZ, can be compiled using the `animateinline` environment. Each iteration of a loop or frame command generates a new animation frame directly from LaTeX code.

The package also supports integration with JavaScript-based playback controls in the resulting PDF, giving the user interactive features such as play/pause buttons and frame sliders.

It is important to note that the effectiveness of the animation may depend on the PDF viewer, as not all readers support embedded multimedia features equally. Adobe Acrobat Reader is generally recommended for full compatibility.

89. `letltxmacro`

Usage: The `letltxmacro` package is designed to provide a more reliable and flexible way to copy and redefine LaTeX macros. It overcomes some of the limitations and edge cases associated with the standard `\let` command, particularly when dealing with macros that may have been defined with fragile or protected constructs. This package is particularly useful when one wants to redefine or extend the behavior of an existing command while preserving its original functionality.

To use it, load the package in the preamble of your document:

```
\usepackage{letltxmacro}
```

Features: The central feature of the `letltxmacro` package is the command `\LetLtxMacro`, which allows one to assign the meaning of one macro to another in a way that respects LaTeX's internal scoping and control sequence structure. Unlike `\let`, which is a TeX primitive and may not handle macros defined with LaTeX's command layer properly, `\LetLtxMacro` ensures that the copied macro works correctly in the LaTeX environment and maintains robustness in moving arguments such as those passed into section headings or captions.

This is particularly important when redefining commands in custom document classes or packages, or when trying to override existing functionality without breaking dependencies elsewhere in the document. With this approach, the original command can be saved, modified, and restored if needed while maintaining LaTeX's expected behavior.

By using `letltxmacro`, users can ensure compatibility and reliability in complex macro manipulations, especially when developing reusable LaTeX code or templates.

90. bm

Usage: The `bm` package is used to produce bold mathematical symbols in LaTeX documents. While the standard `\mathbf` command can be used to bold certain math characters like Latin letters and digits, it does not work with symbols, Greek letters, or complex math constructs. The `bm` package overcomes this limitation by allowing any mathematical expression to be bolded correctly and consistently.

To begin using the package, include the following line in the preamble of your document:

```
\usepackage{bm}
```

Once loaded, you can apply bold styling to math content using the `\bm` command:

```
\bm{\alpha}, \bm{A}, \bm{\nabla}, \bm{x+y}
```

Features: The key feature of the `bm` package is its ability to bold any math symbol or expression, including Greek letters, integral signs, nabla operators, and even entire equations. This makes it especially useful in scientific and engineering disciplines where bold notation often indicates vectors, matrices, or tensors.

Unlike `\boldsymbol` from the `amsbsy` package, which has limited scope, `\bm` is more comprehensive and robust, offering better support for a wider range of mathematical symbols. It also handles font changes and font encodings internally, ensuring that the bold appearance remains consistent across different parts of the document.

91. datetime

Usage: The `datetime` package is used in LaTeX documents to display the current date and time with fine control over their format. It is particularly helpful in documents that require precise timestamping, such as drafts, logs, technical reports, or automatically updated documentation. By default, LaTeX offers only basic support for displaying the date via the `\today` command, which prints the date in a fixed format (e.g., "April 11, 2025"). The `datetime` package significantly expands this functionality by allowing authors to specify and customize the exact appearance of the date and time.

To use the package, include the following in the preamble of your LaTeX document:

```
\usepackage{datetime}
```

Once included, the package allows the author to redefine the `\today` command or use new macros such as `\currenttime` and `\xxivtime` to print the current time in 12-hour or 24-hour formats, respectively.

Features: The `datetime` package provides extensive tools for customizing the way dates and times are printed in a document. It supports options for changing the date format, for example, switching between "11 April 2025" and "2025-04-11,", and for formatting the time using either 12-hour or 24-hour clocks. The package also enables authors to redefine the built-in `\today` command, making it easy to reflect local or institutional date formats.

In addition to formatting, the package can display both the current date and time anywhere in the document, which is particularly useful for version control or for marking when a document was compiled. While not as extensive as its successor `datetime2`, the `datetime` package remains lightweight and highly compatible, making it a solid choice for basic to moderate date/time formatting needs in LaTeX.

92. `bigfoot`

Usage: The `bigfoot` package is designed to provide advanced control over footnote behavior in LaTeX documents. It is particularly useful when a document contains complex footnote structures such as multiple footnote series, footnotes in tables, or footnotes that need custom formatting. Unlike standard footnote commands in LaTeX, which offer limited flexibility, the `bigfoot` package allows authors to manage footnotes with precision, ensuring correct layout and numbering even under complicated conditions.

To use the package, include the following line in your document preamble:

```
\usepackage{bigfoot}
```

Once loaded, the package extends the functionality of the standard `\footnote` command and introduces features such as multiple independent footnote series and customizable placement rules.

Features: The `bigfoot` package enhances the default footnote mechanism by resolving several limitations associated with traditional footnote handling. One of its key features is support for multiple footnote series, which allows users to define distinct categories of footnotes, each with its own numbering style and formatting. This is especially beneficial in academic or legal documents where explanatory notes, citations, and editorial comments must be separated.

The package also handles footnotes in tables more gracefully, preventing layout issues that often arise when standard footnote commands are used within tabular environments. Additionally, `bigfoot` ensures that long or complex footnotes do not interfere with page breaking, preserving the visual integrity of the document.

Authors can also define custom formatting for different footnote series, including placement, font size, and separation from the main text. In essence, `bigfoot` provides a robust and reliable system for managing all aspects of footnote presentation in LaTeX documents.

93. nicematrix

Usage: The `nicematrix` package is used for creating matrices with enhanced formatting options that go beyond the capabilities of traditional environments such as `matrix`, `bmatrix`, or `pmatrix`. It is particularly helpful when authors want to add visual elements, like dotted lines, colored rows, or braces, within matrix structures. This package is ideal for typesetting matrices in teaching materials, research papers, and mathematical textbooks where clarity and visual aids enhance comprehension.

To activate the package, add the following to the preamble:

```
\usepackage{nicematrix}
```

Features: The `nicematrix` package significantly improves how matrices are displayed in LaTeX documents. One of its most useful features is the ability to add vertical and horizontal dotted lines inside a matrix to visually separate or highlight elements. These lines can be added automatically between columns or rows using simple key-value options, avoiding the need for manual drawing commands.

Additionally, `nicematrix` allows the user to add TikZ annotations, such as braces, highlights, or arrows, that interact directly with matrix elements. It also supports diagonal arrows and rectangular frames around submatrices, which are especially valuable when illustrating row operations, block matrices, or steps in a matrix transformation.

Another notable feature is the compatibility with mathematical environments like `align` or `equation`, meaning that matrices can be seamlessly integrated into larger expressions without breaking formatting. Furthermore, the package maintains alignment with equation numbers, making it well-suited for formal mathematical writing.

94. chessboard

Usage: The `chessboard` package is used to draw and customize chessboards within LaTeX documents. It is ideal for creating diagrams of chess positions, especially in instructional or historical analysis contexts.

To use the package, include in the preamble:

```
\usepackage{chessboard}
```

Features: The package provides the `\chessboard` command to render a chessboard with pieces in specified positions. Boards can be customized in size, color, orientation, and annotation. It works in combination with the `skak` package to position pieces via Forsyth–Edwards Notation (FEN). Users can also highlight squares, mark moves, and overlay coordinates, making it well-suited for chess books or educational documents.

95. skak

Usage: The `skak` package enables typesetting chess games and diagrams using LaTeX. It supports algebraic notation and is often used alongside `chessboard` for complete chess presentations.

Include the package in the preamble with:

```
\usepackage{skak}
```

Features: skak provides commands like \mainline, \variation, and \newgame to write and display chess games in algebraic notation. It supports automatic move numbering, inline diagram generation, and setting positions using FEN strings. While skak can display diagrams on its own, it is typically paired with chessboard for full board rendering and greater visual customization.

96. circuitikz

Usage: The circuitikz package is designed for drawing high-quality electrical and electronic circuit diagrams directly within LaTeX documents. It is built on top of the tikz drawing framework, which provides extensive capabilities for creating graphics in LaTeX. circuitikz simplifies the process by providing specialized commands and predefined symbols for a wide range of circuit components. This makes it especially useful for students, educators, and professionals in electrical engineering, physics, and related fields.

To use this package, include the following in the preamble:

```
\usepackage{circuitikz}
```

Features: The circuitikz package provides an extensive library of standardized circuit elements, such as resistors, capacitors, inductors, diodes, transistors, voltage sources, current sources, operational amplifiers, and more. These elements can be easily positioned and connected using coordinate-based drawing commands. The package supports both American and European circuit symbol conventions and allows users to label components, specify orientations, and customize the appearance of diagrams.

In addition to basic circuit elements, circuitikz supports advanced features such as open and closed switches, logic gates, meters, and transformers. The diagrams integrate seamlessly into LaTeX documents, ensuring consistent font use and scaling. This makes it ideal for producing publication-ready circuit schematics within academic papers, theses, textbooks, and lecture notes. The flexibility and precision of `circuitikz` make it a powerful tool for any technical document requiring circuit visualization.

97. chngpage

Usage: The `chngpage` package is used when a document requires local adjustments to the layout of specific pages, especially margins. This is particularly helpful when inserting wide figures, tables, or content that does not fit within the default page layout. Instead of altering the global page geometry using a package like `geometry`, `chngpage` provides an efficient method to apply temporary margin changes in a localized section of the document.

To use the package, include the following in the preamble:

```
\usepackage{chngpage}
```

Features: The core feature of `chngpage` is the `adjustwidth` environment, which allows the user to temporarily change the left and right margins for a block of text or a float (such as a figure or table). The margin changes apply only within the scope of this environment and revert to the original settings afterward. This is especially useful for content that requires extra horizontal space without modifying the layout of the entire document. The environment is flexible and can accept both positive and negative values to either reduce or expand the margins. This makes `chngpage` a lightweight and versatile tool for fine-tuning document appearance while maintaining the integrity of the overall formatting structure.

98. relsize

Usage: The `relsize` package is used to adjust font sizes in a relative manner, rather than specifying absolute font sizes like `\small` or `\Large`. This is particularly useful when you want to slightly increase or decrease the size of a piece of text without disrupting the document's overall typographic consistency. It helps create fine-grained size changes based on the current font size rather than setting a fixed one.

To begin using it, load the package in the preamble with:

```
\usepackage{relsize}
```

Features: The `relsize` package introduces a suite of commands that allow you to scale text up or down in incremental steps. For example, `\relsize{+1}` increases the font size by one relative step, while `\relsize{-1}` decreases it. There are also shorthand commands like `\larger` and `\smaller` that perform a single-step adjustment without requiring arguments. These adjustments are context-sensitive, so the size increases or decreases are based on the current font size, not an absolute base.

The package is particularly useful in situations like emphasizing text with slight changes in size, formatting footnotes, or adjusting fonts in subscripts and superscripts for clarity. It works well in both text and math environments, maintaining consistent typography throughout. As a lightweight solution for relative font sizing, `relsize` is widely appreciated for its precision and ease of use.

99. tocloft

Usage: The `tocloft` package is used to customize the appearance and formatting of the table of contents, list of figures, and list of tables in a LaTeX document. It offers a high level of control over these lists, allowing authors to align them more closely with specific formatting requirements or aesthetic preferences. This is especially useful in theses, books, or formal reports where institutional or publisher guidelines require custom spacing, styles, or labels.

To start using the package, include it in the preamble as follows:

```
\usepackage{tocloft}
```

Features: The `tocloft` package provides a comprehensive set of tools for redefining the layout of entries in the table of contents and other similar lists. It allows you to change font styles, indentations, label widths, and spacing between entries. You can also customize the leader (the dots connecting section titles to page numbers) or even suppress it altogether. Additionally, it enables the renaming of section headers (e.g., changing "Contents" to "Table of Contents") and the reordering or suppression of entries entirely.

Moreover, the package supports the creation of new types of custom lists with their own formatting rules, expanding its use beyond just the default three lists. Whether you are adjusting vertical spacing, aligning numbers, or defining entirely new list types, `tocloft` offers extensive options to tailor your document's structure to meet detailed layout specifications.

100. `url`

Usage: The `url` package is designed to make it easy to include URLs, email addresses, file paths, and other long strings that may not contain spaces in a LaTeX document. This package is particularly useful in academic writing, technical documentation, and Web-related content where hyperlinks and external references must be clearly displayed.

To use the package, include the following in the preamble:

```
\usepackage{url}
```

Features: The core feature of the `url` package is the `\url` command, which formats hyperlinks and similar content using a monospaced font and allows automatic line breaking at appropriate places, such as slashes or dots, without requiring manual intervention. This ensures that long URLs do not extend beyond the margins or overflow text blocks. The command works in both text and footnotes, maintaining legibility and proper spacing.

While the `hyperref` package also defines a `\url` command (with hyperlink capabilities), the `url` package is lighter and especially useful when hyperlinks are not needed, but typographically clean formatting of URLs is still desired. It also integrates well with bibliography styles and is frequently used in BibTeX entries for properly displaying URLs in reference lists.

7.5 Future Directions in LaTeX Publishing

As this volume draws to a close, it is worth considering the evolving landscape of LaTeX publishing. While LaTeX has long been established as the premier tool for producing high-quality technical documents, especially in the domains of mathematics, computer science, physics, and engineering, it is also a living system that continues to grow, adapt, and innovate. The future of LaTeX publishing is being shaped by trends in open science, Web-based collaboration, multilingual typesetting, automation, and multimedia integration.

7.5.1 Online Collaboration and Cloud-Based Editing

One of the most transformative developments in recent years is the rise of online LaTeX platforms such as Overleaf, Authorea, and Papeeria. These cloud-based environments allow authors to write, edit, and collaborate in real time, eliminating the need for cumbersome file exchanges and manual version control. Integration with Git repositories and seamless sharing mechanisms has made LaTeX more accessible and more collaborative than ever before. The future will likely see even tighter integration with institutional repositories, submission portals, and version tracking systems, allowing documents to move fluidly through drafting, review, and publication stages.

7.5.2 Reproducible Research and Literate Programming

Another direction gaining strong momentum is the use of LaTeX in reproducible research workflows. With the increasing emphasis on transparency in computational research, tools such as `knitr`, `Sweave`, and `Pweave` allow authors to embed live code from R, Python, and Julia directly into LaTeX documents. This enables dynamic generation of plots, statistical tables, and results that are automatically updated whenever the underlying data or analysis changes. This paradigm of literate programming aligns perfectly with the needs of modern scientific communication and is likely to become a standard feature in technical publishing.

7.5.3 Support for Multilingual and Global Publishing

The modern research environment is inherently international, and the need to support diverse languages and scripts is more pressing than ever. Traditional `pdfLaTeX` struggled with non-Latin alphabets and right-to-left (RTL) scripts. However, modern compilers such as XeLaTeX and LuaLaTeX provide robust support for UTF-8 encoding and OpenType fonts, enabling seamless typesetting of complex scripts such as Arabic, Chinese, Russian, and Hindi. Packages like `polyglossia`, `xeCJK`, and `bidi` have made multilingual document preparation not only feasible but also easy. In the years to come, we anticipate that LaTeX will be increasingly used to produce accessible and globalized publications.

7.5.4 Interactivity, Multimedia, and Web Integration

As the line between digital publishing and traditional typesetting blurs, LaTeX is beginning to embrace more interactive and multimedia content. Packages like `media9` and `pdfwidgets` enable embedding of videos and interactive forms into PDF outputs. Tools like `LaTeXML`, `TeX4ht`, and `pandoc` offer ways to convert LaTeX into HTML5, EPUB, or JATS XML, paving the way for hybrid publications that are both print-ready and Web-native. Interactive mathematical visualizations, embedded plots, and responsive layouts are becoming possible within the LaTeX ecosystem.

7.5.5 Enhanced Automation and Document Management

Efforts are underway to make package management and document compilation more automated and user-friendly. Modern distributions like TEX Live and MiKTEX already support automatic package installation. Future improvements may include dependency resolution, better sandboxing of packages, and tighter integration with graphical front-ends. Projects like `latexindent` and `linter` tools for LaTeX code formatting and style checking are also helping to make source code cleaner and more maintainable.

7.5.6 Integration with Publishing Pipelines

Journals and academic publishers are increasingly moving toward XML-based formats such as JATS, DocBook, or EPUB for archiving and dissemination. There is growing interest in enabling LaTeX documents to be directly exported into such formats using automated tools. This trend could help unify authoring, submission, and production workflows, where a single LaTeX source file is transformed not only into a beautifully typeset PDF but also into structured data for indexing, accessibility, and digital archiving.

7.5.7 Open Science and FAIR Principles

The rise of open science and the FAIR principles (Findable, Accessible, Interoperable, Reusable) has implications for document preparation. LaTeX authors are beginning to annotate documents with metadata, link to data sets, and integrate persistent identifiers like ORCIDs and DOIs.[1,2] In the future, LaTeX documents may be routinely expected to meet machine-readability standards and be linked to broader research ecosystems.

Exercises for Chap. 7: Advanced LaTeX Packages and Domain-Specific Applications

7.1 Useful LaTeX Packages for Various Fields

1. **Field-Specific Document Creation**: Choose one academic field (e.g., linguistics, economics, or chemistry) and create a short document using at least two LaTeX packages specifically designed for that field. Describe the purpose of each package used.

2. **Comparative Formatting**: Use two different packages to format the same type of content (e.g., tables or diagrams) from different disciplines. Compare the syntax, appearance, and functionality provided by each.

3. **Package Research Task**: Find a LaTeX package related to your area of study that was not discussed in the chapter. Write a brief summary of its features and provide a simple example showing how it enhances document preparation.

---

[1] ORCID (Open Researcher and Contributor ID) is a persistent digital identifier that uniquely distinguishes researches and links them to their scholarly works and affiliations.

[2] DOI (Digital Object Identifier) is a standardized and permanent identifier used to uniquely identify and provide stable access to digital scholarly content.

7.2 Electrical Engineering in LaTeX

1. **Drawing a Basic Circuit**: Use the `circuitikz` package to draw a simple electrical circuit containing a resistor, voltage source, and ground. Compile the document and explain each component's code.

2. **Advanced Diagram with Labels**: Extend your circuit diagram by including labeled current paths, component values, and annotations. Use `circuitikz` or `tikz` features for styling and positioning.

3. **Frequency Response Plot**: Use the `pgfplots` package to plot a frequency response curve for a filter or an amplifier. Include axis labels and legend.

7.3 Developing Your Own LaTeX Packages

1. **Creating a Simple Package**: Write your own ".sty" file that defines a few custom commands and environments (e.g., for theorem formatting or custom notes). Load the package in a LaTeX document and demonstrate its usage.

2. **Package Documentation**: Add documentation comments inside your custom ".sty" file describing the purpose and syntax of each command. Compile a short user manual for your package using the `doc` package.

3. **Advanced Package Behavior**: Modify your package to accept options (e.g., color schemes, font sizes) and respond conditionally using `\newif` or `\ifthenelse`. Demonstrate the use of these options in an example document.

7.4 Commonly Used Packages

1. **Custom Title Page**: Create a customized title page using the `titling` and `geometry` packages. Adjust margins and spacing and include elements like a logo or subtitle.

2. **Enhanced Math Formatting**: Use `amsmath`, `mathtools`, and `physics` together to typeset a system of equations and a derivation involving partial derivatives and vectors.

3. **References and Hyperlinks**: Use the `hyperref` and `cleveref` packages to link equations, figures, and sections in a document. Show how references adapt when content is rearranged or renumbered.

7.5 Future Trends in LaTeX Publishing

1. **Exploring Online Tools**: Research and briefly test a cloud-based LaTeX platform (e.g., Overleaf, Papeeria, or Authorea). Reflect on its advantages and limitations compared to local LaTeX environments.

2. **Markdown-to-LaTeX Workflows**: Explore how tools like Pandoc convert Markdown documents into LaTeX. Write a short Markdown file and convert it into LaTeX. Examine the output and potential use cases for academic publishing.

3. **AI and LaTeX Automation**: Read a recent article or blog post about using AI tools for LaTeX editing, code generation, or layout design. Write a brief summary discussing potential benefits and risks of integrating AI with LaTeX workflows.

Bibliography

1. A collaborative, continuously updated guide covering fundamental and advanced LaTeX topics. LaTeX Wikibook. Available online at: https://en.wikibooks.org/wiki/LaTeX

2. American Mathematical Society: An essential reference for handling complex mathematical environments in LaTeX. User's Guide for the `amsmath` Package. Available online at: https://www.ams.org/publications/authors/tex/amslatex

3. Downes, M.: A must-have reference for typesetting mathematical notation in LaTeX. In: Short Math Guide for LaTeX. American Mathematical Society, Providence (2002). Available online at: https://www.ams.org/arc/tex/short-math-guide.html

4. Downes, M.: A systematic guide to mathematical typesetting, including spacing, delimiters, and multi-line equations. In: A Guide to LaTeX Math Mode. American Mathematical Society, Providence (2017)

Md. Aquib, *Advanced LaTeX*, University
Texts in the Mathematical Sciences,
https://doi.org/10.1007/978-981-96-9322-1

5. Eijkhout, V.: A deep dive into TeX internals, covering macro programming and advanced typesetting techniques. In: TeX by Topic: A TeXnician's Reference. Addison-Wesley, Boston (1992)

6. Flynn, P.: A comprehensive collection of frequently asked questions about LaTeX, TeX, and related tools. The UK TeX FAQ. Available online at: https://texfaq.org

7. Goossens, M., Rahtz, S., Mittelbach, F.: An in-depth guide to including and manipulating graphics in LaTeX. In: The LaTeX Graphics Companion. Addison-Wesley, Boston (1997)

8. Gratzer, G.: A detailed exploration of mathematical typesetting, including AMS-LaTeX and theorem environments. In: More Math into LaTeX, 5th edn. Springer, Berlin (2016)

9. Gratzer, G.: An encyclopedic reference covering LaTeX for mathematical and scientific writing. In: Texts and Math into LaTeX, 6th edn. Springer, Berlin (2023)

10. Knuth, D.E.: The classic reference for TeX, providing deep insights into document preparation and typesetting. In: The TeXbook. Addison-Wesley, Boston (1986)

11. Knuth, D.E.: A fundamental text on TeX's default font system and typography principles. In: Computer Modern Typefaces. Addison-Wesley, Boston (1986)

12. Kopka, H., Daly, P.W.: A user-friendly introduction to LaTeX, covering both basic and advanced document preparation. In: A Guide to LaTeX: Document Preparation for Beginners and Advanced Users, 4th edn. Addison-Wesley, Boston (2003)

13. Kottwitz, S.: A modern beginner-friendly introduction, covering document creation, formatting, and customization. In: LaTeX Beginner's Guide. Packt Publishing, Birmingham (2011)

14. Lamport, L.: The foundational text by Leslie Lamport, the creator of LaTeX, introducing core concepts and usage. In: LaTeX: A Document Preparation System, 2nd edn. Addison-Wesley, Boston (1994)

15. Lehman, P.: A reference manual for handling bibliographies and citations in LaTeX. The `biblatex` Package Documentation. Available online at: http://www.ctan.org/pkg/biblatex

16. Mittelbach, F., Goossens, M.: A comprehensive guide detailing advanced LaTeX usage, including fonts, layouts, and automation. In: The LaTeX Companion, 2nd edn. Addison-Wesley Professional, Boston (2004)

17. Moore, R., Oetiker, T.: A guide to using LaTeX for web publishing, including PDF and HTML conversions. In: LaTeX for the Web. Addison-Wesley, Boston (2000)

18. Oetiker, T., Partl, H., Hyna, I., Schlegl, E.: A widely used introductory document covering the essential aspects of LaTeX. In: The Not So Short Introduction to LaTeX2e. Available online at: https://tobi.oetiker.ch/lshort/

19. Tantau, T.: The definitive manual for the TikZ package, covering advanced diagramming and graphical representations. The TikZ and PGF Packages. Available online at: http://mirrors.ctan.org/graphics/pgf/base/doc/pgfmanual.pdf

20. Tantau, T.: The official guide for Beamer, covering slide design, animations, and professional presentations. User Guide to the Beamer Class. Available online at: http://www.ctan.org/pkg/beamer

21. Voss, H.: A comprehensive resource for creating high-quality vector graphics using PSTricks. PSTricks: Graphics and PostScript for TeX and LaTeX. Available online at: http://www.ctan.org/pkg/pstricks

The manufacturer's authorised representative in the EU is Springer Nature Customer Service Centre GmbH, Europaplatz 3, 69115 Heidelberg, Germany. If you have any concerns regarding our products, please contact ProductSafety@springernature.com

Printed and bound by CPI Group (UK) Ltd, Croydon, CR0 4YY
21/09/2026
02219988-0017